WHAT DO THESE ABBREVIATIONS MEAN:

bb&em? FYI? thi? t-a? NASAD?
MWAI? B.Sc.S.S.? M.C.D?   ?

HOW DO YOU ABBREVIATE:

South Dakota? Atomic weight? Footnote?
Fahrenheit? Net worth? Program modification?

You'll find the answers in this book, which makes
short work of the long list of abbreviations en-
countered every day in every way in business,
science, school and daily life.

THE NEW AMERICAN DICTIONARY OF ABBREVIATIONS

MARY A. DE VRIES has written dozens of
books dealing with writing style and word usage—
including *The Practical Writer's Guide, The New
American Handbook of Letter Writing,* and *The Complete Office Handbook,* all in Signet editions.

THE
NEW AMERICAN
DICTIONARY OF
ABBREVIATIONS

Mary A. De Vries

A SIGNET BOOK

SIGNET
Published by the Penguin Group
Penguin Books USA Inc., 375 Hudson Street,
New York, New York 10014, U.S.A.
Penguin Books Ltd, 27 Wrights Lane,
London W8 5TZ, England
Penguin Books Australia Ltd, Ringwood,
Victoria, Australia
Penguin Books Canada Ltd, 2801 John Street,
Markham, Ontario, Canada L3R 1B4
Penguin Books (N.Z.) Ltd, 182-190 Wairau Road,
Auckland 10, New Zealand 5/91

Penguin Books Ltd, Registered Offices:
Harmondsworth, Middlesex, England

First published by Signet, an imprint of New American Library,
a division of Penguin Books USA Inc.

First Printing, February, 1991
10 9 8 7 6 5 4 3 2 1

 REGISTERED TRADEMARK—MARCA REGISTRADA

Printed in the United States of America

CONTENTS

PREFACE

Unless you have committed an extensive list of abbreviations to memory, it's doubtful that you will recognize or understand all of the abbreviations, acronyms, initialisms, signs, and symbols that inundate contemporary writing in newspapers, magazines, books, reports, and other material. The increasing use of abbreviated language in technical, business, and specialized writing propels readers to the nearest library reference room and an up-to-date book of abbreviations.

Therein lies the problem. It's not always convenient to leave home, work, or school to look in one of the impressive supervolumes of abbreviations that libraries offer; yet smaller, affordable abbreviations dictionaries suitable for desktop use are scarce. The few that exist often do not have enough entries to be useful or may focus on only one area of professional activity. The compilation in the *New American Dictionary of Abbreviations*, on the other hand, is intended to be extensive enough (ten thousand entries) for it to be useful to most people on a daily basis. In addition, the entries were drawn from numerous fields of business and professional activity, as well as from everyday social and business usage, to give the most well-rounded coverage possible; this includes important selected entries for deceased persons (*FDR*) and historical activities and organizations (*WPA*) as well as an extensive collection of contemporary abbreviations, acronyms, and initialisms.

The entries are organized into six major categories to help you locate items faster and easier. These categories are (1) general abbreviations, acronyms, and initialisms, including business and administrative forms (such as *mgr.* for *manager* and *eod* for *every other day*); (2) technical abbreviations and initialisms (such as *eV* for *electron volt* and *ols* for *ordinary least squares*); (3) organizations (such as *CORE* for *Congress of Racial Equality* and *OPC* for *Overseas Press Club*); (4) academic degrees (such as *A.Sc.* for *associate in science* and *M.S.T.* for *master of science in teaching*); (5) states and countries (such as *Kans.* for *Kansas* and *Bulg.* for *Bulgaria*); and (6) signs and symbols (such as ↑ for *gas* and *Fe* for *iron*). For those who are also concerned about the rules for writing abbreviations, acronyms, and initialisms, "Abbreviation Guidelines" immediately following this preface explains how to treat various words and phrases.

Within each of the six parts of the book (except signs and symbols), the entries are listed alphabetically, with small letters preceding capital letters and unpunctuated letters preceding punctuated letters. Signs and symbols are grouped in like categories such as "electrical signs and symbols." To find a particular abbreviation, acronym, or initialism, first pick the proper category and then the logical alphabetical location in that category. Since most abbreviations begin with the same letter as that of the words to which they refer, common sense will usually guide you to the right place. The abbreviation for *millimeter* (*mm*), for instance, is listed in the "Technical Abbreviations" part of the book among the entries beginning with the letter *m*. Occasionally, more than one acceptable abbreviation is given, and a few abbreviations appear in both the general and technical parts of the book.

With phrases of two or more words, the abbreviated form often consists of the first letter of each word in the phrase (initialism), for example: *asap* = *as soon as possible*. In fact, if you're drafting something such as a letter, report, or article, and you find yourself repeating some phrase over and over, you can devise your own shorthand by combining the first letter of each word in the phrase. When I was preparing advance material for this book, I kept repeating the phrase *dictionary of abbreviations*, so to save time I used the initialism *doa* in the draft work and spelled it out only in the final copy.

The rules applied to the spelling, capitalization, and punctuation of the entries in this book are described in "Abbreviation Guidelines." The style used in this book is one that is common in the United States, but as the discussion of the rules reveals, authorities in different countries and even within a country differ in their recommendations; to complicate questions of usage further, individual and organizational users vary greatly in their preferred styles.

Although the trend in most fields is toward less punctuation and the use of small letters for everything except proper nouns, follow the practices and requirements of your employer at work. In fact, whether you are using abbreviations, acronyms, and initialisms socially, at work, or in school, follow three basic rules: be consistent in the style (spelling, punctuation, and capitalization) you select; avoid short forms in formal social writing and in formal, general writing; and when you do use an abbreviation, acronym, or initialism (except for widely known forms that nearly everyone recognizes such as *IRS*), spell it out the first time and enclose the short form in parentheses following the spelled-out version, for example: *New American Library (NAL)*. If you're using this book, a fourth rule might be to turn to "Abbreviation Guidelines" and read the rules and suggestions before checking the individual entries or creating your own abbreviations.

ABBREVIATION GUIDELINES

Formal, General Writing

The use of abbreviations, acronyms, and initialisms in formal, general writing (such as an official letter or a formal document) is decreasing. Even technical terms in such cases are spelled out (*amperes*, not *a* or *amps*). Ordinary words and phrases are always spelled out in formal, general writing (*manager*, not *mgr.; as soon as possible*, not *asap*). Organization names, too, should be spelled out (*General Motors*, not *GM*). In certain cases such as in a formal report, if a name is repeated over and over, the initials may be used if the name is spelled in full the first time followed by the initials in parentheses: *Environmental Protection Agency (EPA); intercontinental ballistic missile (ICBM)*.

There are relatively few exceptions to the rule that words and phrases should be spelled out in formal, general writing. One that is familiar to most people is the use of *RSVP (Répondez s'il vous plaît)* in formal invitations. Also, in an official report or article, the footnotes, tables, and so on may properly use abbreviations to conform to traditional note and tabular style. In addition, writers may use any form of abbreviation or initialism desired in preparing the rough drafts of formal, general material. The only requirement is that the word or phrase be spelled out when the final document is prepared; hence in the final official version, abbreviations such as *disb.* would become *disbursement* and initialisms such as *dsi* would become *data systems inquiry*. Keep a list of any such forms you use in your rough drafts so that you don't forget when preparing final copy (e.g., by *Amer.* did you mean *American* or *America?*).

Business and Technical Writing

Abbreviations, acronyms, initialisms, signs, and symbols abound in technical and scientific writing. A technical discussion of operating systems in the computer field, for instance, would likely refer to *dos* or *DOS*, not to the spelled-out version, *disk operating system*. In fact, it would be spelled out the first time only if the audience had a number of laypersons who were not computer literate. Similarly, a chemical report to experienced chemists would use chemical symbols freely without explanation or definition. (Technical entries appear in the "Technical Abbreviations" section of this book.)

Various business and professional organizations have their own shorthand for business forms (requisitions, order confirmations, authorizations, financial reports, and so on), for record keeping, and for research. Someone in a purchasing department, for example, knows that *bo* means *back order*, not *body odor*. The field of activity, the document in question, and the intended audience will determine whether technical abbreviations and initialisms (such as *r/k* for *radial keratotomy*) or business abbreviations and initialisms (such as *os* for *out of stock*) are used and whether they may be used freely without definitions for the intended audience. (General business and professional entries appear in the "General Abbreviations" section of this book.)

Spelling

Many words and phrases have more than one acceptable form of abbreviation. Which one you use depends on the type of writing you are doing and for whom you are doing it. At work you should use the spellings preferred by your employer. The word *chapter*, for example, can be abbreviated in more than one way: *c.*, *ch.*, or *chap.* All three are correct, but lawyers commonly use *c.* in legal citations, some organizations use *ch.*, and the *Chicago Manual of Style* lists *chap.* for general scholarly text.

In this dictionary, a widely accepted form of spelling is given for each abbreviation; occasionally, more than one popular form is given. If you want to learn all acceptable forms for a particular word or phrase, however, consult a large library reference work. Regardless, one point on which authorities agree is that no matter how you choose to spell an abbreviation, you should use that form consistently throughout a document.

Capitalization

In matters of capitalization, too, it becomes very difficult to define a single correct style. The most one can do is emphasize that the trend in capitalization is toward small (lowercase) letters. This book encompasses that style, although in some cases, both lowercase and uppercase (capital) letters are shown when both are very popular or when different circumstances might cause one to make a different selection for a particular abbreviation. Occasionally, capitals are given only when that style is predominant.

Some things are always capitalized in contemporary writing. The initials of a person's name (*JFK*) are always in full capitals as are the letters for organization names (*YMCA*). Acronyms of official titles or names such as *SALT (Strategic Arms Limitation Talks)* are always in full capitals. Computer languages (*BASIC*) and commands (*DEL*) are commonly in all capitals, and some technical terms such as *J* for *joule* are also in capital letters. Whenever a letter stands for a proper noun, it should be a capital letter, but some terms have the status of both proper and common nouns and thus could be uppercase or lowercase depending on your intended meaning and usage. The abbreviation *OS* (all capitals) refers to an official computer operating system unveiled in the late 1980s. But *os* (lowercase letters) also is used to refer generally to any computer operating system, to the manner of conducting business in a company office or department, or to an item that is out of stock.

Certain abbreviations are not all capitals but may have an initial capital. *Belg.*, for instance, is the short version of *Belgian* and *Belgium; Freud.* is the abbreviated form for *Freudian;* and *Esl* refers to *English as a second language.* In such cases, only the letter that stands for the word that is a proper noun is capitalized.

Sometimes the use of capitals when lowercase letters would seem to be more appropriate merely follows custom; it is simply an exception that persists in many places. Organizations that are concerned with advanced technology sometimes overcapitalize, whereas organizations concerned with less technical or specialized activity tend to use more lowercase letters for the same terms, especially as they become more familiar in society.

The usual recommendation of writing authorities is to follow the requirements of your employer and, when there are no requirements, to follow the current trend. If this trend appears to contradict traditional or previous rules of abbreviation, remember that custom often prevails. Although this is distressing to language purists, history reveals that if society has been breaking or bending a rule for a long time, originally unauthorized modification may become an accepted new rule. In any case, no matter how you choose to capitalize abbreviations, use that style consistently throughout a document.

Punctuation

The decision whether to use or omit periods or other punctuation in abbreviations is no easier than the one about capitalization. In this case, the trend is to use less punctuation. But this increasing tendency is not necessarily a rule, and some organizations still use punctuation more than others do. In the United States, certain words or terms are always punctuated, such as academic degrees *(Ph.D.)* and traditional country or state abbreviations *(N.J.).* According to U.S. custom, titles *(Mr., Mrs., Dr.)* are also punctuated; the British style, by contrast, omits the period.

The names of most countries are spelled out in formal text *(the United States, France, West Germany)* but may be abbreviated in footnotes, tables, and so on to conform to conventional tabular and reference citation style. The Soviet Union, however, is often abbreviated as *USSR* in text material. In informal general writing, country names that are abbreviated as individual capital letters *(U.S.)* rather than as uppercase and lowercase short forms *(W.Ger.)* may be written as abbreviations when used as an adjective *(U.S. currency).* But the names should be spelled out when used as a noun *(the currency of the United States).* When country names are used as an adjective, they should be punctuated *(U.S. currency,* not *US currency; U.K. economics,* not *UK economics).* The *Soviet Union* is usually not abbreviated as *USSR* when used as an adjective; rather, the term *Soviet* is used *(Soviet government,* not *USSR* [or *U.S.S.R.*] *government).*

In the United States, metric weights and measures omit the periods *(m, cm)* and also omit the *s* to form a plural *(mm* can refer to either *millimeter* or *millimeters);* common weights and measures may or may not use the period, depending on the user's required style or preference *(yd* or *yd.);* also, an *s* is used to form the plural in certain cases with common weights and measures *(lbs.,* but *ft.,* not *fts.).* This dictionary also omits the period with metric weights and measures *(mg),* but it uses it after most common weights and measures *(qt.)* unless the abbreviation is a single letter *(c* for *cycle)* in which case the period is omitted. In the style represented in this book, there is always a period after any lowercase abbreviation—metric or otherwise—that might be mistaken for another word; in fact, authorities generally agree on the need for this to avoid confusion. Hence *cot.* for *cotangent* has a period because *cot* without a period could also refer to a type of bed.

True abbreviations such as *admin.* for *administration* are punctuated (abbreviations in all capitals such as [*Mr.*] *T* or *FBI* are not). Some organizations omit the period after any abbreviation that ends with the same letter as the word it represents (such as *acct* [no period] for *account*). This dictionary follows the style of punctuating that type of abbreviation (*acct.*) the same as one in which the end of the word is omitted (*admin.*). But no punctuation is used for an initialism consisting of the first letter of each word in the phrase (*ic* = *i*ntegrated *c*ircuit). The only exception occurs when this type of abbreviation spells another word (such as *ace.* for *a*utomatic *c*ircuit *e*xchange); since *ace* is an actual word in the English language, a period is added to avoid confusion with that word.

When an abbreviation is really a contraction, with an apostrophe, no period is used (*nat'l*, not *nat'l.*). Many words that have prefixes, and in that respect have the character of two words, are treated as if they are two words. No period is used, therefore, after *pe* for *photoelectric* or *av* for *audiovisual*. Certain abbreviated words are currently treated as complete words (*memo* for *memorandum*), and therefore no period is required.

Some organizations add a space before and after an ampersand (*&*) when such space also occurs in the spelled-out term. Other organizations always omit the space for the sake of simplicity and speed in composition. For convenience, this dictionary uses no space before or after an ampersand. Some abbreviations use hyphens or virgules (slash marks); no space is used before or after such punctuation.

Since punctuation styles vary so widely, authorities recommend that you follow the requirements of your employer. Especially, be consistent in the style you employ in a particular document.

Words Always Abbreviated

Some words in the United States are always abbreviated such as personal and professional titles (*Mr.*, *Mrs.*, *Messrs.*, *Dr.*, and so on). Also, *Jr.*, *Sr.*, and *Esq.* are abbreviated after a name in all cases except in certain formal social situations.

Scholarly degrees are abbreviated after a name (*John*

Doe, M.D., not *John Doe, Medical Doctor*). Time designations, too, are abbreviated (*a.m.; B.C.*). In street addresses, compass points following the street name are abbreviated (*110 Wilson Avenue, N.E.*, but *110 West Avenue*), and the U.S. Postal Service prefers two-letter abbreviations for states on envelope addresses (*Phoenix, AZ*).

Numbers

In technical writing, use figures when units of measure are abbreviated (*24 cm*, not *twenty-four cm*). In general, nontechnical writing, numbers up to one hundred and large even numbers are commonly spelled out (*forty-five kilometers; two thousand votes*). Fractions, too, are spelled out in nontechnical writing (*three-fourths*) but are usually written as figures in statistical, tabular, and similar technical material (*¾*). When a number opens a sentence, however, it should be spelled out (*Ninety percent were present*).

Abbreviate numbers over one hundred that are joined by a hyphen except when the first number ends in two zeros or when the second number begins with different digits (*1989–90; 1870–1902; 505–6; 300–307;* but: *from 1989 to 1990* and *between 505 and 506*).

Use figures with *a.m.* and *p.m.* in informal writing (*6:30 a.m.; 7 p.m.*; but *2 o'clock* or *two o'clock*); spell out the number in formal writing such as in an invitation (*half past seven o'clock*). Numbers referred to as numbers should be written as figures (*no. 3 and no. 7*); indefinite amounts should be spelled out (*several dozen people*). Use figures in organization names or indentifications (*Local No. 21*). In technical writing and informal general writing, use figures for ratios and proportions (*10 to 1 odds; 2:1 ratio*).

GENERAL ABBREVIATIONS

a absent; account; acre; adjective; at

A adulterer/adulteress; answer

A-1 first class

aa always afloat; author's alteration(s)

a-a air to air

a&ca additions and amendments

aac average annual cost

aae average annual earnings

aap advise if able to proceed; affirmative action program

AAP affirmative action program

aar after action report; against all risks; average annual rainfall

aarp annual advance retainer pay

aasr airport and airway surveillance radar

aav airborne assault vehicle

ab. about

a/b airborne

a&cb   assault and battery

AB   air base; Assembly Bill; Atlantic Beach

aband.   abandoned

abbr.   abbreviate(d); abbreviation

abcd   above and beyond the call of duty; awaiting bad conduct discharge

abd   all but dissertation

abi   abstracted business information

abortus   aborted fetus

abr.   abridged; abridgment

ac   air conditioning; average cost

a.c.   before meals (Latin *ante cibos*)

a/c   account; account current; air conditioning

a&cc   addenda and carrigenda

acad.   academy

acc.   accept; account(ed); accusative

acc. & aud.   accountant and auditor

accd   accelerated construction completion date

acc. de.   acceptable deception

accel.   accelerate(d); accelerating; acceleration

access.   accessory

acci.   accidental injury

accid.   accident(al)

accom.   accommodation

accomp.   accomplish

accrd. int.   accrued interest

accred.   accredited

acct.   account(ant)(ing)

acctd.   accented

accum.   accumulate

accus.   accusative

accy.   accessary

a-c/d-c   bisexual (slang)

acdu   active duty

acf   accessary clinical findings

ach   arm, chest, height; automated clearinghouse

achiev.   achievement

aci   adult correctional institution; automatic car identification

ack   accidentally killed

ack.   acknowledge; acknowledgment

acl   allowable cabin load

acld   air cooled

acm   active countermeasure

ACM   advanced cruise missile

acn   all concerned notified; assignment control number

acog   aircraft on ground

acous.   acoustics

a&cp   anchors and chains proved

a/c pay.   accounts payable

acpr   acoustical paper

acq.   acquire; acquittal

a/c rec.   accounts receivable

acrg.   acreage

acron.   acronym

acs   autograph card signed

ACS Address Change Service

acsc automated contingency support capability

act. acting; action; actor; actress; actual; actuarial; actuary; actuate; actuating

act. ct. actual count

act./is active in service

activ. activity

actnt. accountant

act./os active out of service

actv. activate

act. val. actual value

act. wt. actual weight

acv actual cash value

acwbcn action will be cancelled

ad active duty; after drain; air dried; after date; athletic director

a&d accounting and disbursing; ascending and descending

Ad Alzheimer's disease

A.D. in the year of our Lord (Latin *Anno Domini*)

ada average daily attendance

ADA assistant district attorney

adap. adapted

adb accidental death benefit

adc active duty commitment; adopted child; advance delivery of correspondence; average daily census

ad cap. for pleasing; made attractive (Latin *ad captandum*)

adcon advance concepts; advise or issue instructions to all concerned

add.   addenda; addendum; address; average daily dose

addict.   addiction

ade   automatic data entry; average daily enrollment

adeda   advise effective date

ad fin.   to the end (Latin *ad finem*)

adhca   advise headquarters of complete action

ad h.1.   at this place (Latin *ad hunc locum*)

ad hom.   to the man (Latin *ad hominem*)

adi   acceptable daily intake; automatic direction indicator

ad id.   both the same; likewise (Latin *ad idem*)

ad ig.   to ignorance (Latin *ad ignorantiam*)

adimd   advise immediately by dispatch

ad inf.   to infinity (Latin *ad infinitum*)

ad init.   at the beginning (Latin *ad initium*)

adinsp   administrative inspection

ad int.   in the interim or meantime (Latin *ad interim*)

adipu   advise whether individual may be properly used (in your installation)

adj.   adjacent; adjective; adjust; adjutant

adl   activities of daily living; authorized data list; automotive discount leasing

ad lib.   at one's pleasure; freely to the degree desired (Latin *ad libitum*)

ad loc.   to or at this place (Latin *ad locum*)

adm   action description memo; average daily membership

ADM   air defense missile; air-launched decoy missile

admad   advise method and date (of shipment)

admap   advise by mail as soon as possible

admin. administration; administrative; administrator

adminord administrative order

adm. admission

Adm. admiral

admx. administrator

ad naus. dull to the point of nausea (Latin *ad nauseam*)

ad neut. until neutral (Latin *ad neutralizandum*)

adnok advise if not correct

adop. adoption

adore. advise date of receipt

adosh advise date of shipment

adpe automatic data processing equipment

adpl average daily patient load

adr asset depreciation range

adrde advise reason for delay

ads. area, date, subject; autograph document signed; automatic door seal

ad saec. to the century (Latin *ad saecutum*)

adsap advise as soon as possible

ad sat. to saturation (Latin *ad saturandum*)

adsc average daily service charge

adsda advise earliest date

ad sec. at suit of—legal (Latin *ad sectam*)

adstadis advise status and/or disposition

adstkoh advise stock on hand

adt any damn thing (placebo)

Adt Atlantic daylight time

adult. adulterant; adulterate; adulteration

ad us.   according to custom (Latin *ad usum*)

ad us. ext.   for extensive use (Latin *ad usum externum*)

adv.   advance; advantage; adverb; advertising

advac   advise acceptance

ad val.   according to value (Latin *ad valorem*)

adv. chgs.   advance charges

adv. frt.   advance freight

adv. mtr.   advertising matter

advof   advise this office

adv. pmt.   advance payment

adw   assault with deadly weapon

ae   account executive; almost everywhere

aea   actual expenses allowable

aec   additional extended coverage; at earliest convenience

aee   absolutely essential equipment

aek   all-electric kitchen

ael   audit error list

aen   advance evaluation note

aep   accrued expenditure paid

aeq   age equivalent

aero.   aerographer; aeronautical; aeronautics

aes   annual expectation of sales

aeu   accrued expenditure unpaid

afc   average fixed cost

afd   alternate full day

aff.   affairs

affd.   affixed; affordable

affec.   affectation; affection; affective

afft.   affidavit

aflt.   afloat

afr   auditor freight receipt

afra   average freight rate assessment

afsd.   aforesaid

aftn.   afternoon

ag.   agricultural; agriculture

a-g   air to ground

AG   adjutant general; attorney general

AG   company; joint stock company (German *Aktien Gesellschaft*)

aga   accelerated growth area

agb   any good brand

agbio.   agrobiology

aggr.   aggregate

agi   adjusted gross income; annual general inspection

agit. bene   shake well (Latin *agita bene*)

agit-prop   agitation and propaganda

agl   above ground level

AGM   air-to-ground missile

agric.   agricultural; agriculture

agt.   agent

agw   actual gross weight

agy.   agency

a/h   at home

a&ch   accident and health; alive and healthy

aha   all have automobiles

ahr   acceptable hazard rate

a.h.v.   at this word (Latin *ad hunc vocum*)

ai   accidentally incurred; artificial insemination; artificial intelligence

a&i   abstracting and indexing; accident and indemnity

A&I   agricultural and industrial (college)

aia   advise if available

aid.   acute infectious disease

aida   attention, interest, desire, action

AIDS   acquired immune deficiency syndrome

aim.   active inert missile

AIM   active inert missile

aima   as interest may appear

aime   average indexed monthly earnings

ain   approved item name

aio   activity, interest, opinion

air.   artist in residence

aircondit   air condition(ed)(ing)

airsurance   air insurance

ais   agreed industrial standards; answer in sentence; average insurance set

AIS   administrative and information services

aj   apple juice

aka   also known as

al   air lock; all lengths; annual leave

a/l   airlift

alc   on the menu (French *a la carte*)

ALCM   air-launched cruise missile

alcoh.   alcohol

alcon   all concerned

ald   a later date; acceptable limit for dispersion

ald.   alderman

alf   alien life force; automatic letter facer

alg.   algebra; algebraic

align.   alignment

alk.   alkali

all.   above lower limit

alloc.   allocate; allocation

allow.   allowance

allus.   allusion

alluv.   alluvial; alluvium

Alp.   Alpine

alpha.   alphabetical

Alps   Alpine Mountains

ALPS   Alternative Loans for Parents and Students

ALR   *American Law Reports*

als   autograph letter signed

ALSAM   air-launched surface-attack missile

alt.   alter(ation(ed)(ing)(native)(nator); altitude

alter.   alteration; alternate

altho.   although

alt. hor.   at alternate hours (Latin *alternis horis*)

alt. noc.   on alternate nights (Latin *alternis noctibus*)

A.M.   before noon (Latin *ante meridiem*)

a/m   auto/manual

a&m agricultural and mechanical; ancient and modern; architectural and mechanical

Am. America(n)

amal. amalgam(ate)(ation)

A-matter advance matter

amb. ambassador; amber; ambient; ambulance

ambig. ambiguity; ambiguous

ambiv. ambivalence; ambivalent

amcl amended clearance

am. cur. a friend at court (Latin *amicus curiae*)

Am. Emb. American Embassy

Am. Engr. *American Engineer*

Amer. America(n)

amf airmail facility

Am. Ind. American Indian

Am. L. *American Lawyer*

AMM antimissile missile

Am. Mach. *American Machinist*

amn. airman

amo advance material order; airmail only

amr automatic message routing

AMS administrative and management services

AMSAM antimissile surface-to-air missile

amsl above mean sea level

amtex air mass-transportation experiment

an. above named; annual

an. before (Latin *ante*); year (Latin *anno*)

a/n acidic and neutral

A&N army and navy

anal. analogy; analysis; analytical

Anal. Chem. *Analytical Chemistry*

anat. anatomy

ANBS armed nuclear bombardment satellite

anc all numbers calling

anch. anchorage

ancr aircraft not combat ready

ang. angiogram; angle; angular

ani automatic number identification

ank. ankle

anlys. analysis

ann. announce(ment)(r); annual(ly); annuity

ann. year (Latin *anno*); years (Latin *anni*)

anniv. anniversary (Latin *anniversarium*)

annot. annotate(d); annotation

annul. annulment

ano above-named officer

anon. nameless (Latin *anonymous*)

ans. answer(ed)(ing)

ant. antenna; anterior; antique; antonym

antag. antagonistic

anthrop. anthropological; anthropologist; anthropology

ant. jentac. before breakfast (Latin *ante jentaculum*)

ant. prand. before dinner (Latin *ante prandium*)

antr apparent net transfer rate

anvo accept no verbal orders

anx. annex

ao access opening; antioxidant; area of operations; accuracy only; account of; arresting officer

a/o account of

aoa about once around; at or above

aob alcohol on breath; angle on the bow; annual operating budget; any other business; at or below

aod as of date

aoe auditing order error

aog aircraft on ground

aoi accent on information; aims of industry; area of interest

aok all okay (everything in good order)

aol absent over leave

aoq average outgoing quality

aoql average outgoing quality limit

aor area of responsibility

a/or and/or

aos acquisition of signal; add or subtract

ap above proof; access panel; action potential; advanced placement; aiming point; as prescribed; attached processor; author's proof; average product

a.p. before a meal (Latin *ante prandium*)

a-p American plan (includes meals)

a/p authority to pay; authority to purchase; allied papers

a&p agricultural and pastoral; anterior and posterior

apart. apartment

apc average propensity to consume

apd action potential duration; aiming point determination

aper.   aperture

api   acceptable periodic inspection

apl   adult performance level

apma   advance payment of mileage authorized

apol.   apologist; apologize; apology

apos.   apostrophe

apost.   apostasy; apostate

app.   apparatus; apparel; apparent; appeal; append-(age)(ed)(ix); appetite; applause; applied; apprentice; approach; approve

appar.   apparatus

appd.   approved

appi   advanced planning procurement information

appl.   applicable; application; applied

appr.   approval; approve(d)

appren.   apprentice

appro.   approval

approp.   appropriation

approx.   approximate(ly)

appt.   appointment

apr   annual percentage rate

Apr.   April

APR   annual percentage rate

aps   average propensity to save

apt.   apartment

apti   actions per time interval

aq   accomplishment quotient; achievement quotient; any quantity

aql acceptable qualifying levels; acceptable quality level; approved quality level

ar achievement ratio; all rail; all risks; allocated reserve; armed robbery; artificial respiration; average revenue

a/r all risks; armed robbery; at the rate of

a&r approved and removed; artists and repertory; assault and robbery; assembly and repair

arb. arbitrary; arbitration

arch. archaic; archipelago; architect(ural)(ure)

ard acute respiratory disease

arf acute respiratory failure

arfo after receipt firm offer

arfor area forecast

argus advanced research on groups under stress

arith. arithmetic

arl acceptable reliability level; average remaining lifetime

ARM adjustable-rate mortgage; antiradar missile; antiradiation missile

aro after receipt of order

arrn arrival notice

art. advanced research and technology; artery; article; artillery; artisan; artist(ic)(ry); automatic reporting telephone

as. alloy steel; at sight

a/s after sight; alongside

a&s accident and sickness; arts and sciences

asap as soon as possible

asc altered state of consciousness; automatic switching center

as&cc   aerospace surveillance and control

ASC   All Saver Certificate

ASCM   antiship capable missile

ase   airborne search equipment

asf   additional selection factor

ash   aerial scout helicopter

asl   above sea level

Asl   American sign language

ASM   air-to-surface missile

asn   average sample number

asp.   affirmative self-protection; automatic system procedure

Asp   American selling price

asr   airport surveillance radar; air-sea rescue; answer and receive; available supply rate

a-s rs   air-sea rescue service

assd.   assigned

assem.   assemble

assist.   assistant

assn.   association

asst.   assist(ance)(ant)

ast   absolute space time

Ast   Atlantic standard time

astrol.   astrology

asu   administrative systems unit; all screwed up (slang)

asw   antisubmarine warfare

a/t   action/time

a&t   acceptance and transfer; assemble and test

At   Atlantic time

A/t   American terms

ata   actual time of arrival; air to air

atar   above transmitted and received

atbm   average time between maintenance

ATBM   advanced technology ballistic missile; antitactical ballistic missile

atbyropt   at buyer's option

atc   acoustical tile ceiling; approved type certificate; automatic temperature control; automatic tint control

atdp   attitudes toward disabled persons

atf   accounting tabulating form; actual time of fall

atg   air to ground

ath   above the horizon

ati   actual time of interception; average total inspection

atiob   as this is our best

Atl.   Atlanta; Atlantic

ATM   automated teller machine

ato   according to others

atp   at any price (French *a tout prix*)

at pres.   at present

att.   attached; attempt; attorney

atten.   attention

attn.   attention

atto.   attorney

atv   all-terrain vehicle

ATV   all-terrain vehicle

au.   author

auc   average unit cost

Aug.   August

aul   above upper limit

AUM   air-to-underwater missile

aun   without annotation (Latin *abesque ulla nota*)

aureq   authority is requested

auth.   authentic(ate)(ity); author; authority; authorization; authorize(d)

auto   automobile

AUTOCAP   Automobile Consumer Action Program

autog.   autograph

autopilot   automatic pilot

auv   administrative-use vehicle

aux.   auxiliary

av   acid value; assessed valuation; audiovisual

av.   avenue; average

AV   Authorized Version

ava   audiovisual aids

avail.   available; availability

avc   average variable cost

avdth   average depth

ave.   avenue

avfr   available for reassignment

avg.   average

avge.   average

avm   automatic voting machine

AVM   automatic voting machine

avs   area vocational school

avt   adult vocational training

av. temp.   average temperature

aw   above water; acid waste; actual weight; air to water; atomic warfare

a/w   actual weight; all-water; all-weather

a&w   alive and well

awa   absent without authority

awd.   award

awe.   advise when established; average weekly earnings

awiy   as we informed you

awk.   awkward

awl.   absent without leave

awn   awaiting maintenance

awol   absent without leave; absent without official leave

AWOL   absent without official leave

awy.   airway

ax.   axiom(atic)

ayr   all-year 'round

az.   azure

b.   born; brother

ba   blind approach

b/a   billed at; budget authorized

bac.   bacilli; bacillus; bacteria(l)

bach.   bachelor

bact.   bacteria; bacteriological; bacteriologist; bacteriology; bacterium

ba&f   budget, accounting, and finance

bag.   baggage

bak.   bakery

bal   blood alcohol level

bal.   balance; balcony

ban.   bond anticipation note

bar.   barometer; barometric

barb.   barbarian; barbecue; barber; barbiturate

basd   basic active service data

bath.   bathroom

batt.   batter(y); batteries

bb   ball bearing; below bridges; blood bank

b/b   bail bond

b&cb   bed and board; bed and breakfast

b to b   back to back

bba   born before arrival

bbb   banker's blanket bond; bed, breakfast, and bath

bb&em   bed, breakfast, and evening meal

bbp   boxes, barrels, packages; building-block principle

bbq   barbecue

bc   back course; bad check; between centers; bills for collection; birth control; budgeted cost; building center; bulk carrier

b/c   bales of cotton; bills for collection; birth control; broadcast

b&c   buildings and contents

B.C.   before Christ

bcs.   because

bcwp   budget cost of work performed

bcws   budget cost for work schedule

bdi both days included

b&e breaking and entering

bef blunt end first

beg. begin(ning)

bel. below

b&ent&pl breaking and entering and petty larceny

beq. bequeath

bev. bevel; beverage

bexec. budget execution

bf backfeed; boldface

b.f. genuine; in good faith; without fraud or deception (Latin *bona fide*)

b/f black female; brought forward

b&f bell and flange

bg back gear; before girls; block grant; business girl

b&g buildings and grounds

bgl below ground level

bi background investigation

b&i bankruptcy and insolvency

bib. bibliography; biblical

Bib. Bible (Latin *Biblica*)

bibliog. bibliography

bif buyer induced failure

bio. biographical; biography; biological; biology

biog. biographer; biographical; biography

biol. biological; biologist; biology

bionics biology and electronics

bior business input-output rerun

bip   balanced in plane; books in print; borough-interborough problems

bir   basic incidence rate

bis   best in show

Bish.   bishop

bi-w   biweekly

biz   business

b&j   bone and joint

bk   below the knee

bk.   bank; book

bkcy.   bankruptcy

bkfst.   breakfast

bkg.   banking; bookkeeping

bkgd.   background

bkpt.   bankrupt

bkt.   basket; bracket

bl   bank larcency

b/l   basic letter; bill of lading; blue line; blueprint

bldg.   building

bldr.   builder

blk.   black; block(ing)

bll   below lower limit

bls.   bales

blvd.   boulevard

bm   birthmark; board measure; book of the month

b/m   bill of material

bmoc   big man on campus

bno   but not over

bo   back order; blackout; body odor; branch office

b/o   back order; brought over; budget outlay

boa   born on arrival

bol   bill of lading

bom   business office must

bomb.   bombardment

bop.   balance of payments; best operating procedure

bow.   born out of wedlock

bp   back pressure; beautiful people; before present; behavior pattern; below proof; bills payable; birthplace; blood pressure; blueprint; boiling point

b/p   baking powder; bills payable; blood pressure; blueprint

b&p   bare and painted

b of p   balance of payments

bpl.   birthplace

bpu   base production unit

bq   beauty quotient

br   bank rate; bill of rights; builder's risk

b/r   bills receivable

b&r   budget and reporting

brc   business reply card

brf.   brief(ing)

brig.   brigantine; ship's prison (slang)

brkt.   bracket

brm   business reply mail

BRM   business reply mail

bro.   brother (general)

Bro.   Brother (religious)

Bros. Brothers
brp bathroom privileges
brt. bright
brt. fwd. brought forward
brz. bronze
bs backspace
b&s brandy and soda
bsa body surface area
bsh. bushel
bsi basic shipping instructions
bskt. basket
bst brief stimulus therapy
b/st bill of sight
bs&cw basic sediment and water
bt body temperature; bulk transport
b&t bath and toilet
b of t balance of trade
bta best time available; better than average
btf balance to follow
b/tf balance transferred
btm bottom
bto big-time operator
btp body temperature and pressure
bts back to school
btv basic transportation vehicle
btw. between
btwn. between
bu. bureau

bud. budget

build. building

bul below upper limit

bull. bulletin

bur. bureau

bus. business

bus. hrs. business hours

bus. mgr. business manager

bv blood vessel

b/v book value; brick veneer

BVD Bradley, Vorhees & Day (suits of underwear)

bw best of winners; birth weight; body weight

b.w. please turn over (German *bitte wenden*)

b/w black and white; bread and water

bwcdi best we can do is

bwia better walk if able

bwoc big woman on campus

bw-tv black and white television

byo bring your own

byt bright young things

c about; calorie; candle, carat; cent; century; chapter; child

c. chapter

C Centigrade; cold

ca about; civil authorities; current assets

c/a capital account; current account

c&a classification and audit

cab.   cabin(et); taxicab

cad.   cadet; cash against documents; computer-aided design; contract-award date

CAD   computer-aided design

cad/cam   computer-aided design/computer-aided manufacturing

CAD/CAM   computer-aided design/computer-aided manufacturing

caf   clerical, administrative, and fiscal; cost and freight; cost, assurance, and freight

caf.   cafeteria

cal   computer-aided learning

CAL   computer-aided learning

cal.   calendar; caliber; calorie

can.   cancel(ed)(ing)(lation)

canv.   canvas

cap.   capacity; capital; capital letter; capitol; capsule; client assessment package; computer-aided production

CAP   computer-aided production

caps.   capital letters

Capt.   captain

car.   carat; carton

card.   cardinal (general)

Card.   cardinal (religious)

carp.   carpenter; carpentry; carpet(ing)

cartog.   cartographer; cartographic; cartography

cat.   catalog; caterpillar tractor

cath.   cathartic; cathedral

catv   cable television; community antenna television

CATV   community antenna television

cav.   warning; writ of suspension (Latin *caveat*)

cav. emp.   let the buyer beware (Latin *caveat emptor*)

cb   chairman of the board; citizen's band (radio); collective bargaining

c&b   collating and binding

c of b   confirmation of balance

CB   citizen's band (radio)

cbb   commercial blanket bond

cbd   cash before delivery

cbdn   can be done

cb/l   commercial bill of lading

cbr   crude birth rate

cbx   computerized branch exchange; computerized business exchange

CBX   computerized branch exchange; computerized business exchange

cc   carbon copy; chief complaint; color code; command and control

c/c   center to center; current account

c&cc   carpets and curtains; consultation and concurrence

c of c   cost of construction

c to c   center to center

ccm   counter-countermeasures

ccp   credit card purchase

c/cut   crosscut

ccw   carrying a concealed weapon; counterclockwise

ccy.   currency

cd   certificate of deposit; civil defense; compact disc

c-d countdown

c/d carried down; cash against documents; certificate of deposit

c&d carpets and drapes; collection and delivery

CD certificate of deposit

cdp critical decision point

cds. cards

cdst central daylight saving time

cdt central daylight time

ce career education; counterespionage; critical examination

c/e custom entry

c&e commission and exchange; customs and excise

C.E. Christian Era

c&ed clothing and equipment development

cei contract end item

cent. century; hundred (Latin *centum*)

ceo chief executive officer

CEO chief executive officer

cert. certificate; certify

cf. compare (Latin *confer*)

c/f carried forward

c&f clearing and forwarding; cost and freight

cf&c cost, freight, and commission

cfi cost, freight, and insurance

cfo calling for orders

CFP certified financial planner

cge. carriage

cgo.   cargo

ch.   chair; chapter; chief

c&h   cocaine and heroin; cold and hot

chap.   chapter

char.   character

chf   congestive heart failure

chf.   chief

chg.   change; charge

choc.   chocolate

chp   comprehensive health plan

ch. ppd.   charges prepaid

chr.   character

chrg.   charge

chs.   chapters

ci   coefficient of intelligence; cost and insurance; counterintelligence

c/i   certificate of insurance

c&i   cost and insurance; cowboys and Indians

C&I   Currier and Ives (art)

cia   cash in advance

CiP   Cataloging in Publication (Library of Congress)

cir.   circle; circuit; circular

cit.   citation

cj   clip joint

ck.   cask; check; cork

ckd   completely knocked down

ckt.   circuit

cl   carload; center line

c/l   carload lot; cash letter; combat loss

class.   classification

c&lc   capital and lowercase (small) letters

cldy.   cloudy

cleo   clear language for expressing orders

cler.   clerical

cli   central life interests; cost-of-living index

CLI   cost-of-living index

clin./d.   clinical death

clk.   clerk; clock

clo   cod liver oil

clor   container loaded at owner's risk

clws.   clockwise

cm   court-martial

c.m.   cause of death (Latin *causa mortis*)

c/m   current month

c of m   certificate of merit

CM   Common Market

cmd.   command

Cmdr.   commander

cn   contract number

c.n.   tomorrow night (Latin *cras nocte*)

cna   code not allocated

cnc   computer numerical control

C-note   one hundred dollar bill

cns   central nervous system

co   crossover; cutoff; cutout

co.   company; county

c/o   care of; carried over; cash order; complains/complaints of

c-o-b   close of business

cod.   cash on delivery; cause of death

c.o.d.   cash on delivery

c-o-d   cargo on deck

COD   cash on delivery

C.O.D.   cash on delivery

coed   female college student

coed.   coeducation

cof   cause of failure

c/offer   counteroffer

coh   cash on hand

coin.   complete operating information; counterinsurgency

col.   colonial; colony; color; column

Col.   colonel

cola   cost-of-living adjustment; cost-of-living allowance

COLA   cost-of-living adjustment; cost-of-living allowance

collab.   collaborate; collaboration; collaborator

coll. agy.   collection agency

colloq.   colloquial(ism)

colo.   colophon

col. p.   color page

com.   comedy; comma; command; commercial; commission; committee; common; communication; communism

Com.   Communist

comb.   combat; combination; combine; combustion

combo   combination

comkd   completely knocked down

comp.   compiler; compiled by

compend.   compendious; compendium

compt.   comptroller

comrel   community relations

comsat   communications satellite

cond.   condenser; condition; conductor

conf.   confer(ence); confidential

cong.   congress

Cong.   Congress (U.S.)

conj.   conjugal; conjugate; conjunction

conn.   connection

cons.   consider; consist

conserv.   conservation(ist); conservatory

consgt.   consignment

consid.   consideration

consol.   consolidated

const.   constant; constitution(al); construct(ion)(or)

constr.   construct(ion)(or)

cont.   contact; content; continent(al); continue; contract; control

cont.   against (Latin *contra*)

contax   consumers and taxpayers

contr. bon. mor.   contrary to good manners (Latin *contra bonos mores*)

cont. rem.   continue the remedy (Latin *continuetur remedia*)

contrib.   contribution; contributor

coop. cooperation

co-op cooperative

coord. coordinate; coordination; coordinator

cop customer owned property; policeman (slang)

c-o-p change of plea

copr. copyright

coq cost of quality

cor. corner; cornet; correction

cor. body (Latin *corpus*)

cords. corduroy trousers

corp. corporal; corporation

corres. correspond(ence)(ent)(ing)

corresp. correspond(ence)(ent)(ing)

co career officer

cos cash on shipment

cosecy company secretary

cosmo. cosmopolitan

cost. costume

cot. cotton

cp cerebral palsy; code of practice; command post

c/p carport; change package; composition/printing; control panel

c&p carriage and packing; collated and perfect

cpa closest point of approach; cost planning and appraisal; critical path analysis

CPA certified public accountant; critical path analysis

cpaf cost plus award fee

cpe central programmer and evaluator; customer provides equipment

cpf   cost per flight

cpi   consumer price index

CPI   consumer price index

Cpl.   corporal

cpm   critical path method

cpo   cost proposal outline

cpr   cardiopulmonary resuscitation

cps   creative problem solving

CPS   certified professional secretary

cpt   continuous performance task

cq   class quotient

CQ   call to quarters

cr   carriage return; clinical research

cr.   credit; creek; crown

c/r   company risk; correction requirement

c&r   cops and robbers

crb   central radio bureau; chemical, radiological, biological

cr. bal.   credit balance

crf.   capital recovery factor; change request form; cross-reference file

crim.   criminal(ist); criminologist; criminology

CRIS   Carrier Route Information System

crit.   critic(al)(ality)(ism)

cr/m   crew member

crt   cathode ray tube

CRT   cathode ray tube

cru   clinical research unit

cs   caesarean section; capital stock; center section; current series

c/s   cases

c&s   clean and sober

c of s   chief of staff

C.S.   keeper of the seal (Latin *Custos Sigilli*)

C/S   call signal

c&sc   caps and small caps (capital and small capital letters)

c-sect.   cesarean section

c/sgnd.   countersigned

csi   contractor standard item

c/smp.   countersample

cso   central signoff

cst   cargo ships and tankers; central standard time; combined station power; convulsive shock therapy

ct   cellular therapy; central time; central timing; corrected therapy

ct.   cent; court

ct.   hundred (Latin *centum*)

c/t   certificate of title

c&t   classification and testing

ctf.   certificate

ctgf   clean tanks, gas free

ctl   constructive total loss

ctn.   carton

cto   cancelled to order

ct. ord.   court order

ctp.   central transfer point; close to profit

ctr. center; counter

ctv cable television; color television

ctw. counterweight

cty. city; county

cu clinical unit

cub. control unit busy

cul. culinary

cult. cultural; culture

cup. cupboard

cur. curiosity; currency; current

curr. currency; current

curric. curriculum

cust. custard; custodian; custody; custom(er)

cuv current-use value

cv capital value; carrier vehicle; collection voucher

cvli cash-value life insurance

cvr cockpit voice recorder

cw caseworker; chemical warfare; child welfare; clock-wise

c/w counterweight

c&w country and western

cwd clerical work data

cwe current working estimate

cwm commerical waste management

cwo cash with order

CWO chief warrant officer

cwp communicating word processor

cw&s crushed, washed, and screened

cwt counterweight; hundredweight

cx central exchange; chest X-ray; correct copy

CX central exchange

cy calendar year; current year

czy. crazy

d daughter; day; degree; died

D democrat(ic)

da days after acceptance; delayed action; deposit account; discharge afloat; district attorney; do not answer; documents against acceptance; documents attached; doesn't answer

d/a deposit account

DA district attorney

dac data acquisition and control; data assistance and control; deductible average clause

dacks Dacron slacks

dacum designing a curriculum

dad daddy

dad. dispense as directed

daf discharge afloat

daff. daffodil

dafm discard at failure maintenance

dai death from accidental injuries

DAI death from accidental injuries

dalpo do all possible

dam. damage

dao duly authorized officer

dap   data analysis package; data automation proposal; do anything possible; documents against payment

dard   data acquisition requirements document

das   delivered alongside ship

dat   day (date) after tomorrow

datanet   data network

datran   data transmission

datrec   data recording

datrix   direct access to reference information

dats   data accumulation-transmission sheet

dax   dachsund

db   day book; delayed broadcast; distribution board; double bed

db.   debit

d/b   documentary bill

d&b   dead and buried

dba   doing business as/at

dbacc   debit accounting

d/ba   draw bar

dbb   dinner, bed, breakfast

dbbal   debit balance

dbd   death by drugs

dbi   database index; development-at-birth index

DBI   development-at-birth index

dbk.   debark; drawback

dbl.   double(r)

dblb   double room with bath

dbls   double room with shower

db. rts.   debenture rights

dbs   damn bloody soon (slang); direct broadcast satellite

dbsr   double-bed sitting room

dbt.   debit

dc   data collection; dead center; deck cargo; deviation clause; digital computer; direct credit; double column; down center

d/c   deviation clause; double column; drift correction

d&c   dilation and curettage

dci   double column inch; driving car intoxicated

dco   draft collection only

dcp   development cost plan

dd   days after date; deferred delivery; delayed delivery; double draft; drydock; due date

d'd   deceased

d/d   dated; delivered at dock; demand draft; developer/demonstrator; domicile to domicile; due date

d&d   deaf and dumb; drunk and disorderly; dungeons and dragons (game)

d to d   dawn to dusk; dusk to dawn

D&D   Dungeons and Dragons (game)

ddc   data documentation costs; deck decompression chambers

ddd   deadline delivery date

ddf   design disclosure format

ddr   direct debit

ddt   digital data transmission

ddt&e   design, develop, test, and evaluate

ddw   displaying a deadly weapon

de deflection error; direct elimination; direct entry; double entry

d/e date of establishment

dealer prep. dealer preparation

deb. debenture; debit

deb. stk. debenture stock

dec. deceased; deciduous; decimal; decision; decorate; decrease

Dec. December

decaf. decaffeinated

decel. deceleration

decid. deciduous

declar. declaration

deco direct energy conversion operation

decomp. decomposition

decor. decorate; decoration; decorative

ded date expected delivery

ded. dedicate(d); deduct(ed)(ion)

de d. in d. from day to day (Latin *de die in diem*)

deduct. deduction

dee jay disc jockey

deek duck decoy

def. defeat(ed); defect(ion)(or); defend(ant); defense; defer(red); definite; definition; deflect(ing)(ion); defrost(er)(ing); defunct

def. art. definite article

defic. deficiency; deficit

deg. degenerate; degree

degen. degeneration

del. delegate; delegation; delete; deletion; deliberate; deliberation; delineate(d); delineation; deliver(y)

del. acct. delinquent account

delcap delayed capacity

dele. delete

deleg. delegation

del. ent. delete entirely

deli delicatessen

delib. deliberate; deliberation

delin. delineate(d); delineating; delineation

delinq. delinquency; delinquent

delmes delay message

delu. delusion

dely. delivery

dem. demand; democracy; democrat(ic); demolish; demolition; demonstrate; demonstration; demote; demotion

demo demolition; demonstration

democ. democracy

demod. demodulator

den. denotation; dental; dentist(ry)

dens. density

dent. dental; dentist(ry); denture

dep do everything possible

dep. depart(ment)(ure); depend(ency)(ent); depose; deposit(or); depot; deputy

depart. department; departure

depend. dependent; dependency

depo. deposit

depr.   depreciation; depression

dept.   depart(ment)(ure)

der.   derivation; derivative

deriv.   derivation; derivative

derm.   dermatitis; dermatology

deros   date eligible for return from overseas

des.   descend(ed)(ing); desert; design(er); designate: designation; desire; dessert

desc.   descend(ant)

descr.   description

dest.   destination; destroy(er); destruction

det.   detach(ment); detail; detect(ive)(or); determinant; determine

detl.   detail

detox.   detoxification

Deut.   Deuteronomy

dev.   develop(er)(ment); deviate; deviation; deviator

devel.   develop(er)(ment)

dew.   dewpoint

d. ex m.   godlike device; god from a machine (Latin *deus ex machina*)

df   damage free; dead freight; decontamination factor; dispostion form

d/f   defogging; direct flow

d&f   determination and finding

d. forg.   drop forging

dfq   dry frequency

dfr   decreasing failure rate; dropped from rolls

d/g   dangerous goods; directional gyroscope

dh   dead heat; designated hitter

d&h   daughter and heiress

dhw   double-hung windows

di   daily inspection; direction indicator; document identifier

DI   drill instructor

dia   date of initial appointment; due in assets

diacrit.   diacritic(al)(ly)

diag.   diagnose; diagnosis; diagnostic; diagonal; diagram

dial.   dialect(ical)(ician)(ics)

diam.   diameter

diaph.   diaphragm

dib   dead in bed (sexually)

dic   data item category; defense identification code

d&ic   dependency and indemnity compensation

dickel   dime and nickel

dict.   dictate(d); dictation; diction(ary)

die.   died in emergency room

DIE   died in emergency room

diet.   dietary; dietetic(s); dietician

dif.   differ(ence)(ential); diffuse; diffuser

diff.   differ(ence)(ential); diffuse; diffuser

dig.   digest(ion)(ive)

dik   drug identification kit

dimin.   diminish; diminution; diminutive

din.   dinner

dino.   dinosaur

dio.   diode

dioc. diocesan; diocese

dip. diptheria; diploma; diplomat

diph. diphtheria

diplo. diploma(cy); diplomat(ic)

dir. direct(ion)(or)

dis delivered into store

dis. discount(ed)

disab. disable(d)

disb. disburse(ment)

disc. discount

disco discotheque

discon disorderly conduct

discon. disconnect

discr. discriminate; discrimination

dishon. dishonest(y); dishonorable; dishonorably

disord. disorder(ly)

disp. dispatch; dispensary; dispenser; display; disposal; disposition

disp. dispense (Latin *dispensa*)

displ. displacement

diss. dissent(er); dissertation

dist. distance; district

div. diverse; divide(d)(nd); divisible; division; divorce(d)

divvy divide

diw dead in water

diy do it yourself

dj disc jockey; dust jacket

D-J Dow-Jones (average)

djd   degenerative joint disease

dk   don't know; drop kick

dk.   dark; deck; dock

d&k   dining and kitchen

dkt.   docket

dl   data link; day letter; demand loan; driver's license

d/l   data link; demand loan

DL   day letter

d. lat.   difference in latitude

dlb   dead-letter box

dlc   direct left control; down left center

dld   deadline date

dld.   delivered

dlet.   delete

dlo   dead-letter office; difference in longitude; dispatch loading only

DLO   dead-letter office

dlp   date of last payment

dlr   double-lens reflex

dlrs.   dollars

dls   debt-liquidation schedule

dls.   dollars

dls./shr.   dollars per share

dlvd.   delivered

dlwg   daily weight gain

dlx.   deluxe

dly.   daily; delay; dolly

dm   data management; diagnostic monitor; draftsman

d/m   date and month; day and month; density/moisture

dmc   direct manufacturing cost

dmd.   demand; diamond

dmy.   dummy

dn   debit note

d/n   debit note

D/N   debit note

dna   did not attend; does not answer

DNA   deoxyribonucleic acid

dnc   direct numerical control

dnd   died a natural death

dnf   did not finish

dnka   did not keep appointment

dnl   do not load

dnm   data name

d/note   debit note

D-note   five hundred dollar bill

dnp   do not publish

dnr   does not run; do not renew

do.   days off; delivery order; direct order; ditto; drop-out; dual ownership

do.   same as before (Latin *dictum*)

d-o   dropout

d/o   delivery order; disbursing officer

doa   date of arrival; date of availability; dead on arrival; direction of approach; disposal of assets

dob   date of birth

doc   died of other causes; direct operating cost

doc. doctor; document(ary)(ation)

Doc. doctor

dod. date of death; died of disease

doe. date of enlistment

dof degrees of freedom; delivery on field

doh direct operating hours

doi dead of injuries

dol. dollar

dollies dolophine pills

dols. dollars

dom date of marriage; dirty old man

dom. domain; dominion

Dom. of the Lord (Latin *Dominicus*)

dom. ex. domestic exchange

don. until (Latin *donec*)

donk. donkey

dor date of rank

dos date of sale

dot. draft on Treasury

dow died of wounds

doz. dozen

dp data processing; deal pending; departure point; dew point; displaced person; distribution point

d/p delivery papers; documents against payment

d&p developing and printing

dpa deferred payment account

dplx. duplex

dpm documents per minute

dpob date and place of birth

dpp deferred payment plan

dpty. deputy

dq definite quantity; direct question

dr date register; delivery room

dr. debit; differential rate; dram; drill; drive

Dr. doctor

d/r deposit receipt

dr&a data reporting and accounting

drain. drainage

dram. drama(tic)(tist)

drapes draperies

drc down right center

drftmn. draftsman

dri data-rate indicator

drk. dark

dros date returned from overseas

drq discomfort relief quotient

drvr. driver

drzl. drizzle

ds days after sight; dead-air space; debenture stock; domestic service; double strength

d.s. document signed

d&s demand and supply; distribution and supply

DSC Distinguished Service Cross

dsg. designate

dso direct shipment order

dspch. dispatch(er)

dspn.   disposition

dsq   discharged to sick quarters

D-squad   death squad

ds&r   data storage and retrieval; document search and retrieval

dss   documents signed; dry surface storage

dst   daylight saving time

dstl.   distill

dstn.   destination

dt   dead time; double time

d of t   deed of trust

dta   daily travel allowance

dtc   design to cost; direct to consumer

dtf   daily transaction file

dtl.   detail(ed)

dto   detailed test objective; dollar trade-off

dtp   desktop publishing

DTP   desktop publishing

d/tr   documents against trust receipt

dtx.   detoxification

du   density unknown; diagnosis undetermined; duodenal ulcer

dub.   dubious (Latin *dubius*)

duct.   ductile

dudat   due date

dui   driving under the influence (of alcohol/drugs)

dulc.   sweet (Latin *dulcis*)

duod.   duodenum

dup.   duplicate; duplicating; duplication

dupl.   duplicate; duplication

dur.   duration

dur.   hard (Latin *duris*)

dv   direct vision; distinguished visitor; double vision

d/v   declared value

d&v   diarrhea and vomiting

D.V.   God willing (Latin *Deo volente*)

dvr.   driver

dw   deadweight; delivered weight; double weight; dumbwaiter

d/w   dock warrant

dwb   double with bath

dwc   deadweight capacity

dwd   died while drinking

dwf   divorced white female

dwi   driving while intoxicated

dwm   dangerous waste material; divorced white male

dwp   deepwater port

dwr.   drawer

dx.   deluxe; diagnosis; duplex

dy.   delivery; duty

dyb   do your best

dy. bf. hl.   day before holiday

dyd.   dockyard

dyf   damned young fool

dy. fl. hl.   day following holiday

dyke   bulldyke

dyn.   dynamic(s); dynamo

dyna.   dynamite

dyu   do your utmost

dz.   dizziness; dizzy; dozen; drizzle

ea   enemy aircraft

ea.   each

e/a   enemy aircraft; experimental aircraft

eac   estimate at completion

ead   equipment allowance deduction; estimated availability date

ead.   the same (Latin *eadem*)

eaf   emergency action file

eal   estimated average life

Eal   English as an additional language

eam   electronic accounting machine

eaon   except as otherwise noted

eap   equivalent air pressure

ear.   estimate after release

eas   estimated air speed

eat.   estimated arrival time; earnings after taxes

EAT   estimated arrival time

eaw   equivalent average words

e/b   eastbound

ebit   earnings before interest and taxes

ec   extended coverage; extension and conversion

ec.   economics

e.c.   for example (Latin *exempli causa*)

e&c engineering and construction

ecc equipment classification control; error correction code

ecd estimated completion date

ece extended coverage endorsement

ecom electronic computer-originated mail

ECOM electronic computer-originated mail

econ. economic(s); economist; economy

e con. on the contrary (Latin *e contrario*)

ecr energy consumption rate

ed extra dividend

ed. edit(or)(ion); edited by; editorial; educate(d); education

e&d exploration and development

eda early departure authorized

edac error detection and correction

edd estimated delivery date; expected date of delivery

edit. editing; edition; either; editorial

ed. note editorial note; editor's note

edoc effective date of change

eds estimated date of separation

eds. editors

edt eastern daylight time

ee errors excepted; eye and ear

e/e electrical/electronic

e&e eye and ear

e to e end to end

EE Early English

eeo   equal employment opportunity

eep   emergency essential personnel

eer   energy efficiency ratio

eet   estimated elapsed time

ef   each face; extremely fine

efa   essential fatty acids

e&fc   examined and found correct

eff.   effect(ive); efficiency

effect.   effective

eft   earliest finish time

e.g.   for example (Latin *exempli gratia*)

egp   embezzlement of government property

e&h   environment and heredity

ehp   extrahigh potency

ehw   extreme high water

ei   emotionally impaired; environmental illness

e/i   endorsement irregular

e by i   execution by injection

ej   elbow jerk

el   each layer; educational level; extra line

elab.   elaborate(d); elaborating; elaboration

elas.   elastic(ity)

elcar   electric car

elec.   electric(al)(ian)(ity)

elect.   election; elector(al)(ate)

elem.   element(ary)

elev.   elevate(d); elevation; elevator

elig.   eligible

ellip.   elliptic(al)

elong.   elongate

eloq.   eloquent(ly)

elw   extreme low water

em   emergency maintenance; enlisted man

emb.   embargo; embark(ation); embassy

emend.   emendate(d); emendation; emendator(y)

emend.   corrected or edited (Latin *emendatis*)

emerg.   emergency

emerit.   retired with honor (Latin *emeritus*)

emig.   emigrant; emigration

emis   emergency medical services

emis.   emission

emot.   emotion(al)

emp.   emperor; empire; empress

e.m.p.   as or in the manner prescribed (Latin *ex modo prescripto*)

emp. agy.   employment agency

empl.   employ(ee)(er)(ment)

empro   emergency proposal

emr   educable mentally retarded

emt   emergency medical team

emul.   emulsion

enam.   enamel(ed)

enc.   enclose(d); enclosure; encumbrance

encl.   enclose(d); enclosure

ency.   encyclopedia

end. endorse(ment)

end mo. end of month

end wk. end of week

end yr. end of year

eng. engine; engineer(ing)

Eng. English

engin. engineering

Engl. English

engr. engineer

engrv. engrave(r); engraving

enl. enlist

enrt en route

ent ear, nose, and throat

env. envelop(e); envoy

environ. environment(al)(alism)(alist)

eo end of operation

eo by authority of his or her office (Latin *ex officio*)

eoa effective on or about; examination, opinion, advice

eob expense operating budget

eod every other day

eoe equal opportunity employer

e&oe errors and omissions excepted

eof end of flight

eoh equipment on hand

eohp except as otherwise herein provided

eol end of life

eom end of message; end of month; every other month

eooe   error or omission excepted

eop   end of passage

eoq   end of quarter

eos   eligible for overseas service

eot   end of transmission

eov   end of volume

ep   extended play; external publication; extreme pressure

e.p.   first edition (Latin *editio princeps*)

e/p   endpaper

e&p   exploration and production

epa   economic price adjustment

epd   earliest practicable date

epicen.   epicenter

epid.   epidemic

epig.   epigram

epilog.   epilogue

eps   earnings per share; emergency power supply

ept   excess profits tax

epte   existed prior to entry

Eq.   Equator

EQ   educational quotient; ethnic quotient

eqi   environmental quality index

eqn.   equation

eqt   equivalent training

eq. tr.   equip. trust

equil.   equilibrium

equip.   equipment

equiv. equivalent

e/r editing/reviewing; en route

ERA Equal Rights Amendment

erc equipment record card

erect. erection

erot. erotic(a)(ally)(ism)

err. error; erroneous

err. & app. errors and appeals

ert estrogen replacement therapy

ESA Endangered Species Act

esc electronic service charge

esc. escape; escort; escrow

esd estimated shipping date

Esk. Eskimo

Esl English as a second language

ESL English as a second language

esp. especially

e&sp equipment and spare parts

Esq. Esquire

est eastern standard time; electroshock therapy

est. estate; estimate(d); estimation

estab. establish(ed)(ment)

est. wt. estimated weight

et eastern time; educational therapy; elapsed time; electric/electronic typewriter; extraterrestrial

eta estimated time of arrival

et al. and elsewhere (Latin *et alibi*); and others (Latin *et alia*)

etc.   and so on; and so forth (Latin *et cetera*)

etd   estimated time of departure

etiol.   etiology

eto   estimated takeoff

etoc   expected total operating cost

etp   estimated turning point

et seq.   and following (Latin *et sequens*)

etsp   entitled to severance pay

et ux.   and wife (Latin *et uxor*)

etv   educational television

ETV   educational television

eu   emergency unit

eua   examination under anesthetic

euph.   euphemism

Eur.   Europe(an)

Eurasia   Europe and Asia

ev   earned value; exposure value

evac.   evacuate; evacuation

eval.   evaluate; evaluation

evap.   evaporate; evaporation

eve.   evening

evol.   evolution(ary)(ist)

evs   expected value saved

ew   early warning

e/w   equipped with

ewl   evaporative water loss

ewr   early warning radar

ex   example; extra(neous); former; without

exacct   expense account

ex. af.   of affinity (Latin *ex affinis*)

exag.   exaggerate(d); exaggeration

exam.   examination; examine(r)

ex cath.   from the seat of authority (Latin *ex cathedra*)

exch.   exchange

excl.   exclude; exclusion; exclusive

ex con.   ex (former) convict

ex cp.   ex (without) coupon

ex div.   ex (without) dividend

exec.   execute(d); execution; executive; executor

exhib.   exhibit(ion)(or)

exhib.   let it be shown (Latin *exhibeatur*)

ex int.   ex (without) interest

ex lib.   from the library of (Latin *ex libris*)

ex n(ew)   excluding new shares

ex off.   by authority of his or her office (Latin *ex officio*)

exord   exercise order

exp.   expansion; expenditure; expense; export; express

ex p.   on one side only (Latin *ex parte*)

exper.   experiment(al)

expo   experimental order

ex r   ex (excluding) rights

ext.   extend; extension; exterior; external; extinguish-(er); extra

e-z   easy

f   family; farthing; father; female

f.   folio; following page

F   Fahrenheit

fa   fatty acid; first aid

f/a   friendly aircraft

f&ca   fire and allied (insurance); fore and aft

faa   free of all average

fab.   fabric(ate)(ation); fabulous

fac   fast as can

fac.   facade; facial; facility; facsimile; factor(y); faculty

fact.   factory

fam.   familiar(ization); family

fao   finish all over

fAp   full American plan

faq   fair average quality; free at quay

fas   free alongside ship

fat.   fixed asset transfer

fath.   fathom

fau   fixed asset utilization

fav.   favor(able)(ite)

fax   facsimile (transmission/machine)

fb   freight bill; fullback

f/b   feedback; female black; front to back

fc   fixed cost; follow copy; free and clear

f/c   free and clear

f&cc   fire and casualty (insurance)

fd   fatal dose; free delivery

f/d   father and daughter; free dock

f&d   freight and demurrage

f&e   facilities and equipment

Feb.   February

fed.   federal; federated; federation

Fed. Reg.   *Federal Register*

Fed. Rep.   *Federal Reporter*

fel   front-end loader

fem.   female; feminine

fert.   fertility; fertilization; fertilizer

fest.   festival

feud.   feudal(ism)(istic)

ff   far afield; folded flat; form feed

ff.   folios; following pages

f/f   face to face; flip-flop

f&f   fittings and fixtures; furniture and fixtures

f to f   face to face; foe to foe; friend to friend

ffa   free for all; free from alongside; for further assignment

ffwd   fast forward

fga   foreign general average; free of general average

fi   fire insurance; fixed interval

fic   freight, insurance, carriage

fict.   fiction; fictitious

fifo   first in, first out

fig.   figuratively; figure

fih   free in harbor

filo   first in, last out

fin.   finance; financial; financier; finish

fina   following items not available

fio   for information only; free in and out

fis   free in store; freight, insurance, and shipping (charges)

fix.   fixture

fka   formerly known as

fl   flight level; flow line; focal length; forklift

fl.   flourished (Latin *floruit*)

f&l   fuel and lubricants

flex.   flexible

flt. pln.   flight plan

fluc.   fluctuate

f&m   foot and mouth (disease)

fmr   fair market rent

fn.   footnote

f/n   freight note

fna   for necessary action

fo   fade out; firm offer; firm order; free out; full out terms

f/o   for credit of; firm offer; for orders

fob   free on board

foc   free of charge; free on car

fod   free of damage

fol.   folio; follow(ing)

fol.   leaf (Latin *folium*)

fold.   folding

foq   free on quay

for free on rail; free on road

for. foreign(er); forest(er)(ry)

for'd forward

for. lang. foreign language

fos free on station

fot free on truck

fow free on wharf

fp fire policy; fixed price; floating policy; fully paid

fpaa free from particular average

fpo fixed price open

fq fiscal quarter

Fr. Father (religious); French

f/r fixed response; freight release; front to rear

fract. fraction

freq. frequency; frequent(ly)

Freud. Freudian

Fri. Friday

frict. friction

frig. refrigerator

front. frontispiece

frt. fwd. freight forward

fruc. fruit (Latin *fructus*)

fs factor of safety; fire station; flight service; foreign service

f/s financial statement; first stage

fsbo for sale by owner

fs&q functions, standards, and qualifications

ft free of tax; free trade; full terms

f-t   follow through

f&t   fire and theft (insurance)

fta   failure to appear

fti   federal tax included

ftka   failed to keep appointment

fufo   fly under, fly out

fund.   fundamental(ism)(ist)

f/up   follow-up

fur.   furlong; further

fut.   future

fv   forward visibility; future value

fv.   back of the page (Latin *folio verso*)

f/w   female white

f&w   feed(ing) and water(ing)

fwd   front-wheel drive

fwd.   forward

fwh   flexible working hours

fx   foreign exchange

fy   forever yours

FY   fiscal year

fyi   for your information

FYI   for your information

fyr   for your reference

FYR   for your reference

g   gender; glucose

ga   go ahead; ground to air

g/a   general average; ground to air

g&a   general and administrative

g/a/g   ground to air to ground

gai   guaranteed annual income

gall.   gallery

gaq   general air quality

gar   gross annual return

gar.   garage; garrison

garb.   garbage

gav   gross annual value

g/av   general average

gaw   guaranteed annual wage

g/bl   government bill of lading

gbo   goods in bad order

gc   general cargo; good condition; good conduct

Gct   Greenwich civil time

gdp   gross domestic product

GDP   gross domestic product

gds.   goods

ge   gross energy

gen.   gender; general; genus

Gen.   general

gen. av.   general average

gen. prac.   general practice

gen. pub.   general public

gent.   gentlemen

gep   gross energy product

ger.   gerund

gfa   good fair average

g-force   gravity force

gg   gamma globulin; ground to ground

g-g   ground to ground

gi   government issue; gross income; gross inventory

GI   American soldier (from the term *government issue*)

gim   general information management

Gk.   Greek

gl   general liability; ground level

gloss.   glossary

Gmat   Greenwich mean astronomical time

Gmt   Greenwich mean time

gne   gross national expenditure

GNE   gross national expenditure

gni   gross national income

GNI   gross national income

gnp   gross national product

GNP   gross national product

gnw   gross national welfare

GNW   gross national welfare

goi   gross operating income

govt.   government

gov't   government

gp   galley proofs; general practice; general purpose; government property

gpa   grade-point average

gpi   general price index

GPI   general price index

gpm   graduated payment mortgage; gross profit margin

GPM   graduated payment mortgage

gr.   grain; great; gross

gram.   grammar

g/r/n   goods received note

gro.   gross

gs   gold standard; ground speed

gsi   ground-speed indicator

gsl   guaranteed student loan

gt   grand total

Gt   Greenwich time

gtc   good till canceled

gtw   good this week

guar.   guarantee

guo   government use only

gv   ground visibility

g/w   gross wt.

gwp   gross world product

GWP   gross world product

gyn.   gynecology

H   hot

ha   heir apparent

h.a.   in this year (Latin *hoc anno*)

hab. corp.   may you have the body (Latin *habeas corpus*)

halluc.   hallucination

hb   halfback; handbook

h/b   handbook

h'back   hatchback

h/back   hardback

hbd   herein before described

hbk   hardback

h/board   hardboard; headboard

hc   hard copy; hydrocarbon

h.c.   tonight (Latin *hac nocte*)

h/c   held covered

h&c   heroin and cocaine; hot and cold

hca   held by civil authorities

hcap.   handicap

hcl   high cost of living

h-d   heavy duty; high density

hdc   holder in due course

hdkf.   handkerchief

hdl.   handle

hdqrs.   headquarters

h/duty   heavy duty

hdv   high dollar value

hdwe.   hardware

h/f   held for

hfm   hold for money

hfr   held for release

hg   high grade

h/h   hard of hearing; house to house

hi fi   high fidelity

hifo   highest in, first out

hi lo   high low

hist.   historical; history

h.l.   in this place (Latin *hoc loco*)

hlg.   halogen

h&m   hit and miss

hmo   health maintenance organization

HMO   health maintenance organization

h.n.   tonight (Latin *hac nocte*)

ho   holdover

hol.   holiday

hon.   honey; honor(able)(arium)(ary)(ed)

hp   high performance; high potency; high pressure

hq   headquarters

hr.   hour

h/r   heart rate

hs   half strength

ht   half title; halftone; high tension; high tide

h.t.   at this time (Latin *hoc tempore*); under this title (Latin *hoc titulo*)

htc   headline to come

h/w   husband and wife

hwy.   highway

hy   high yield

ia   immediately available

i&a   indexing and abstracting

iae   in any event

iatd   is amended to delete

iatr   is amended to read

iaw   in accordance with

ibid.   in the same place (Latin *ibidem*)

ic   in charge; in command; international communications

i/c   in charge; in command; intercom

ICBM   intercontinental ballistic missile

ic&cc   invoice cost and charges

icl   incoming correspondence log

ico   in case of

icv   improved capital value

icw   in connection with

id   identification; immediate delivery; import duty; item description

id.   the same (Latin *idem*)

id. ac   the same as (Latin *idem ac*)

ident.   identification; identify; identity

i.e.   that is (Latin *id est*)

i-e   internal-external

if nec.   if necessary

ifo   in favor of; in front of

igr.   therefore (Latin *igitur*)

iho   in-house operation

iia   if incorrect, advise

iip   index of industrial production; individualized instructional planning

il   incoming letter

i/l   import license

illus.   illusion; illustrate(d); illustration; illustrator

ilt   in lieu thereof

i&m   improvement and modernization

immed.   immediate

immig.   immigrant; immigration

imp.   imperative; imperfect; imperial; import, improve-(ment)

i/n   item number

in d.   daily (Latin *in diem*)

indef.   indefinite

individ.   individual

inf.   infinity

inf.   below (Latin *infra*)

info.   information

in init.   in the beginning (Latin *in initio*)

in litt.   in correspondence (Latin *in litteris*)

in loc.   in the place (Latin *in loco*)

in loc. cit.   in the place cited (Latin *in loco citato*)

in-out   input-output

in pr.   in the first place (Latin *in principio*)

in re   in regard to

in s.   in the original place (Latin *in situ*)

int.   interest

int. al.   among other things (Latin *inter alia*)

INTELPOST   international post

intelsat   international communications satellite

interj.   interjection

int. noct.   during the night (Latin *inter noctem*)

in trans.   in transit (Latin *in transitu*)

introd. introduction

i/o in and/or over; input/output; instead of

i&o input and output

iont in order not to

IOU I owe you

iow in other words

i/p input

ipa including particular average

i.q. the same as (Latin *idem quod*)

IQ import quota; intelligence quotient

i.q.e.d. that which was to be proved (Latin *id quod erat demonstrandum*)

i-r infrared

i&r information and retrieval; intelligence and reconnaissance; interchangeability and replaceability

IRA individual retirement account

IRBM intermediate range ballistic missile

iro in rear of

irp initial receiving point

irr internal rate of return

ISBN International Standard Book Number

isr information storage and retrieval

it. information technology; item

ita initial teaching alphabet

ital. italics

itc installation time and cost

iv increased value; intravenous; invoice value

i.v. under the word (Latin *in verbo*)

i/v   increased value
ivo   in view of
iw   index word
i/w   interchangeable with

j.   journal
j.   law (Latin *jus*); of law (Latin *juris*)
j/a   joint account
Jan.   January
jb   job blank (form)
JC   Jesus Christ; Julius Caesar
J.C.   Jesus Christ; Julius Caesar
jd   juvenile delinquency
jds   job data sheet
je   job estimate
J. Ed.   *Journal of Education*
j/f   jigs and fixtures
JFK   John Fitzgerald Kennedy
jnl.   journal
jnt. stk.   joint stock
jo   job order
July   July
June   June

k   kindergarten
k&b   kitchen and bathroom
kia   killed in action

KIA   killed in action

k-j   knee jerk

ko   keep off; keep out

k-o   knockout

KO   knockout

kog   kindly old gentlemen

k size   king size

l.   line

l/a   letter of advice; letter of authority

lab.   label(ing); labor(atory)

lam.   laminate

lang.   language

lat.   lateral; latitude

Lat.   Latin

lav.   lavatory

law.   lawyer

lax.   laxative

lb   landing barge; letter box; lifeboat

lb.   pound

l&b   land and buildings

lc   lowercase (small letters)

l.c.   in the place cited (Latin *loco citato*)

lcl   less than carload lot

l/cr.   letter of credit

l/e   lifetime earnings

lex.   lexical; lexicographer; lexicography; lexicon

lib. liberal(ism); liberation(ist); libertarian(ism); liberty; librarian; library

lic. license

lifo last in, first out

lin. lineal; linear

lit. liter; literacy; literal(ly); literary; literate; literature; litter; little

l/o letter of offer

loc letter of credit

loc. primo cit. in the place first cited (Latin *loco primo citato*)

lo-lo load on-load off

lov limit of visibility

lp long play

LP long play

lr letter report; long range

l/r left/right; lower right

l to r left to right

lrp long-range planning

l.s. place of the seal (Latin *locus sigilli*)

l.s.c. in the foregoing place cited (Latin *loco supra citato*)

ls&d liquor store and delicatessen

lst local standard time

lst. wk. last week

lt language translation; local time; low temperature; low tension

Lt. lieutenant

LT letter message (telegram)

ltc long-term care

Lt. Col.   lieutenant colonel

ltd.   limited

ltm   long-term memory; long-term mortgage

ltr.   letter

lub.   lubricant; lubricate; lubrication

lux.   luxurious; luxury

lv.   leave

lw   lightweight; low water

l&w   living and well

m   male; married; masculine; noon (Latin *meridies*)

M   money supply

ma   machine account; mental age; monthly account

m&ca   maintenance and assembly

mach.   machine(ry); machinist

mad.   mind-altering drug; mutual(ly) assured destruction

MAD   mutual(ly) assured destruction

mag.   magazine

mag.   great (Latin *magnus*)

mag. op.   major work (Latin *magnum opus*)

mai   minimum annual income

MAIL   Mail Addressing Improvement Link (service)

maitre d'   head waiter (French *maitre d'hotel*)

maj.   major(ity) (general)

Maj.   major (rank)

malt.   malted milkshake

mar.   marine; maritime; married; minimal acceptable rate

Mar.   March

mart.   maintenance analysis and review technique

MART   maintenance analysis and review technique

masc.   masculine

masc.   male (Latin *masculus*)

mat.   material; materiel

math   mathematics

math.   mathematician

max.   maximal; maximum

May   May

mayo.   mayonnaise

m.b.   mix well (Latin *misce bene*)

m/b   male black

mbb   mortgage-backed bonds

mbe   minority business enterprise

mbo   management by objectives

MBO   management by objectives (technique)

mbt   mean body temperature

mc   marginal cost; master of ceremonies

m/c   my home or house (Spanish *mi casa*)

m&c   manufacturers and contractors; morphine and cocaine

MC   master of ceremonies; member of Congress

md   muscular dystrophy

m-d   manic-depressive

m/d   market day; memorandum of deposit; month(s) after date

m&e   mechanical and electrical

meas. measure(ment)

mech. mechanic(al); mechanism

med. medal(ist)(lion); median; medic(al)(ation)(ine); medieval(ism)(ist); medium

medex medical expert

MEDLARS Medical Literature Analysis and Retrieval System

mei marginal efficiency of investment

mem. member; memoirs; memorial

mes mutual energy support

Mesd. Ladies (French *Mesdames*)

Messrs. Gentlemen (French *Messieurs*)

met. metal(lic); metaphor; metropolitan

m. et n. morning and evening or night (Latin *mane et nocte*)

metro. metropolitan

mex military exchange

mf maintenance factor; male to female (ratio)

m/f male or female

m&f male and female

M-F Monday through Friday

mfg. manufacturing

mfr. manufacture(d)(r)

mgr. manager

Mgr. Monseigneur (French *Monsignor*); Monsignore (Italian *Monsignor*)

mhr maximum heart rate

mi manual input; mentally ill; middle initial

mia missing in action

MIA   missing in action

mic   military-industrial complex

midwk.   midweek

mike   microphone

mil.   mileage; military; million

mimeo.   mimeograph(ed)

min.   minimum; minister; minor(ity); minute

mini.   miniskirt

minr   minimum room rate desired

MIRV   multiple independently targeted (targetable) re-entry vehicle

misc.   miscellaneous

mj.   marijuana

mkt.   market

Mlle.   Miss (French *Mademoiselle*)

Mlles.   Misses (French *Mesdemoiselles*)

m.m.   with the necessary changes (Latin *mutatis mutandis*)

Mme.   Missus (French *Madame*)

Mmes.   Ladies (French *Mesdames*)

mo   mail order; method of operation; money order

mo.   month(ly)

m.o.   mode or way of operating or working (Latin *modus operandi*)

mod. pres.   in the manner prescribed (Latin *modo prescripto*)

moe   measure of effectiveness

m-o-m   middle of month; milk of magnesia

Mon.   Monday

mono.   mononucleosis; monopoly; monotype

mop.   mother of pearl; mustering-out pay

mor   middle of the road

mor. dict.   as directed (Latin *more dicto*)

mor. sol.   in the usual manner (Latin *more solito*)

mort.   mortal(ity); mortgage; mortician; mortuary

mos.   months

mov.   movable; movement; moving

mp   marginal product(ion)

m&p   materials and processes

MP   member of Parliament; military police; mounted police

mpi   marginal propensity to invest

mr   marginal revenue

mrp   machine-readable passport; maximum retail price

ms   months after sight; multiple sclerosis

ms.   manuscript

m/s   months after sight

MS   multiple sclerosis

mss.   manuscripts

mst   mean solar time; mountain standard time

mt   mountain time

m/t   mail transfer; manual transmission

MTN   multilateral trade negotiations

mtr   marginal tax rate

mus.   museum; music

Mus.   Muslim

m&v   meat and vegetables

mvp   most valuable player

m/w   male white

myst.   mysteries; mysterious; mystery; mystic(al)(ism)(s)

myth.   mythological; mythologist; mythology

n   note; number; noun

n.   note; number; noun

na   not applicable; not authorized; not available

n/a   not applicable

nad   not on active duty

nAe   no American equivalent

nag.   net annual gain

nai   no action indicated

n.a.n.   unless it is otherwise noted (Latin *nisi aliter notetur*)

nap.   not at present

narc.   narcotic(s); narcotics agent or officer

narco.   narcotic(s); narcotics hospital or treatment center; narcotics agent or officer

natl.   national

nat'l   national

n/a/v   net asset value

n.b.   note well (Latin *nota bene*)

n/b   no brands; northbound

nc   nuclear capability; numerical control

n/c   no charge; numerical control

NC   numerical control

ncad   net cash against documents

ncd   no can do

nci   no cost item

nco no-cost option; noncommissioned officer

NCO noncommissioned officer

NCOA National Change of Address (service)

nd next day; no date; no decision; no discount

nde near-death experience

ne not exceeding

n/e no effects

nec not elsewhere classified

nec. necessary

nei not elsewhere included; not elsewhere indicated

nem. dis. no one dissenting (Latin *nemine dissentiente*)

neol. neologism

nep new edition pending; not elsewhere provided

ne. rep. do not repeat (Latin *ne repetatur*)

nes not elsewhere specified

nf no funds

n/f no funds

n&f near and far

nfa no further action

nfb no feedback

nfd no further description

nfr no further requirement

nft no fixed time; no forwarding time

ng no go; no good; not given; not good

ni net income

nie not elsewhere included

nimby not in my backyard

nis not in stock

nit   negative income tax

nk   not known

nl   new line; no liability; not licensed; not listed

NL   night letter (telegram)

n/m   no mark

NM   Night Message (telegram)

nmc   no more credit

nmi   new model introduction; no middle initial

n/n   no number; not to be noted

nnp   net national production

NNP   net national production

no.   number

n/o   no orders

noa   not otherwise authorized

nob.   not on board

noct.   by night; nocturnal (Latin *nocte*)

noe   not otherwise enumerated

nohp   not otherwise herein provided

noi   not otherwise identified

nok   next of kin

nol. con.   do not want to contend (Latin *nolo contendere*)

nol. pros.   do not want to prosecute (Latin *nolle prosequi*)

nom.   nominative; nominal

nom. std.   nominal standard

non cul.   not culpable or guilty (Latin *non culpabilis*)

non obs.   notwithstanding (Latin *non obstante*)

non pros.   does not prosecute (Latin *non prosequitur*)

non seq.   it does not follow (Latin *non sequitur*)

no op. no opinion

nop not otherwise provided for

nos no salt added; not otherwise specified

Nov. November

np no place; no publisher; notary public; note payable

n.p. no place; no publisher

n/p net proceeds

NP notary public

ns new series; not specified

NS new style

N.S. new style

nspf not specifically provided for

n/t new terms

n&t nose and throat

nta net tangible assets

nte not to exceed

ntep not to exceed price

ntepq not to exceed price quoted

ntp no title page

nts not to scale

num. number(ed)(ing); numerical; numerologist; nu-
merology

nv new version

n&v nausea and vomiting

nw net worth

nw/m net words per minute

nyp   not yet published

nyr   not yet returned

NYT   *New York Times*

o/a   on account; on or about

oac   on approved credit

ob.   died (Latin *obiit*)

ob-gyn   obstetrician-gynecologist

obit.   obituary

obj.   object(ive)

ob. s.p.   died without issue (Latin *obiit sine prole*)

obt.   he died (Latin *obiit*)

oc   office copy; on camera; open charter

o.c.   in the work cited (Latin *opere citato*)

o/c   overcharge

Oct.   October

o/d   on demand; overdraft

o&d   origin and destination

odc   other direct costs

oe   omissions excepted; omissions expected; open end

o/e   on examination

OE   Old English

o/h   overhaul

ok   correct; okay

oka   otherwise known as

o&m   operation and maintenance

omc   owner may carry (mortgage)

OMC   owner may carry (mortgage)

on a/c   on account

ono   or near offer

oo   office of origin; on order

o/o   on order; order of

o&co   owned and operated

ooa   on or about

o/o/o   out of order

oos   out of stock

oot   out of town

op   old prices; open policy; out of print

op. cit.   in the work cited (Latin *opere citato*)

or.   owner's risk; speech or discourse (Latin *oratio*)

o/r   on request

OR   operating room

os   old series; operating system; out of stock

o.s.   old series

o/s   out of service; out of stock

OS   old style

O.S.   old style

o.s.p.   died without issue (Latin *obiit sine prole*)

o&u   over and under

ovc   other valuable consideration

ow   out of wedlock

owc   owner will carry (mortgage)

OWC   owner will carry (mortgage)

p. page

pa particular average; pending availability; private account

p.a. by the year (Latin *per annum*)

p-a public address (system)

p/a per annum; power of attorney

p&a price and availability; professional and administrative

PAC political action committee

pam. pamphlet

pap. papacy; papal; paper

par. paragraph; parallel

para. parachute; paragraph; parallel

pass. passage; passenger; passive; passport

pass. here and there (Latin *passim*)

pat. patent; patrol; pattern

pax. private automatic exchange

PAX private automatic exchange

p/b paperbook; passbook; pushbutton

pbx private branch exchange

PBX private branch exchange

pc percent; personal computer; petty cash; prices current

p/c percent(age)

p&c put and call

PC personal computer

pct. percent

pd postdate(d); postage due

pd. paid

p.d.   by the day (Latin *per diem*)

p/d   postdated

p&d   pickup and delivery

pdq   pretty damn quick

pe   printer's error

p/e   price-earnings (ratio)

p&e   planning and estimating

per.   period(ic)(icity); person(al)(ate)

p/f   portfolio

PFC   private first class

pg.   page

p&h   postage and handling

pi   personal income; private investigator; productivity index

p&i   principal and interest

PI   private investigator; productivity index

pin.   personal identification number

PIN   personal identification number

pins.   person(s) in need of supervision

pit.   principal, interest, and taxes

pkg.   package

pl.   plural; plate

p/l   payload

p&l   profit and loss

PLC   public limited company

pl&pd   personal loss and personal damage

pls.   please

pm   post mortem

p.m.   afternoon and night (Latin *post meridiem*)

pms   postmenstrual syndrome; premenstrual syndrome

PMS   postmenstrual syndrome; premenstrual syndrome

pmt.   payment

pn   part number; promissory note

p/n   part number; please note; promissory note

p.n.g.   an unacceptable person (Latin *persona non grata*)

p/o   part of

PO   post office

P.O.   post office

pod.   payable on death; port of debarkation; port of departure

pol. sci.   political science

pops   popular concerts; popular tunes

por   payable on receipt

pos   point of sale

posslq   person(s) of opposite sex sharing living quarters

POW   prisoner of war

pp   parcel post

pp.   pages

p. pa.   by proxy (Latin *per procura*)

ppd.   prepaid

P.P.S.   additional postscript (Latin *post postscriptum*)

p&q   peace and quiet

pr.   pair; printer

p/r   payroll

pref.   preface; preferred

pre-op   preoperation(al)

prep.   preparation; preparatory; prepare; preposition

pres.   present

prf.   preface or introduction (Latin *praefatio*)

princ.   principle; principal

prob.   probability; probable; probably; problem(atic)-(atical)

proc.   procedure; proceedings

prod.   product(ion)

prof.   profession(al); professor

pron.   pronoun

prop art   propaganda art

pro tem.   for the time being (Latin *pro tempore*)

P.S.   written after (Latin *post scriptum*)

PSI   pollution standards index

Pst   Pacific standard time

pt   physical therapy; private terms

Pt   Pacific time

pto   please turn over

pub.   public(ation); publicity; publish(ed)(er)(ing); published by

pur.   purchase(r); purchasing; pursuant; pursuit

pvt.   private (general)

Pvt.   private (military)

pw   prisoner of war

p/w   parallel with

px   please exchange

pyt   pretty young thing

Q   question; query

q&a   question and answer

q/c   quick change

qcd   quit-claim deed

q.e.   which is (Latin *quod est*)

q.e.d.   that which was to be proved or demonstrated (Latin *quod erat demonstrandum*)

q.e.f.   that which was to be done (Latin *quod erat faciendum*)

q.e.i.   that which was to be discovered (Latin *quod erat inveniendum*)

qli   quality-of-life index

QLI   quality-of-life index

qr.   quarter

quant.   quantity

q.v.   which see (Latin *quod vide*)

r   recto; reigned

r/a   return(ed) to author

rad   released from active duty; returned to active duty

radn.   radiation

rai   random access and inquiry

rap   frank talk (slang)

rap.   repartee or witty retort (French *repartie*)

r/b   reentry body

r&b   rhythm and blues; room and board

rbi   request better information

rbt.   rabbit

rc   radio code; rate of change; reverse course

r/c   reconsign(ed)

r&c   rail and canal

rca   replacement-cost accounting

rcd.   received

rd   required date

r&d   research and development

R&D   research and development

rdd   required delivery date

rdt   reserve duty training

rdt&e   research, develop(ment), test, and evaluate(evaluation)

RDT&E   research, develop(ment), test, and evaluate (evaluation)

rdy.   ready

re   revised edition

r/e   rate of exchange

rec.   receipt; receive; record; recreation

recon.   reconcentration; reconciliation; recondite; recondition; reconnaissance; reconsign(ed)(ment); reconstruct(ed)(ion); reconversion; reconvert(ed); reconvey(ance)(ed)

ref.   refer(ee)(ence); reform(atory); refraction; refresher

refrig.   refrigerate; refrigeration; refrigerator

reg.   region; register; regular; regulate; regulation

relig.   religion; religious

rep.   report; representative

repr.   reprint(ed)

res.   rescue; research(er); reservation; reserve; reservoir; resign; resistant; resolution

ret rational emotive therapy

rev. reverse(d); review(ed); revise(d); revision; revolution

Rev. reverend

rev. a/c revenue account

rev. ed. revised edition

rfb request for bid

RFD rural free delivery

rfi ready for issue

rfo request for factory order

rin report identification number

riv. river; rivet(ed)

rje remote job entry

rkg radiocardiogram

rkt. rocket

r/l radio location

r&l rail and lake

rm raw material

rm. ream (paper); room

rna ribonucleic acid

RNA ribonucleic acid

ro receive only

r/o roll out; rule out

r&o rail and ocean

roa received on account; return on assets

robrep robbery report

roc return on capital

roi return on investment

rom.   roman (type style)

romv   return on market value

rop   run of paper; run of press

rotn.   rotation

rp   relay paid; role play(ing)

r&r   rape and robbery; rest and recreation; rest and recuperation; rock and roll

rsg   receiving stolen goods

RSVP   please reply (French *répondez s'il vous plaît*)

R.S.V.P.   please reply (French *répondez s'il vous plaît*)

rt   radio telephone; reaction time; real time; receive-transmit; round trip

rtb   return to base

rte   ready to eat (foods)

rts   radar tracking station

rtw   ready to wear

rub.   rubber

rv   recreation vehicle; reentry vehicle

r/v   reentry vehicle

RV   recreation vehicle; reentry vehicle

r/w   read/write; right of way

r&w   rail and water

r-w-r   rail to water to rail

ry   railway; relay

s   son

/s/   signed

sa   subject to approval

s/a   storage area

sac   sacral; sacrament(al); sacred

sae   self-addressed envelope

sai   sell or sold as is

s.a.l.   according to the rules of art (Latin *secundum artis leges*)

SALT   Strategic Arms Limitation Talks

salv.   salvage

sam   served available market; student accountability model

SAM   student accountability model

sanr   subject to approval—no risks

sap.   soon as possible

sar   search and rescue; short-term acquisition and retrieval

sare   self-addressed return envelope

sas   so and so; surface to air to surface

sase   self-addressed stamped envelope

sat.   satellite; systematic assertive therapy

Sat.   Saturday

sav.   savings

sax.   saxophone

saxist   saxophonist

sb   small business; switchboard

s/b   should be; surface based

sbn   standard book number(ing)

sbo   specific behavioral objectives

sbs   small business satellite

s-b-s   side by side

sc   separate; small caps (small capital letters); statistical control

sc.   to wit; namely (Latin *scilicet*)

s/c   single column

s&c   search and clear; shipper and carrier

scan.   suspected child abuse and neglect

scat.   supersonic commercial air transport

SCAT   supersonic commercial air transport

scc   specific clauses and conditions

scd   security coding device

sch.   schedule; school

sci.   science; scientific; scientist

Sci. Am.   *Scientific American*

sci-fi   science fiction

scil.   to wit; namely (Latin *scilicet*)

scrip.   scriptural; scripture

script   manuscript

script.   scriptural; scripture

scrn.   screen(ing)(s)

scs   satellite control system; space command station

sculpt.   sculpture

sd   standard deviation; sudden death

s.d.   without date (Latin *sine die*)

s&d   search and destroy; song and dance

sdbl   sight draft bill of lading

sds   sudden death syndrome

se   single entry; standard error; straightedge

s&e   services and equipment

sec. second(ary); secret; section; security

sec. according to (Latin *secundum*)

sec. art. according to art (Latin *secundum artem*)

sec. leg. according to law (Latin *secundum legem*)

sec. nat. according to nature (Latin *secundum naturam*)

sec. reg. according to the rules or regulations (Latin *secundum regulam*)

sect. section; sector

sec'y secretary

sed. sedative; sediment(ation)

s.e.e.o. excepting errors and omissions (Latin *salvis erroribus et omissis*)

seg. segment(ation)(ed)(s); segregate; segregation(ist)

sel socioeconomic level; sound-exposure level

sel. select(ed)(ee)(or)

sep. separate; separation

Sept. September

seq. the following (Latin *sequens*); it follows (Latin *sequitur*)

ser. serial; series

serv. service

sess. session

sf safety factor; salt free; science fiction; sinking fund; standard form

s.f. near the end (Latin *sub finem*)

s/f shift forward; store and forward

s&f stock and fixtures

s&fa shipping and forwarding agent

sfrr sinking fund rate of return

sgd.   signed

sgo   surgery, gynecology, and obstetrics

Sgt.   sergeant

sh   sexual harassment

s/h   shorthand

ship.   shipment; shipping

shr.   share

s.h.v.   under this work (Latin *sub hoc voce*)

s&i   stocked and issued

sid   sudden infant death

sig.   signal(ing); signature

sig. nom. pro.   sign with the proper name (Latin *signa nomine proprio*)

s-i-l   sister-in-law

sim.   similar; simile; simulate

simp.   simple

si n. val.   if of no value (Latin *si non valet*)

sip.   standard inspection procedure

sit.   stopping in transit

SI unit   International System of Units (French *Systeme International unit*)

siw   self-inflicted wounds

skel.   skeletal; skeleton

sl   sales letter; standard label

s.l.   according to law (Latin *secundum legem*); no place of publication (Latin *sine loco*)

s-l   short-long

s/l   self-loading

s&l   savings and loan

sla   single-line approach

slc   straight-line capacity

s.l. et a.   without place and year (Latin *sine loco et anno*)

slr   self-loading rifle; single-lens reflex

sm   secondary memory; service module; servomechanism; strategic missile

s-m   sadist-masochist; sadomasochism

s&cm   sadism and masochism

sma   subject-matter area

smat   see me about this

smaze   smoke and haze

sm. caps   small capitals (small capital letters)

smist   smoke and mist

smm   standard method of measurement

smo   senior medical officer

smog   smoke and fog

smp   social marginal productivity; sound motion picture

s.m.p.   without male issue (Latin *sine mascula prole*)

smsa   standard metropolitan statistical area

SMSA   standard metropolitan statistical area

smt   ship's mean time

smust   smoke and dust

sn   serial number; service number; stock number

s.n.   according to nature (Latin *secundum naturam*); without name (Latin *sine nomine*)

s/n   serial number; service number; stock number

snlr   services no longer required

sns   sympathetic nervous system

so.   seller's option; senior officer; sex offender; shipping order; ship's option; shop order; south(ern); standing order; supply office(r)

s-o   shutoff

s/o   shipping order; son of

soa   state of the art

sob.   see order blank

s-o-b   son of a bitch (slang)

soc.   society; social(ist)

soc. sci.   social science

soc. sec.   social security

sol.   solution (Latin *solutio*)

solv.   solvent

son.   sonata

sop.   soprano; standard operating procedure

sor   specific operating requirements

s-o-r   stimulus-organism-response

sot.   shower over tub

sota   state of the art

sov   special orientation visit

sow.   sent on their way

sp   self-propelled; selling price; single purpose; special purpose; standard practice; starting point; stop payment

sp.   species; spelling

s.p.   without issue (Latin *sine prole*)

s&p   systems and procedures

sp. del.   special delivery

spe   special-purpose equipment

spec. special(ly)(ty); specie(s); specific(ally)(ation); specimen; spectacle; speculation

spi scientific performance index

s.p.l. without legitimate offspring (*sine prole legitima*)

s.p.m. without male issue (Latin *sine prole mascula*)

sp. n. new species (Latin *species nova*)

sp. nov. new species (Latin *species nova*)

spp. species (Latin *species*)

s.p.s. without surviving issue (Latin *sine prole supersite*)

sq. squadron; square

sqc statistical quality control

sqd. squad

sqr supplier quality rating

sr scientific research; standard range; stimulus response; surveillance radar

Sr. sister (religious)

srac short-run average cost

SRAM short-range attack missile

srm standard reference missile

SRM short-range missile

sro single-room-occupancy hotel

srs short-run supply

ss sample size; single signal; single source; social security; solid state; stainless steel; steamship; supersonic; suspended sentence

ss. namely (Latin *scilicet*); written above (Latin *supra scriptum*)

s/s same size

s to s ship to shore; station to station

ssi   small-scale integration

SSM   surface-to-surface missile

ssp   subspecies

ssr   secondary surveillance radar

ssv   ship-to-surface vessel

st   stock transfer; surface tension; survival time

st.   saint; stanza; state; street

st.   let it (copy crossed out) stand (Latin *stet*)

s&t   science and technology

sta.   station(ary)(ery)

stab.   stabilizer

stag.   stagger(ed)

stat.   statistic(al); statuary; statue; statute

stat.   immediately (Latin *statim*)

std   salinity, temperature, depth; sexually transmitted disease

std.   standard

std. by   stand by

sten.   stencil

steno.   stenographer; stenography; stenotype

STEP   supplemental training and employment program

stereo   stereophonic

stet   let stand what has been crossed out

stew.   steward(ess)

st. ex.   stock exchange

sti   service and taxes included

stmt.   statement

sto   standard temperature and pressure; standing order

stp   seawater treatment plant; solar thermal power; standard temperature and pressure

sts   ship to shore

stud.   student

stv   subscription television

subj.   subject; subjunctive

subset   subscriber set

suc.   succeed; success(or)

sud   sudden unexpected/unexplained death

sui. rep.   suicide report

sum.   take (Latin *sume*)

Sun.   Sunday

sup.   above (Latin *supra*)

supp.   supplement

suppl.   supplement

supra cit.   cited above (Latin *supra citato*)

supv.   supervise; supervisor

surg.   surgeon; surgery; surgical

surv.   survey(ing)(or)

sv   sailing vessel; security violation

s.v.   under the word (Latin *sub verbo*)

s/v   surrender value

s.v.p.   if you please (French *s'il vous plaît*)

S.V.P.   if you please (French *s'il vous plaît*)

sw   seawater; shipper's weights; shortwave; stock width

s-w   shortwave

s/w   seaworthy; standard weight

s&w   salaries and wages; surveillance and warning

swm   standards, weights, and measures

swoc   subject word out of context

syd   sum of the year's digits

sym.   symbol(ic)(ism); symmetric(al); symmetry; symphonic; symphony

symb.   symbol(ic)(ism)

syn.   synagogue; synonym(ous); syntax; synthetic

sync.   synchronize; synchronous

syph.   syphilis

syr.   syrup

sys.   system(atic)(atization)(atize)(ic)(s)

sz.   size

t   temperature

T   temperature

ta   target area; teaching assistant; time and attention; travel allowance

t.a.   as the records show (Latin *testantibus actis*)

t-a   toxin-antitoxin

t/a   trading as

t&ca   taken and accepted; tonsils and adenoids

t of a   'terms of agreement

tab.   table; tablet; tabulate(d); tabulation; tabulator

tac   try and collect

tac.   tactic(al)(s)

tah   temperature, altitude, humidity

targ.   target

taut.   tautology

taw   twice a week

tax.   taxation; taxes; taxonomy

tb   time base; trial balance; tuberculosis

t&cb   top and bottom

TB   tuberculosis

tba   to be announced; to be approved; to be assigned; to be audited

tbb   to be billed

tbe   to be edited; to be executed

tbn   to be named; to be noted

tbo   to be ordered

tbr   to be rented

tbsn.   tablespoon

tbsp.   tablespoon

tc   terra cotta; total cost; true course

t/c   tabulating card

tcb   take care of business

tcp   traffic control panel

td   technical director; time delay; time of departure; touchdown

t/d   table of distribution; time deposit

tdb   total disability benefit

tdp   technical development plans

tdpfo   temporary duty pending further orders

tdrs   tracking and data relay satellite

tds   temperature, depth, salinity

te   table of equipment; technical exchange; tenants/tenancy by the entirety; trial and error

t&e   testing and evaluation; training and evaluation; travel and entertainment; trial and error

tech.   technic(al)(ian)(s); technique(s); technological; technology

tel.   telegraph; telephone; television

tele.   television

telecom.   telecommunication

telecon   telephone communication

telly   television

temp.   temper(ature)(ed)(ing); temporary

ten. com.   tenants/tenancy in common

term.   terminal; terminate; terminology

tf   till forbidden

t/f   true/false

t/g   tracking and guidance

t&h   transportation and handling

theat.   theater; theatrical

theol.   theologian; theological; theologist; theology

thi   temperature-humidity index

tho'   though

thou.   thousand

thro'   through

thro' b/l   through bill of lading

Thrs.   Thursday

thru   through

t/i   target identification

tifr   total investment for return

'til   until

tio take it off; time in office

tip. truly important person

tks. thanks

tl time limit; time line; total load; transmission line; truck load(ing)

t/l total loss

tlc tender loving care

TLC tender loving care

tly. tally

tm trademark

t/m test and maintenance

tmp total mind power

tntc too numerous to count

to telephone order; turn off

t/o takeoff

toc table of contents

tod time of day; time of delivery

toe. term of enlistment; total operating expense

tof time of flight

tol. tolerance

too. time of origin

tor time of receipt

tow. tug of war

tp title page

t/p test panel

tr. transpose

t/r transmit/receive

trad. traditional

trag.   tragedy

trans.   transitive; translated; transportation; transaction

trav.   travel

treas.   treasure(r); treasury

trgt.   target

ts   time sharing; traffic signal; typescript; type specification

t&s   toilet and shower

tsvp.   please turn over (French *tournez s'il vous plaît*)

t&t   time and temperature

Tues.   Tuesday

tut.   tutor(ial)

tv   television; total volume

TV   television

tvc   total variable cost

twds.   tradewinds

twp.   township

typ.   typical; typing; typist; typographer; typography; typewriter

type.   typewriter; typewriting

tyvm   thank you very much

U.   university

uaf   unit authorization file

ual   upper acceptance limit

UAM   underwater-to-air missile

uas   upper air space

uc   uppercase (capital letters)

ucb unless caused by

ucc universal copyright convention

ucs universal character set

ufa until further advised

ufn until further notice

ufo unidentified flying object

UFO unidentified flying object

ug underground

ugt. urgent

u.i. as below (Latin *ut infra*)

u/i unit of issue

uis urban industrial society

u/l upper limit

u&lc upper and lowercase (capital and small letters)

ult. at or of the last (Latin *ultimo*)

univ. universal; university

unodir unless otherwise directed

unoind unless otherwise indicated

uo undelivered orders

u/o used on

u&o use and occupancy

up. underproof(ed)(ing); unpaged; upper

upc universal production code

upd. unpaid

urb. urban

urg. urgent

us. unconditional stimulus; under seal; undersize; uniform sales *u.s.*   as above (Latin *ut supra*)

u/s   unserviceable

usc   under separate cover

usea   undersea

USM   underwater-to-surface missile

usu.   usual(ly)

usurp.   to be used (Latin *usurpandus*)

u.s.w.   and so forth (German *und so weiter*)

ut   universal time

u/t   untrained

ut dict.   as ordered (Latin *ut dictum*)

ut inf.   as below (Latin *ut infra*)

ut sup.   as above (Latin *ut supra*)

u-v   ultraviolet

uw   unconventional warfare; underwater; underwriter

u/w   underwater; under way; underwriter; used with

ux.   wife (Latin *uuxor*)

v.   verb; verse; verso

var.   variable; variant; variation; variety

vb.   verb(al)

vc   valuation clause; visual communication

veg.   vegetable; vegetarian(ism); vegetation

veh.   vehicle; vehicular

ven.   veneer(ing); venerable; venereal

vent.   ventilate; ventilating; ventilation; ventilator; venture

verb. et lit. word for word; exact (Latin *verbatim et literatim*)

vesp. evening (Latin *vesper*)

vet. veteran; veterinarian; veterinary

v. et. also see (Latin *vide etiam*)

vf vertical file

vg very good

vho very high output

vhp very high performance

v.i. see below (Latin *vide infra*)

vib. vibrate; vibration; vibratory

vic. vicinity

vid. see (Latin *vide*)

vip very important person; very important people

vis. viscera; visible; visibility; visual

vit. vital; vitamin

vit. stat. vital statistics

viz. namely (Latin *videlicet*)

vlr very long range

voc. vocal(ist); vocation(al)

voc. ed. vocational education

vol. volume; volunteer

vop valued as in original policy

vot voluntary overtime

voy. voyage

vr variable response

vs very soluble

vs. versus

v.s.   see above (Latin *vide supra*)

vsi   very seriously ill; very slight imperfection; very slight inclusion

vsl   variable safety level

vt   variable time

v.v.   conversely (Latin *vice versa*)

v&v   verification and validation

vy   various years

wa   warm air; will advise; with average

wae   when actually employed

waf   with all faults

war.   warrant; with all risks

warr.   warranty

WASP   white Anglo-Saxon Protestant

wats   wide-area telephone service

WATS   Wide Area Telecommunications Service

w/b   westbound

wc   working capital; workers' compensation

w/c   with corrections

wca   worst-case analysis

w/d   wind direction

w/e   weekend

Wed.   Wednesday

wf   wrong font

w/f   white female

w&f   water and feed

wgt.   weight

wh   water heater; withholding

w/h   withholding

wi   wrought iron

wia   wounded in action

WIA   wounded in action

wip   work in process; work in progress

wit.   witness

wittos   women in the transition of separation

wk.   walk; weak; week; work; wreck

wl   water level; working level

w/m   white male

wnb   will not be

wo   wait order; without; work order; write out; written order

w/o   without

woh   work on hand

wop   with other property; without papers

wor   without our responsibility

wp   will proceed; word processing; working paper; working party

w/p   without prejudice

wpa   with particular average

wpc   water pollution control

wpi   wholesale price index

WPI   wholesale price index

wr.   write out

w/r   water and rail

w&r   water and rail

w. ref. with reference

ws weather station; working space

w&t wear and tear

ww warehouse warrant; waterworks; wrong word

w/w wall to wall

w/wo with or without

xch exchange

xcp without coupon

xd ex (without) dividend

xi ex (without) interest

xin without interest

xn excluding new (shares)

xp express paid

xpr ex (without) privileges

xref cross-reference

xrt ex (without) rights

xs cross-section; extra strong

xsect cross-section

ya young adult

yap young aspiring professional

yb yearbook

ycw you can't win

yd. yard

yl yield limit; young lady

y/o years old

yob   year of birth
yod   year of death
yr.   year
ytd   year to date
yumpie   young upwardly mobile professional
yuppie   young urban professional

z   zero; zone
zeg   zero economic growth
zn.   zone
zo   zero output
zof   zone of fire

TECHNICAL ABBREVIATIONS

a ampere; arc; atto (prefix: one quintillionth)

A absolute

Å angstrom

aac automatic aperture control

aai azimuth angle increment

aao amino-acid oxidase

aas aortic arch syndrome

aat auditory attending task

aavd automatic alternate voice/data

a/b acid/base (ratio)

ab-a abampere

abact. abacterial

abamp absolute ampere

abm automated batch mixing

ABM automated batch mixing

abp absolute boiling point; actual block processor

ABP actual block processor

abs.   absolute

ac   alternating current; automatic analog computer; axiocervical

aca   acetic acid

acb   air circuit breaker

acc   accumulator

ACC   accumulator

accw   alternating current continuous wave

acd   acid citrate dextrose

ACD   acid citrate dextrose

ACDMS   Automated Control of Document Management System

ace.   alcohol-chloroform-ether; automatic circuit exchange

aces   automatic control evaluation simulator

acet.   acetone

acetl.   acetylene

acf   advanced communication function

acg   apex cardiogram

ACG   apex cardiogram

achrom.   achromatism

acia   asynchronous communications interface adapter

acid.   acidosis

ACL   Audit Command Language

acls   automatic carrier landing system

acm   area-composition machine; automatic coding machine

ACMS   Advanced Configuration Management System

acn   automatic celestial navigation

acous. coup.   acoustic coupler

acp   azimuth change pulse

acpu   auxiliary computer power unit

acr   abandon call and retry

acre.   automatic checkout and readiness equipment

acs   alternating-current synthesizer

acsg   alternating-current signal generator

ACSS   analog computer subsystem; Automated Color-Separation System

acu   address control unit; automatic calling unit

acw   alternating continuous waves

ac/w   acetone/water

a/d   analog to digital

ADABAS   Adaptable Data Base System

adac   automatic direct analog computer

adacx   automatic data acquisition and computer complex

ADAIS   Aerodynamic Data Analysis and Integration System

adaline   adaptive linear neuron

ADAPS   Automatic Display and Plotting System

adar   analog-to-digital-to-analog recording

adat   automatic data accumulation and transfer

adc   analog-to-digital converter

ADC   analog-to-digital converter

ADCSP   Advanced Defense Communications Satellite Program

add.   airborne digital decoder

addar   automatic digital data acquisition and recording

addm   automated drafting and digitizing machine

ADDR address

ADDS Automatic Direct Distance Dialing System

ade automatic data entry

ADEMS Advanced Diagnostic Engine Monitoring System

ADES Automatic Digital Encoding System

adf automatic direction finder

adi automatic direction indicator

ADIOS Automatic Digital Input-Output System

ADIS Automatic Data Interchange System

ADJ adjust

adl automatic data link

ADL automatic data link

adma automatic drafting machine

adp automatic/advanced data processing

adpe automatic data processing equipment

ADPO Automatic Data Processing Operations

ADPS Automatic Data Processing System

adr analog-to-digital recorder

ADR adder

adrt analog data recording transcriber

adtn automatic digital test unit; auxiliary data-translation unit

ADV advance

advm adaptive delta voice modulation

aei azimuth error indicator

aep auditory-evoked potential

aer auditory-evoked response

aerodyn.   aerodynamics

aex   automatic electronic exchange

af   audiofidelity; audiofrequency; autofocus

afa   azimuth follow-up amplifier

afc   automatic frequency control

afm   antifriction metal

afpa   automatic flow process analysis

afr   acceptable failure rate; air-fuel ratio; automatic field/format recognition

aft.   automatic fine tuning

agc   automatic gain control

agd   axial gear differential

a/g   albumin/globulin (ratio)

agt   antiglobulin test

agw   actual gross weight

agz   actual ground zero

ah   ampere hour

a-h   ampere-hour

Ah   ampere-hour; hyperopic astigmatism

ahm   ampere-hour meter

ahp   air horsepower; aviation horsepower

ahs   ablative heat shield

ai   azimuth indicator

aich   automatic integrated container handling

AIDS   Advanced Integrated Data System

AILS   Advanced Integrated Landing System

aimo   air mold

AIMS   Automatic Industrial Management System

air. average injection rate

air hp. air horsepower

airmap air monitoring, analysis, and prediction

ais automatic interplanetary system

AIS Advanced Information System

ait autoignition temperature

aiu advanced instrumentation unit

aiw auroral intrasonic wave

alairs advance low-altitude infrared-reconnaissance sensor

albi air-launched booster intercept

alcc algebraic components and coefficients

alcid alcohol and acid

alcom algebraic compiler; algebraic computer

aldep automated layout design program

aldp automatic language-data processing

ALERT Automatic Linguistic Extraction and Retrieval Technique

ALGOL Algebraically Oriented Language; Algorithmic Language

alit automatic line insulation tracker

allcat all critical atmospheric turbulence

allp audiolingual language programming

alp. assembly language program; autocode list processing; automated language processing

ALP assembly language program

alphanumeric alphabetical and numerical

als automatic line supervision

alt. alternator; altimeter

altac   algebraic translator and compiler

altran   algebraic translator

alu   arithmetic and logic unit

am.   amplitude modulation; auditory memory

a/m   ampere per meter; auto/manual

A/m   ampere per meter

amc   automatic message counting

AMC   automatic message counting

am/fm   amplitude modulation/frequency modulation

ami   acute myocardial infarction

ammeter   amperemeter

amp   average mean pressure

amp.   ampere; amplification; amplifier; amplitude

amp. hr.   ampere hour

ampl   a macroprogramming language

ampp   advanced microprogrammable processor

AMPS   Automatic Message Processing System

amp-turns   ampere-turns

amr   automatic message routing

AMR   automatic message routing

amu   atomic mass unit

amw   actual measurement weight

anacom   analog computer

ane   acoustic noise environment

ang.   angiogram; angle; angular

ani   automatic number identification

anl   automatic noise limiter

anov   analysis of variance

ans autonomic nervous system

ant. d anterior diameter

antilog. antilogarithm

ant. pit. anterior pituitary

ao axio-occlusal

aoa abort once around

aoc automatic output control

aoi angle of incidence

aor angle of reflection

aos add or subtract; angle of sight

aosp automatic operating and scheduling program

ap attached processor

a/p after perpendicular; angle point

apa axial pressure angle

apache. analog programming and checking

apar automatic programming and recording

a-part. alpha particle(s)

APAS Automatic Performance Analysis System

apc aperture current; automatic performance control; automatic phase control

apdl algorithmic processor description language

aper. aperture

apex. assembler and process executive

apf animal protein factor

api air position indicator

apl a programming language

apld automatic program locate device

apmi area precipitation measurement indicator

apn average peak noise

apoth. apothecaries; apothecary

app automatic priority processing

APP automatic priority processing

apr aerial photographic reconnaissance

aps accessory power supply; auxiliary power supply; auxiliary propulsion system

apt. automatically programmed tools

APT Automatic Programmed Tools

apth. apthong

apti actions per time interval

apu auxiliary power unit

ar achievement ratio; address register; aspect ratio; auditory reception

AR address register

arccos. arccosine

arccot. arccotangent

arccsc. arccosecant

arcos arc cosine

arcsec. arcsecant

arcsin. arcsine

arctan. arctangent

arda analog recording dynamic analyzers

are. air reactor experiment

ARE air reactor experiment

arm. armature

arpl a retrieval-process language

ARQ automatic repeat request; automatic request for correction

art. automatic reporting telephone

aru analog remote unit; audio response unit

asc automatic sequence control; automatic switching center; auxiliary switch closed

ASCII American Standard Code for Information Interchange

asdi automated selective dissemination of information

asfx assembly fixture

asi air-speed indicator; azimuthal speed indicator

ASKA Automatic System for Kinematic Analysis

aslo assembly layout

aslt advanced solid logic technology

asm auxiliary-storage management

asmbl. assemble

assmblr. assembler

asn average sample number

aso auxiliary switch open

asp. attached support processor; automatic switching panel; automatic system procedure

asr answer-send-receive; automatic send-receive

ast absolute space time

ASTIP Army Scientific and Technical Information Program

ast. t astronomical time

asv acceleration switching valve; automatic self-verification

at. ampere-ton; ampere-turn; atmosphere

At ampere-ton; ampere-turn

atan arc tangent

ate. altitude transmitting equipment; automatic test equipment

atl analog threshold logic

ATLAS Automatic Tabulating, Listing, and Sorting System

atm. atmosphere

at. m atomic mass

at/m ampere turns per meter

At/m ampere turns per meter

atmos. atmosphere; atmospheric

atm. press. atmospheric pressure

at. no. atomic number

atoms. automated technical order maintenance sequence

atp adenosine triphosphate

atpd ambient temperature and pressure—dry

atps ambient temperature and pressure—saturated (with water vapor)

atr advanced test reactor

atrid automatic target recognition, identification, and detection

ats absolute temperature scale

ATS Acoustic Transmission System; Acquisition and Tracking System

atu atomic time unit

at. vol. atomic volume

at. wt. atomic weight

au angstrom unit; astronomical unit

Au gold

audre audio response; automatic digit recognizer

AUTODIN   automated digital network

autosate   automobile data systems analysis technique

autostrad   automated system for transportation data

AUTOVON   automatic voice network

av   acid value; aortic value

av.   average; avoirdupois

ava   automatic voice alarm

avc   automatic volume control

avd   automatic voice data; automatic voltage digitizer

avdp.   avoirdupois

avi   air velocity index

avl   average length

avo   ampere-volt-ohm

avr   aortic valve replacement

av. temp.   average temperature

aw   atomic weight

a/w   actual weight

awf   acceptable work-load factor; adrenal weight factor

awu   atomic weight unit

ax.   axial; axes; axiom; axis

axfl   axial flow

axgrad   axial gradient

az.   azimuth

azi.   azimuth

azm.   azimuth

azr   automatic zero reset

b   bit

ba   binary add

BA   binary add

bac   binary asymmetric channel

BAC   binary asymmetric channel

badc   binary asymmetric dependent channel

BADC   binary asymmetric dependent channel

bal   blood alcohol level

BAM   basic access method

bao   basal acid output

bapl   baseplate

bar.   barometer; barometric; base address register; buffer address register

BAR   buffer address register

bas   basic air speed

BASIC   Beginner's All-Purpose Symbolic Instruction Code

basicpac   basic processor and computer

b-a test   blood-alcohol test

bau   basic assembly unit; British absolute unit

baw   bare aluminum wire

bb   ball bearing

bbj   ball-bearing joint

bbl.   barrel

bbls./day   barrels per day

bbp   building-block principle

bbt   basal body temperature

bc   binary code; binary counter; bioconversion

bcb   binary-code box

bcc   beam-coupling coefficient

bcd   binary-coded data; binary-coded decimal

b/cd   barrels per calendar day

bcdc   binary-coded decimal counter

bcm   basic control monitor

bd.   baud

bdl   baseline demonstration laser

bdl.   bundle

bdu   basic device/display unit

bem   behavior engineering model

BEM   behavior engineering model

bene.   benzine

besi   bus electronic-scanning indicator

bev.   bevel

bev   billion electron volts

BeV   billion electron volts

bex   broadband exchange

b-f   beat-frequency

bfbaln   buffer boundary alignment

bfe   beam-forming electrode

bfl   back focal length

bfr   biologic false reactor; blood-flow rate; bone-formation rate

bfr.   buffer

bft   biofeedback training

bgh   bovine growth hormone

BGTT   Borderline Glucose Tolerance Test

bhp   boiler horsepower; brake horsepower

bhr   basal heart rate

bi   bacteriological index; burn index; buffer index

bi.   binary

BI   binary

b/i   battery inverter

bicarb.   (sodium) bicarbonate

bidec   binary-to-decimal converter

bil.   billion

bim   beginning-of-information marker

bin.   binary

bioact.   bioactive; bioactivity

bionics   biology and electronics

bir   basic incidence rate

BISAM   Basic Indexed Sequential-Access Method

bisync   binary synchronous computer

bit.   binary digit

biu   basic information unit

bivar.   bivariant

bix   binary information exchange

bizmac   business machine computer

BIZNET   (American) Business Network

bjf   batch-job format

bksp.   backspace

bl   baseline

bl.   bale

blc   boundary-layer control

blkcut   block count

blodi   block diagram

bls   binary light switch

blsw   barrels of load salt water

blsw/d   barrels of salt water per day

blt   blood type; bottom-loading transporter

BLT   bottom-loading transporter

bm   basal metabolism; board measure; body mass; bone marrow; buffer mark; buffer modules

BM   buffer mark; buffer modules

bmep   brake mean effective pressure

bmp   brake mean power

bmr   basal metabolic rate

bms   balanced magnetic switch

bn   binary number (system)

BN   binary number (system)

bno   barrels of new oil

bof   beginning of file

BOF   beginning of file

boi   branch output interrupt

BOI   branch output interrupt

bolt.   beam-of-light transistor

bopd   barrels of oil per day

bos   basic operating system

bot   beginning of tape

BOT   beginning of tape

bo&w   barrels of oil and water

bp   back pressure; blood pressure; boiling point

b/p   blood pressure

bpa   broadband power amplifier

bpcd   barrels per calendar day

bpd barrels per day; boxes per day

bpg break pulse generator

bph barrels per hour

bpi bits per inch; bytes per inch

bpm barrels per minute

bps bits per second; bytes per second

BPS Basic Programming Support (system); Basic Programming System

bpt boiling point

bpu base production unit

br. branch

BR branch

brdf bidirectional reflectance distribution function

brs break request signal

BRS break request signal

Br. std. British standard

bs backspace (character); binary subtraction

BS backspace (character)

BSAM Basic Sequential Access Method

bsbg burst and synchronous bit generator

bsc basic message switching center; binary synchronous communication

bscn bit scan

bsd bit storage density

bsdc binary symmetric dependent channel

bse base support equipment

BSG British standard gage

bsh. bushel

bsic   binary-symmetric independent channel

bssp   broadbank solid-state preamplifier

bsw/d   barrels of salt water per day

btb   bus tie breaker

btdl   basic transient diode logic

bte   battery terminal equipment

btf   barrels of total fluid

bti   bank-and-turn indicator

btj   ball-tooth joint

btl   beginning tape level

btlv   biological threshold limit valve

btp   body temperature and pressure

btr   bus transfer

btu   basic transmission unit; British thermal unit

Btu   British thermal unit

BTU   British thermal unit

bu   base unit

bu.   bushel

buic   backup interceptor control

bup   backup plate

burd   biplane ultralight research device

burp.   backup rate of pitch

bv   biological valve; breakdown voltage

bvd   beacon video digitizer

bvp   beacon video processor

bvw   binary voltage weigher

bwa   backward-wave amplifier; bent-wire antenna

bwc basic weight calculator; broadband waveguide oscillator

bw/d barrels of water per day

bw/h barrels of water per hour

bw/m barrels of water per minute

bwo backward-wave oscillator

bwos backward-wave oscillator synchronizer

bwpd barrels of water per day

bwph barrels of water per hour

bwpm barrels of water per minute

bwv back-water valve

bxs. boxes

by. billion years

c calorie (large); carbohydrates; centi (prefix: one hundredth); coefficient; computer; cycle; speed of light

C calculated weight; candle; Celsius; Centigrade; cold

ca channel adapted

c/a center angle

caa computer amplifier alarm

cab. coronary artery bypass

cac cardiac-accelerator center

cacb compressed-air circuit breaker

cad. cartridge-activated device; computer-aided design

CAD computer-aided design

cad/cam computer-aided design/computer-aided manufacturing

CAD/CAM computer-aided design/computer-aided manufacturing

CADPOS Communications and Data Processing Operations System

cadss combined analog-digital systems simulator

cafe. corporate average fuel economy

cafga computer applications for the graphic arts

cai computer-aided instruction

CAI computer-aided instruction

caiop computer analog input-output

cal computer-aided learning; conversational algebraic language

cal. calorie (small)

CAL computer-aided learning; Conversational Algebraic Language

calc. calculate

CALC calculator

calm. collected algorithms for learning machines

cam. central-address memory; computer-addressed memory; computer-aided manufacturing

CAM computer-aided manufacturing

cama centralized automatic message accounting

camel. computer-assisted machine loading

CAN cancel (character)

cap. computer-aided production

CAP computer-aided production

car. computer-assisted retrieval

CAR computer-assisted retrieval

card. compact automatic retrieval device; compact automatic retrieval display

CARR carriage

case. common-access switching equipment; computer-automated support equipment

cat. computer-assisted teaching; computer-assisted training

CAT computer-assisted teaching; computer-assisted training

cau command arithmetic units

caw cam-action wheel; channel address word

cax community automatic exchange

cb circuit breaker; container base

c-b circuit breaker

c/bale cents per bale

cbe chemical binding effect; circuit-board extractor

cbfm constant bandwidth frequency modulation

cbi computer-based information

c/bush. cents per bushel

cbx computerized branch exchange; computerized business exchange

CBX computerized branch exchange; computerized business exchange

ccb command control block; convertible circuit breaker

ccc central computer complex; command control console; computer-command control

ccd charge-coupled device; computer-controlled display

cce carbon-chloroform extract

ccgt closed-cycle gas turbine

cci circuit-condition indicator

ccib computerized central information bank

ccmc coincident-current magnetic core

ccmd continuous-current monitoring device

cco current-controlled oscillator

ccr command control receiver; computer character recognition; control circuit resistance

ccs column code suppressor

cc&s central computer and sequencer

ccv closed-circuit voltage

cd. cord

Cd coefficient of drag

cda chain data address

cdb current data bit

cdc call-directing code

cdce central data-conversion equipment

cdcm carbon-dioxide concentration module

cdd central data display

cdek computer data-entry keyboard

cdi course-deviation indicator

cdl common display logic

cdp communications data processor

cdpc central data-processing computer

cdt command-destruct transmitter; control differential transmitter

cdu central display unit

ce carbon equivalent; circular error; compass error

c-e chloroform-ether

c of e coefficient of elasticity

cea circular error average

ced computer-entry device

cel. celluloid; cellulose

cemad coherent echo modulation and detection

cep circle of equal probability; circle of error probability

cet cumulative elapsed time

cev cryogenic explosive valve

cew circular electric wire

cf centrifugal force

cfa crossed-field amplifier

cfc chlorofluorocarbon

cfcb card feed circuit breaker

cff computer forms feeder; critical flicker frequency

cfp computer forms printer

cg center of gravity; centigram

c of g center of gravity

cgc critical grid current

cgf center-of-gravity factor

cgh computer-generated hologram

cgl center-of-gravity locator; corrected geomagnetic latitude

cgr captured gamma ray

cgt corrected geomagnetic time

cgtt cortisone glucose tolerance test

cgv critical grid voltage

c-h candle-hour

c/h cards per hour

char. character

CHAR character

chr candle-hour

cht cylinder head temperature

ch. v check valve

ci coefficient of intelligence

CIAPS Customer-Integrated Automated Procurement System

cic cardioinhibitor center; command input coupler

cicu computer-integrated converter unit

cid cubic-inch displacement

cie coherent infrared energy

cil control interpreter language

cim communication-interface module; computer-input on microfilm

CIOCS Computer Input/Output Control System

cisam compressed index sequential access method

ciu computer interface unit

c/km cents per kilometer

ckos countersink other side

ckts countersink this side

cl centiliter

cla communication line adapter

clcs current-logic-current switching

CLENE Continuing Library Education Network and Exchange

clics computer-linked information for container shipping

clip. compiler language for information processing

clj control joint

cll circuit load logic

CLOC Computerized Logging and Outage Control

CLODS Computerized Logic-Oriented Design System

clp command language processor

CLP command language processor

clr center of lateral resistance; computer language recorder

CLR computer language recorder

cls. coils

CLS close

clt communication line terminal

clu central logic unit

cm center of mass; centimeter; communications multiplexer

c/m communications multiplexer; control and monitoring; cycles per minute

cm^2 square centimeter

cm^3 cubic centimeter

cm^3/hr. cubic centimeters per hour

cm^3/min. cubic centimeters per minute

cm^3/sec. cubic centimeters per second

cmc code for magnetic characters; coordinated manual control

CMC code for magnetic characters

cmi computer-managed instruction

CMI computer-managed instruction

c/min. cycles per minute

cml circuit micrologic; current mode logic

CMND command

cmo computer microfilm output

CMP compare

cmps centimeters per second

cmrg cerebral metabolic rate of glucose

CMS Conversation Monitor System

cm/s centimeters per second

CMTCS Computer Management Transaction Control System

cmw critical minimum weight

c/n carbon to nitrogen (ratio); carrier to noise (ratio)

cnc computer numerical control; consecutive number control

CNC computer numerical control

cnl circuit net loss

cno computer nonoperational

cnr carrier-to-noise ratio; composite noise rating

cnsl console

cnt. count(er)

cnv contingent negative variation

co carbon monoxide; cardiac output; coenzyme; corneal opacity

coax. coaxial

COBOL Common Business-Oriented Language

CODES Computer-Oriented Data Entry System

codic computer-directed communications

coed. computer-operated electronic display

coef. coefficient

cof coefficient of friction

COINS Computerized Information System

col computer-oriented language

COL Computer-Oriented Language

colt. computerized on-line test

com   computer output on microfilm

comat   computer-assisted training

comet.   computer-operated management evolution technique

COMET   computer-operated management evolution technique

COMICS   Computer-Oriented Managed-Inventory Control System

compac   computer program for automatic control

compact.   compatible algebraic compiler and translator

cop.   coefficient of performance; computer optimization package

co Q   coenzyme Q

cordat   coordinate data

cos.   cosine

cosfad   computerized safety and facility design

cosmfa   computerized service for motor freight activities

costar.   conversational on-line storage and retrieval

cot.   card or tape reader; cotangent

cotan.   cotangent

cov   cutout valve

covers   coversed sine

coxsec   coexsecant

cp   candlepower; capillary pressure; carotid pulse; center of pressure; central processor

c/p   control panel

cpa   critical-path analysis

cpb   charged-particle beam

cpba   competitive protein-binding analysis

cpc computer production control

c-p cycle constant-pressure cycle

cpdd command-post digital display

cpe circular probable error

cpf conditional peak flow

cph characters per hour; cycles per hour

cpi characters per inch

cpkg cents per kilogram

cpl characters per line; common program language

cpm cards per minute; characters per minute; commutative principle of multiplication; condensed particulate matter; counts per minute; critical path method; cycles per minute

cp/m control program/microcomputers

CPM critical path method

cpp critical path plan

cpps critical path planning and scheduling

cpr cardiopulmonary resuscitation

cps central processing system; characters per second; critical path scheduling; cycles per second

CPS Central Processing System; Conversational Programming System

cpsac cycles-per-second alternating current

cpsi causing pressure shut in

cpt critical path technique

CPT critical path technique

cpu central processing unit

CPU central processing unit

cr cardiorespiratory; carriage return; cathode ray; center of resistance; character reaction; compressions ratio; control relay; critical ratio

c-r cognitive restructuring

cram. card random-access method

cras coder and random-access switch

crbbb complete right bundle branch block

crf control relay forward; corticotropin-releasing factor

crm critical reaction measure; crucial reaction measure

crmr continuous-reading meter relay

cro cathode-ray oscilloscope

crom control read-only memory

Crp C-reactive protein

crr constant ratio roll

crt cathode-ray tube

CRT cathode-ray tube

crtu combined receiving and transmitting unit

cru combined rotating unit

crv central retinal vein

crvf congestive right ventricular failure

crysnet crystallographic computing network

cs conditional stimulus; cryptographic system

c/s call signal; cycles per second

csc cosecant

csd constant-speed drive; convection suppression device; cortical spreading depression

csdc computer signal data converter

csect control section; cross section

csei concentrated solar-energy imitator

csk countersink

csl computer-simulation language; computer-sensitive language

csl. console

CSMP Continuous System Modeling Program

CSMPS Computerized Scientific Management Planning System

cso chained sequential operation

csocr code-sort optical-character recognition

csoro conical span on receive only

csp constant-speed drive

csr circumsolar radiation

css computer system simulator

cssb compatible single sideband

cssl continuous system simulation language

cssm compatible single-sideboard modulation

cst channel status indicator; channel status table; convulsive shock therapy

csts computer science time sharing

csu central statistical unit; circuit-switching unit; constant-speed unit

csw continuous seismic wave

ct contrast threshold; control transformer; current transformer

ct. circuit

cta call time adjustor

ctc carbon tetrachloride

ctdh command and telemetry data handling

cte coefficient of thermal expansion

ctf cytotoxic factor

ctk capacity-ton kilometer

ctl checkout testing language; complementary transistor logic

CTL checkout testing language

ctm capacity ton mile; centrifugal turning moment; communications terminal modules

ctn. cotangent

ctocu central technical order control unit

ctpt. counterpart; counterpoint

ctr computer to reader

ctrl. control

CTRL control

cts contralateral threshold shift

ctu centigrade thermal unit; central terminal unit

ctw. counterweight

ctx computer telex exchange

cu control unit; cubic

cua central unit assembly; computer unit assembly

cub. control unit busy

cu cap. cubic capacity

cue. computer update equipment; correction update extension

cum central unit memory

CUTS Computer-Utilized Turning System

cv coefficient of variation

cva costovertebral angle

cvd chemical vapor deposition; current voltage diagram

cvi cerebrovascular insufficiency

CVIS Computerized Vocational Information System

cvp central venous pressure

cvr cerebrovascular resistance; continuous video recorder; crystal video receiver

cvs   cardiovascular system

cvsd   continuously variable slope delta (modulation)

cvt   constant-voltage transformer; controlled variable time

cw   call waiting; continuous wave; cubic weight

c/w   chainwheel; counterweight

cwfm   continuous-wave frequency modulated

cwo   continuous-wave oscillator

cwp   communicating word processor

CWP   communicating word processor

cw sig. gen.   continuous-wave signal generator

cwt   centum weight; counterweight; hundredweight

cwv   continuous-wave video

cx   central exchange; control transmitter

CX   central exchange

cy.   cycle; cylinder

cyb.   cybernetics

cyc.   cycle

cyl.   cylinder(s)

cys.   cystine

czd   calculated zenith distance

CZm   compass azimuth

d   day; deci (prefix: one tenth)

da   deka (prefix: ten); density altitude; drift angle

d/a   digital to analog

d to a   digital to analog

daa   data-access arrangement; direct-access arrangement

dac   data acquisition and control; data assistance and control; digital-to-analog converter; digital arithmetic center; direct-air cycle; dynamic amplitude control

dacbu   data acquisition and control buffer unit

dacon   digital-to-analog converter

d/a convert.   digital-to-analog converter

dadsm   direct-access device for space management

daf   delayed auditory feedback

dafc   digital automatic frequency control

daft.   digital-to-analog function table

dag   dekagram

dagc   delayed automatic gain control

dal   dekaliter

dalr   dry adiabatic lapse rate

dam.   dekameter; direct-access method

DAM   direct-access method

dam^2   square dekameter

dam^3   cubic dekameter

dap   data-analysis package; data-automation proposal; digital audio processor

dapr   digital automatic pattern recognition

dare.   data automatic reduction equipment; data automation research and experimentation

dart.   datagraphic automated retrieval technique

DART   datagraphic automated retrieval technique

das   data analysis station; dekastere

dasd   direct-access storage device

datac   digital automatic tester and classifier

datacom   data communications

datacor　data correction; data correlator
datan　data analysis
datanet　data network
datap　data transmission and processing
datar　digital automatic tracking and ranging
datel　data and telecommunications
datin　data inserter
datran　data transmission
datarec　data recording
datrix　direct access to reference information
dau　data adapter unit
dav　data above voice
db　decibel; diode block
dB　decibel
dbam　database-access method
DBAM　database-access method
dbc　diameter bolt circle
dbcu　data bus control unit
dbd　double-base diode
dbhp　drawbar horsepower
dbi　database index
db/m²　decibels per square meter
db meter　decibel meter
DBMS　Data Base Management System
db/mW　decibels per milliwatt
DBOS　Data-Based Operating System
dbrn　decibels above reference noise
dbt　dry bulb temperature

dBu   decibel unit

d-bug   debug(ged) (ging)

dbur   data bank update request

dc   digital computer; direct current; directional coupler; drift correction

dcb   data control block

dccu   data communications control unit

dcd   differential current density

dcdt   direct-current differential transformer

dce   data-conversion equipment

dcf   direct centrifugal flotation

dcr   data conversion receiver; direct cortical response

dctl   direct coupled transistor logic

dcu   display and control unit

dcx   double convex

dd   digital data; digital display

dda   digital differential analyzer

ddc   direct digital control

ddce   digital data-conversion equipment

ddd   digital data distributor

ddda   decimal digital differential analyzer

dde   direct data entry

ddg   digital display generator

ddi   digital data indicator; discrete digital input

ddis   data display

ddl   data definition language; data description language; digital data link

ddm   data demand module

ddnc   direct digital numerical control

ddp   digital data processor; distributed data processing

ddr   direct debit

dds   digital display scope; digital dynamics simulator

ddt   digital data transmitter

ddu   data diagnostic unit; data display unit

de   display element

decb   data event control block

decit   decimal digit

deco   decreasing consumption of oxygen

decu   data-exchange control unit

dedl   data element description list

dee   digital-events recorder

dees   dynamic electromagnetic environment simulator

dei   design engineering identification

deis   design engineering inspection simulator

del.   delete

DEL   delete (character)

deltic   delay line time compression

de/me   decoding memory

DES   Data Exchange System

deu   data-exchange unit; digital evolution unit

d/f   defogging; direct flow

dfa   digital fault analysis

dfc   data format converter; discriminant function coefficient

dfd   data function diagram

dfg   digital function generator; diode function generator

dfr   decreasing failure rate

dg   decigram

dgs   designated ground zero

dhdd   digital high-definition display

dhe   data-handling equipment

dhllp   direct high-level language processor

dhn   dynamic hardness number

dhp   developed horsepower

diam.   diameter

dian   digital analog

dias.   defense-integrated automatic switch

dic   data-insertion converter; data item category; digital integrated circuit; digital integrating computer

dice.   direct-installation coaxial equipment

did.   data item description

dida   differential in-depth analysis

didad   digital data display

di/do.   data input/data output

dif   discriminant function

dif.   differential

dif-amps   differential amplifiers

diff. calc.   differential calculus

diff. diag.   differential diagnosis

digicom   digital communications

digital IC   digital integrated circuit

dig. r-o   digital readout

diob   digital input-output buffer

diox.   dioxygen

dip. dual in-line package

dir digital instrumentation radar

dir. coup. directional coupler

disac digital simulator and computer

disc. direct-injection stratified charge

dis. int. discrete integrator

dis./min. disintegrations per minute

dis./sec. disintegrations per second

ditar digital telemetry analog recording

diu data interface unit; digital interface unit

div data in voice; digits in voice

div. divide; division

dks dekastere

dl data link; deciliter

d/l data link

dlc data-link control; direct-lift control

d lock dial lock

dlra door-lock rotary actuator

dlt data-loop transceiver; dry long tons

dlu digitizer logic unit

dm decimeter; delta modulation; demand meter

dm² square decimeter

dm³ cubic decimeter

dma direct memory access

d-max. density maximum

dmb dual-mode bus

dmbc direct material balance control

dmc digital microcircuit

dmcl   device media control language

DMCL   device media control language

dmd   disk memory drive

dmed   digital message entry device

d-min.   density minimum

dml   data-manipulation language

DML   data-manipulation language

dmo   demetallized oil

dmpi   desired mean point of impact

dms   digital multiplex switching

DMS   Data Management System; Disk Monitoring System

dna   deoxyribonucleic acid

DNA   deoxyribonucleic acid

dnc   direct numerical control

dnl   dynamic noise limiter

dnm   data name

d/n   dextrose/nitrogen (ratio)

do.   diamine oxidase; dissolved oxygen

doa   dissolved oxygen analysis

doc   data-optimizing computer

DOCUS   Display-Oriented Computer Usage System

DOES   Disk-Oriented Engineering System

doh   direct operating hours

dohc   double overhead cam; dual overhead cam

do./it.   digital output/input translator

dol   display-oriented language

dop   developing-out paper

dor   digital optical recording

dos   disk operating system

DOS   Disk Operating System

dosim.   dosimetry

dov   data over voice

dp   data processing; dew point; diametral pitch; diffusion pressure

dpa   diagnostic prescriptive arithmetic

dpars   data processing automatic record standardization

dpc   data processing computer; data processing control

dpe   data processing equipment; digital processing effects

dpm   data processing machine; disintegrations per minute

dpu   data processing unit

dq.   deterioration quotient

dr.   dram

dri   data rate indicator; data reduction interpreter

drip.   digital ray and intensity projector

drl   data retrieval language

dro   destructive readout

drod   delayed readout detector

dron   data reduction

drs   data-reduction system

drt   data-review technique

dru   digital register unit; digital remote unit

ds   data set

DS   data set

d/s   dextrose in saline

dsa   data set adapter; discrete sample analyzer

dscb   data set control block

dse   data-storage equipment

dsi   data systems inquiry

dso   data set optimizer

dsorg   data set organization

dsr   digit-storage relay

ds&r   data storage and retrieval

DSRS   Data Storage and Retrieval System

dte   data terminal equipment; diagnostic test equipment

dtl   diode transistor logic

dtmf   dual-tone multifrequency

dtol   digital test-oriented language

dtp   data tape punch

dtr   data terminal ready; distribution tape reel

DTR   data terminal ready

dtu   data-transfer unit

du   digital unit

dual.   dynamic universal assembly language

duv   data under voice

dv   dependent variable

dvd   direct-view device

dvg   digital video generator

dvl   direct voice line

dvm   digital voltmeter

dvom   digital volt ohmmeter

dw   deadweight

dwc   deadweight capacity

dwt   deadweight ton; pennyweight

dxc   data exchange control

dyn.   dyne

dyncm   dyne centimeter

dyno.   dynamometer

dysac   digitally simulated analog computer

dystac   dynamic storage analog computer

eaa   essential amino acid

eal   electromagnetic amplifying lens

eap   equivalent air pressure

ear.   electronic analog resolver

e/at.   electrons per atom

eau   extended arithmetic unit

eax   electronic automatic exchange

eb   electron beam

ebcdic   extended binary-coded decimal interchange code

EBCDIC   Extended Binary-Coded Decimal Interchange
Code

ebr   electron-beam recording

ebt   electron-beam technique

ec   electronic computer

eca   electronic control amplifier; electronics control
assembly

ecam   extended communications access method

ecc   equipment-classification control; equipment-config-
uration control; error-correction code; execute control cycle

ec&d   electronic components and devices

ecg   electrocardiogram

ECG   electrocardiogram

ecm   extended core memory

e/cm^3   electrons per cubic centimeter

ecr   energy consumption rate

ecs   error-correction signals; extended core storage

ect   electroconvulsive therapy

ectl   emitter-coupled transistor logic

edac   error detection and correction

edc   electronic digital computer; error detection and correction

edd   electronic data display

eddf   error detection and decision feedback

edge.   electronic data-gathering equipment

edi   electron-diffraction instrument

EDIS   Engineering Data Information System

edm   electromagnetic discharge measuring

edo   error-detection output

edp   electronic data processing

EDP   electronic data processing

edpm   electronic data processing machine

EDPS   Electronic Data Processing System

EDRS   Engineering Data Retrieval System

edtv   extended-definition television

edu   electronic display unit

eec   electronic engine control

eed   elastic energy density

eeg   electroencephalogram

EEG electroencephalogram

ee/ha ewe equivalents per hectare

eer energy-efficiency ratio

ees electronic environment simulator

efc earth fixed coordinate

efd electro fluid dynamics

efi electronic fuel injection

efl effective focal length

efr effective filtration rate

egd electrogasdynamics

egg. electrogastrogram

egr exhaust gas recirculation

egt exhaust gas temperature

ehd electrohydradynamics

ehf extra high frequency; extremely high frequency

ehp effective horsepower

ei electromagnetic interference; electronic interface; exposure index

eic equipment installation and checkout

eie end-item equipment

eil electron injection laser

eis end interruption sequence

ekg electrocardiogram

EKG electrocardiogram

ekv electron kilovolt

ekw electrical kilowatt

elc extra low carbon

eld electric load dispatcher

elf.   extra low frequency; extremely low frequency

elint   electronic intelligence

elm.   energy-loss meter

elra   electronic radar

elt   emergency locator transmitter

elv   extra low voltage; extremely low voltage

em   electromagnetic; electron microscope

e/m   (specific) electron mass

e of m   error of measurement

emcon   emission control

emf   electromotive force

emi   electromagnetic interference

emm   electromagnetic measurement

Emos   Earth's mean orbital speed

emp   electromagnetic pulses

emr   electromagnetic resonance

ems   expected mean squares

emt   equivalent megatonnage

emu.   electromagnetic unit

emux   electronic multiplexer

emv   electron megavolt

endor   electron nuclear double resonance

eniac   electronic numerical integrator and computer

enr   equivalent noise resistance

eo   end of operation

EO   end of operation

e-o   electro-optical

eob   end of block (character)

EOB   end of block (character)

eocp   engine out of commission for parts

eoe   earth orbit ejection

eof   end of file

EOF   end of file

eoj   end of job

EOJ   end of job

eolb   end-of-line block

EOLB   end-of-line block

eom   end of message

EOM   end of message

eomi   end of message incomplete

eoms   end-of-message sequence

eop   earth orbit plane; end of part

eor   end of record; end of run

EOR   end of record; end of run

eot   end of tape; end of transmission

EOT   end of tape; end of transmission

eou   electro-optical unit

ep   epithelial cell; extreme pressure

epc   edge-punched card; electronic program control; engine performance computer

epe   electronic parts and equipment

epi   electronic position indicator

epl   extreme-pressure lubricant

epm   explosions per minute

epnd   effective perceived noise decibels

epr   electronic-propulsion rocket; engine-pressure ratio

eps electron proton spectrometer

epu electrical power unit; electronic power unit; entry processing unit

eput events-per-unit time

eqfm equal-flow manifold

er echo ranging; external resistance

erd emergency return device

erf error function

erg. electroretinogram

erom erasable read-only memory

eropt error options(s)

erp effective radiated power

erpf effective renal plasma flow

ert electrical resistance temperature; estrogen replacement therapy

eru emergency reaction unit

erx electronic remote switching

es ejection sound

esc extended core storage

esc escape (character)

ESC escape (character)

esd echo-sounding device; estimated standard deviation

esg electronic-sweep generator

esh equivalent solar hour

eshp equivalent shaft horsepower; established standard horsepower

esi emergency stop indicator; externally specified index

esl expected significance level

esm electronic-support measures

esp   electromagnetic surface profiler; electrosensitive programming; external static pressure

esr   electron skin resonance

esrc   electronics recovery control

ess   empty solution set

essu   electronic selective switching unit

est   electroshock therapy

esu   electrostatic unit

et   effective temperature; equation of time

etb   end-of-transmission block (character)

ETB   end-of-transmission block (character)

etc   effluent treatment cell

etcg   elapsed-time code generator

eti   elapsed-time indicator

eto   ethylene oxide

et OH   ethyl alcohol

etw   end-of-tape warning

etx   end of text (character)

ETX   end of text (character)

eu   electron unit

euv   equivalent ultraviolet; extreme ultraviolet

ev   electron volt; exposure value

eV   electron volt

eva   electron velocity analyzer

evco   electron vibration cutoff

evt   effective visual transmission

exa   extended X-ray absorption

excp   execute channel program

extm   extended telecommunications module

ez   electrical zero

e/z   equal zero

f   farad; fathom; feedback; feet

F   Fahrenheit; farad; fathom; feedback

fa   fatty acid; folic acid; free aperture

f-a   fuel-air (ratio)

faccm   fast-access charge-coupled memory

fact.   fully automatic compiler translator

FACT   Fully Automatic Compiler Translator

fae   fine-alignment equipment

fai   frequency azimuth intensity; fresh-air intake

fain.   functional air index number

fair.   fast-access information retrieval

fap   fixed action pattern; floating arithmetic package

far.   floor-area ratio

faro   flow(ed) (ing) at rate of

fas   fetal alcohol syndrome

fast.   fully automatic switching teletype

fath.   fathom

fau   fine-alignment unit; forced-air unit

fax   fuel air explosion

f-b   full-bore

f/b   feedback; front to back (ratio)

fbc   fully buffered channel

fbm   board foot measure

fboe   frequency band of emission

fbp   final boiling point

fc   foot-candle

fca   frequency control and analysis

fcc   flat conductor cable

fcd   failure-correction coding; function circuit diagram

fci   fuel-coolant interaction

fcpl   face plate

fcs   forged carbon steel

fcsm   fire-control system module

fcsm   functional simulation

fcu   fare-calculation unit; fire-control unit; fuel-control unit

fcv   fill-and-check valve

fd   focal distance

f&d   faced and drilled

fdau   flight-data acquisition unit

fdb   field dynamic braking

fde   field decelerator

fdm   frequency division multiplexing

FDOS   Floppy Disk Operating System

fdr   field data recorder; flight data recorder

fds   fixed disk storage

fe   format effective

FE   format effective

fec   forward error correction; forward exchange control

fel   front-end loader

felv   feline complex leukemia virus

fet   field-effect transistor

ff   form feed

FF   form feed

ffa   free of fatty acid

ffd   functional flow diagram

ffp   ferromagnetic fine particles

ffwd   full-speed forward

ffwm   free-floating wave meter

fhd   fixed-head disk

fhp   fractional horsepower

fi   field independence; field independent; field ionization; fixed interval

fif   ferric ion free

fild   federal item logistics data

fir.   fuel-indicator reading

FIRST   Fast Interactive Retrieval System

fj   flush joint

fk   flat keel

fl   flow line; fluid loss; fluorescent level; focal length

f&l   fuel and lubricants

FL   foot-lambert

flang   flowchart language

flbin   floating-point binary

fldec   floating-point decimal

fl. dr.   fluid dram

flea.   flux logic element array

fl./mtr.   flow meter

flop.   floating octal point

fl. oz.   fluid ounce

fl. pt.   fluid pint

flr   flow rate

fl./rt.   flow rate

flt. ld. sim.   flight-load simulator

fm   frequency modulation

FM   frequency modulation

f/m   feet per minute

fmcw   frequency-modulated continuous wave

fme   frequency measuring equipment

fmfb   frequency-modulation feedback

fmr   ferromagnetic resonance

fms   frequency multiplexed subcarrier

fmu   force measurement unit

fnp   fusion point

formac   formula-manipulation compiler

FORTRAN   Formula Translation

fov   field of view

fpc   flat plate collection

fpcc   flight-propulsion-control coupling

fpdi   flight-path-deviation indicator

fph   feet per hour

fpm   facility power monitor; feet per minute; fissions per minute; frequency pulse modulation

fpp   facility power panel; floating-point processor

fpr   feet per revolution

fps   feet per second

fr   fast release; field relay; flow rate

f&r   feed and return; force and rhythm

frd   formerly restricted data

frf   frequency response function

frm   frequency meter

fs   file separation

FS   file separation

f/s   feet per second

fsd   functional sequence diagram

fsp   fiber saturation point

ft.   feet; foot

f/t   freight ton

ft.^{2}   square feet; square foot

ft.^{3}   cubic feet; cubic foot

ft.^{3}/d   cubic feet per day

ft.^{3}/day   cubic feet per day

ft.^{3}/m   cubic feet per minute

ft.^{3}/min.   cubic feet per minute

ft.^{3}/s   cubic feet per second

ft.^{3}/sec.   cubic feet per second

ftbm   board foot measure

ftc   fast time constant

ft.-c   foot-candle

fte   full-time equivalency; full-time equivalent

ftg.   fitting

ft./hr.   feet per hour

ft. H$_2$0   conventional foot of water

fti   fixed-time indicator; frequency-time indicator; frequency-time intensity

ft.-lb.   foot-pound

ft.-lbf foot-pound force

ft./min. feet per minute

ft./sec. feet per second

fufo fly under, fly out

fup fusion point

fur. furlong

fus far ultraviolet spectrometer

fw formula weight

fwb four-wheel brake

fwd four-wheel drive; front-wheel drive

fwr full-wave rectifier; full-wave reflector

fwt. featherweight

g glucose; gram; gravity (acceleration of)

G gauss; giga (prefix: one billion)

ga gas amplification

gac granular-activated carbon

gal. gallon

gal. cap. gallon capacity

gal./min. gallons per minute

gal./sec. gallons per second

galv. galvanometer

gan gyrocompass automatic navigation

gard gamma atomic radiation detector

gaser gamma-ray laser

gasid gas and acid

gasohol gasoline and alcohol

gasphyxiation gas and asphyxiation

g-at.   gram-atom

gatac   general assessment tridimensional analog computer

g at. wt.   gram atomic weight

gawr   gross axle weight rating

Gb   gilbert

gbiu   geoballistic input unit

gc   geographical coordinates; gigacycle; gyrocompass

g cal.   gram calorie

gcd   great circle distance

gcf   greatest common factor

gcip   guidance correction input panel

g/cm^3   grams per cubic centimeter

gcmps   gyrocompass

gcr   great circle route

gc/s   gigacycles per second

gc/sec.   gigacycles per second

gcte   guidance computer test equipment

gcu   generator control unit

gd   gravimetric density

g/d   gallons per day

GDHS   Ground Data Handling System

gdl   ground dynamic laser

gdp   graphic display processor

gdt   graphic display terminal

gdu   graphic display unit

gdwnd   gradient wind

gecom   general compiler

GECREF   Geographic Reference (system)

GEOIS   Geographic Information System

germ.   ground-effect research machine

gert   graphical evaluation and review technique

GERT   Graphical Evaluation and Review Technique

gev   gigaelectronvolt

GeV   gigaelectronvolt

gew   gram equivalent weight

gf   growth fraction

gfci   ground-fault circuit interrupter

gfi   gas-flow indicator; ground-fault interrupter

g-force   gravity force(s)

gg   gamma globulin

ggc   ground guidance computer

g gr.   great gross

gh   grid heading; growth hormone

g/hphr   gallons per horsepower hour

g/hr.   gallons per hour

ghrf   growth-hormone-releasing factor

ghx   ground heat exchange

GHz   gigahertz

gi   gastrointestinal

gif   growth-hormone-inhibiting factor

gill   gill

g ion   gram ion

giq   giant imperial quart

GIRL   Generalized Information Retrieval Language

GIS   Geographic Information System; Global Information System

gj   gigajoule

g/l   grams per liter

glasphalt   glass and asphalt

glassteel   glass and steel

gln.   glutamine

glr   gas-liquid ratio

glu   glutamic acid

glv   globe value

gly   glycine

gm   group mark

GM   group mark

g/m   gallons per minute

gm-aw   gram atomic weight

g/m²   grams per square meter

gmv   gram molecular volume

gmw   gram molecular weight

g-n   glucose-nitrogen (ratio)

goa   gyroscope output amplifier

goof.   general on-line oriented function

gor   gas-oil ratio

gox   gaseous oxygen

gpa/d   gallons per acre per day

gpate   general-purpose automatic test equipment

gpc   gallons per capita; general-purpose computer

gpc/d   gallons per capita per day

gpd   gallons per day

gpdc   general-purpose digital computer

gpg   grains per gallon

gph   gallons per hour

gpl   generalized programming language; grams per liter

gpm   gallons per minute

gpr   general-purpose register

gps   gallons per second

gpss   general-purpose systems simulator

gpu   ground power unit

gr.   grain; gross

g-r   gamma ray

grm   gaseous radiation moniter

grp   ground relay panel

grtm   gross-ton mile

gr. wt.   gross weight

gs   ground speed

g/s   gallons per second

gsd   grid sphere drag

gsi   glide scope indicator; ground speed indicator

gsr   galvanic skin reflex; galvanic skin response

gss   guidance-system simulator

gt   gross tonnage; gross ton

g/t   grams per ton

gta   gas-tungsten arc

gtf   glucose tolerance factor

gtm   gross ton mile

gtow   gross takeoff weight

gtw   gross ton weight

GULP   General Utility Language Processor

gv   grid variation

GV   gigavolt

Gv   gigavolt

gvt   gravity vacuum tube

gvw   gross vehicle weight

gw   gigawatt; ground wave

g/w   gross weight

Gw   gigawatt

GW   gigawatt

gwh   gigawatt hour

GWh   gigawatt hour

gwh/day   gigawatt hours per day

GWh/day   gigawatt hours per day

gz   ground zero

h   hectare; hecto (prefix: one hundred); height; hour

H   henry

ha   hectare; hour angle; hour aspect; humic acid

haat   height above average terrain

had.   head acceleration device

hads   hypersonic air data sensor

hal.   halogen(ic)

hams.   hour angle of the mean sun

hamt   human-aided machine translation

hao   high-altitude observation

haw   highly active waste

Hb   hemoglobin

hc   hydrocarbon

hcd   high current density

hcf   highest common factor

hdtv   high-definition television

hed   high-energy detector

hei   halographic exposure index

hem.   hybrid electromagnetic wave

hep   high-energy phosphate

hepa   high-efficiency particulate air (filter)

hepaf   high-efficiency particulate air filter

hepl   high-energy pulse laser

herfs   high-energy-rate forging systems

hess   human-engineering systems simulator

hf   high frequency; hyperfocal

HF   high frequency

hfc   high-frequency current

hfdf   high-frequency direction finder

hfg   heavy free gas

hfo   high-frequency oscillator

hg   hectogram; heliogram; hydrostatic gage

hgb   hemoglobin

hgo   hepatic glucose output

hhp   hydraulic horsepower

hi   high intensity; humidity index

hic   hybrid integrated circuit

hipar   high-power acquisition radar

hi-T   high torque

hl   hectoliter

hlg.   halogen

hll high-level language

hlttl high-level transistor-translator logic

hm hectometer

hm² square hectometer

hm³ cubic hectometer

hmw high molecular weight

holog. hologram; holograph

hp high pressure; horizontal parallax; horsepower

hpa high-power amplifier

hpf highest possible frequency

hph horsepower-hour

hre high-resolution electrocardiography

hri height-range indicator

hrl horizontal reference line

hrs high-resolution spectrometer

hscp high-speed card punch

hscr high-speed card reader

hsct high-speed computer terminal

hsda high-speed data acquisition

hsi heat-stress index

hsm high-speed memory

hsp high-speed printer

hsr high-speed reader

hsro high-speed repetitive operation

hsv heat-suppression valve

hta heavier than air

htl high threshold logic

hto high-temperature oxidation

htu   heat transfer unit

hv   high velocity; high voltage

hvac   high-voltage alternating current

hvdc   high-voltage direct current

hvf   high-viscosity fuel

hvps   high-voltage power supply

hycol   hybrid computer link

hz   hertz

Hz   hertz

ia   impedance angle; international angstrom

iad   integrated automatic documentation

iae   integral absolute error

ial   international algebraic language

iam   interactive algebraic manipulation

iao   intermittent aortic occlusion

ias   immediate access storage

iat   inside air temperature

iavc   instantaneous automatic volume control

ibg   interblock gap

ibol   integrated business-oriented language

ibp   initial boiling point

ibt   initial boiling-point temperature

ibw   information bandwidth

ic   input circuit; integrated circuit

i/c   intercom

ica   ignition control additive

icc   integrated circuit computer

icd   interface control document

icff   intercommunication flip-flop

icm   interference control monitor

icr   iron-core reactor

ictv   integrated circuit television

id   inside diameter

idac   interim digital-analog converter

idb   integrated data base

idf   integrated data file

idg   integrated drive generator

IDIMS   Interactive Digital Image Manipulation System

idp   information data processing; input data processing; integrated data processing

ids   intermediate drum storage

idu   intermittent drive unit

ie   ion exchange

iec   integrated electronic control

if.   information feedback; interferon; intermediate frequency

ifcr   interface control register

ifpm   in-flight performance monitor

ifr   internal function register

i-fr   image-to-frame ratio

ifss   infinite solution set

ig   inertial guidance

i gal.   imperial gallon

igor   injection gas-oil ratio

igpm   imperial gallons per mile; imperial gallons per minute

ihp indicated horsepower

ihph indicated horsepower hour

ihp/hr. indicated horsepower per hour

iia integrated irradiance analyzer

iid impact ionization diode

il interpretative language

ild instructional logic diagram

ildf integrated logistic data file

ilf inductive loss factor

ilp instant linear programming

im impulse modulation; intensity modulation

imac integrated microwave amplifier converter

imep indicated mean effective pressure

imitac image input to automatic computers

imp. indeterminate mass particle

imp. gal. imperial gallon

in. inch

in.^{2} square inch

in.^{3} cubic inch

ina international normal atmosphere

indac industrial data acquisition and control

INDN indication

INDR indicator

inga inspection gage

in.H_2O conventional inch of water

in./in. inch per inch

inmi international nautical mile

inph. interphone

inr   impact noise rating; impact noise ratio

INS   Inertial Navigation System; Integrated Navigation System

ins./hr.   inches per hour

ins./lb.   inches per pound

ins./sec.   inches per second

INT   initial

intran   input translator

i/o   input/output

i&o   input and output

ioau   input/output access unit

iob   input-output buffer

ioc   input-output channel; input-output controller

i/p   input

ipa   intermediate power amplifier; internal power amplifier

ipfm   integral pulse frequency modulation

ipl   information-processing language

IPL   information-processing language

ipm   impulses per minute; inches per minute; incidental phase modulation

ipmin   inches per minute

ipr   inches per revolution

ips   inches per second

ipu   input preparation unit

ipy   inches per year

ir   infrared

i&r   information and retrieval

irm   infrared measurement

irr　infrared rays

irt　infrared temperature

iru　inertial reference unit; infrared unit

is.　interim storage

isar　information storage and retrieval

ise　integral square error

iseq　input sequence

isr　information storage and retrieval

is&r　information storage and retrieval

istse　integral square time square error

itae　integrated time and absolute error

itm　information transfer module

itse　integral time square error

ivd　interpolated voice data

ivds　independent variable depth sonar

ivp　initial vapor pressure

ixc　interexchange

J　joule

jcl　job-control language

J/deg.　joule per degree

jdl　job-description language

jds　job data sheet

jem　jet-engine modulation

j/f　jigs and fixtures

jg. di.　joggle die

J/kg　joules per kilogram

jol job-organization language

jpt jet pipe temperature

k about one thousand (computer storage capacity); karat (carat); Kelvin; kilo (prefix: one thousand); knot

K about one thousand (computer storage capacity)

kb keyboard; kilobit; kilobyte

kbar kilobar

kbe keyboard entry

kbm keyboard monitor

kbps kilobits per second

kb/s kilobits per second

kbtu kilo British thermal unit

kc kilocycle

kcal kilocalorie

kcps kilocycles per second

kc/s kilocycles per second

kc/sec. kilocycles per second

ke kinetic energy

ketol ketone alcohol

kev kiloelectronvolt; one thousand electron volts

keV kiloelectronvolt

kg kilogram

kG kilogauss

kg cal. kilogram calorie

kg/cm kilograms per centimeter

kg-f kilogram-force

kg/ha kilograms per hectare

kg/hl   kilograms per hectoliter

kg/hr.   kilograms per hour

kgm   kilogram meter

kg/m²   kilograms per square meter

kg/m³   kilograms per cubic meter

kg/ms   kilograms per meter second

kgps   kilograms per second

kg/s   kilograms per second

kgU   kilograms of Uranium

khp   kilohorsepower

khz   kilohertz

kHz   kilohertz

kilohm   kilo-ohm

KΩ   kilohm

kj   kilojoule

kJ   kilojoule

kK   kilokelvin

kl   kiloliter

km   kilometer

km²   square kilometer

km³   cubic kilometer

km/h   kilometers per hour

km/l   kilometers per liter

kmph   kilometers per hour

kmps   kilometers per second

kmw   kilomegawatt

kmwhr   kilomegawatt-hour

kn   kilonewton; knot

kobol   keystation on-line business-oriented language

kov   key-operated valve

kp   keypunch

kPa   kilopascal

kp/ft.²   kips (thousand pounds) per square foot

kp/in.²   kips (thousand pounds) per square inch

kph   kilometers per hour; knots per hour

kpl   kilometers per liter

kpps   kilopulses per second

kpr   knots per revolution

kr   kiloroentgen

krad   kilorad

ksia   thousand square inches absolute

ksr   keyboard send and receive

ksu   key service unit

kt   karat (carat); kiloton

kv   kilovolt

kV   kilovolt

kva   kilovoltampere

kVa   kilovoltampere

kV/a   kilovolts per ampere

kvah   kilovolt-ampere-hour

kvam   kilovolt ampere meter

kvar   kilovar; kilovolt ampere reactive

kvarh   kilovar hour

kvm   kilovolt meter

kvp   kilovolt peak

kw   kilowatt

kW kilowatt

kwh kilowatt hour

kWh kilowatt hour

kwhr kilowatt hour

kwm kilowatt meter

kwr kilowatt reactive

l line; liter; locus

L lambert

la linoleic acid

lac load accumulator

LAC load accumulator

lad. language-acquisition device; lunar atmosphere detector

LAN local area network

lap. left atrial pressure

las low-alloy steel

lasa large-aperture seismic array

lascr light-activated silicon-controlled rectifier

lat lowest astronomical tide

lat. ht. latent heat

lb line buffer

lb. pound

lb. ap. apothecaries' pound

lb. avdp. avoirdupois pound

lbbb left bundle branch block

lb. cal. pound calorie

lb. chu pound centigrade heat unit

lbf pound-force

lb.-f pound-force

lbf-ft. pound-force foot

lb.-f ft. pound-force foot

lbf/ft.^{2} pound-force per square foot

lbf/ft.^{3} pound-force per cubic foot

lbf/in.^{2} pound-force per square inch

lb. ft. pound foot

lb. in. pound inch

lbl. label

LBL label

lbm lean body mass

lb. m pound mass

lbr laser beam recorder

lbs. pounds

lbs./bhp.-hr. pounds per brake horsepower hour

lbs./ft.^{2} pounds per square foot

lbs./ft.^{3} pounds per cubic foot

lbs./hr. pounds per hour

lbs./in.^{2} pounds per square inch

lbs./in.^{3} pounds per cubic inch

lbs./m pounds per minute

lbs./s pounds per second

lbs. t pounds thrust

lc liquid crystal; low calorie; low carbon

l-c launch control

lcd liquid crystal display; lowest common denominator

LCD liquid crystal display

lcf   least common factor; lowest common factor

lcl   lower control limit; lowest charge level

lcm   large-core memory; least common multiple; lowest common multiple

lcp   language conversion program

lcs   large-core storage; launch-control simulator

lcu   launch-control unit

lcv   low calorie valve

lcx   launch complex

ld   lethal dose; line of departure; low density

l-d   low density

l/d   length to diameter (ratio)

ldc   latitude data computer

ldp   logistics data package

lds   large disk storage

ldt   logic design translator

le   limit of error

led.   light-emitting diode

lee.   laser energy evaluator

leg.   liquefied energy gas

leg. wt.   legal weight

lel   lower explosive limit

lep   large electron positron; lowest effective power

leu.   leucine

lf   line feed; low frequency

lfa   last field address

lfc   low-frequency current

lfo   low-frequency oscillator

lft linear feet; linear foot

lg large grain; long grain; low grade

lgp low ground pressure

lg. tn. long ton

l/h labor hour; liters per hectare; low to high

LH₂ liquid hydrogen

lha local hour angle

lhams lower hour angle of the mean sun

lhats lower hour angle of the true sun

lHe liquid helium

lhr lumen hour

l/hr. liters per hour

li line item; longitudinal interval

lic linear integrated circuit

lidar light detection and ranging

lih light intensity high

lil light intensity low

lim light-intensity marker; line-insulation monitor; line interface module

linac linear accelerator

lines/m lines per minute

lines/mm lines per millimeter

lines/s lines per second

lin. ft. linear feet; linear foot

lin. yd. linear yard

lipl linear information programming language

LIPL linear information programming language

lisp. list processor

ll lower limit

l/l line by line; lower limit

lli latitude and longitude indicator

lll low-level logic

llr line of least resistance

llw low-level waste

lm lumen

l/m lines per minute

lmc liquid-metal cycle

lmf language media format

lm/ft.^{2} lumens per square foot

l/min. liters per minute

lmlr load memory lockout register

l/mm lines per millimeter

lm/m^2 lumens per square meter

lmo lens-modulated oscillator

lms least mean square; lumen second; lunar mass spectrometer

lm/s lumens per second

lmt length, mass, time

lmtd logarithmic mean temperature difference

lm/w lumens per watt

lm/W lumens per watt

lna low-noise amplifier

lng. length

LNG length

lnp lunar neutron probe

lnr low noise receiver

lo   longitudinal optic

lob.   line of balance

lobar   long baseline radar

loc   locus of control

lo-d   low density

lof   lowest operating frequency

log.   logarithm

logal   logical algorithmic language

logcom   logistic communication

lop.   line of position

lordac   long-range accuracy

los   line of sight; loss of signal

lot.   large orbiting telescope

lotis   logic, timing, sequencing

lov   limit of visibility

loxygen   liquid oxygen

loz   liquid ozone

lp   latent period; light perception; linear programming; low pressure

lpa   low-power amplifier

lpc   linear-power controller; low-pressure chamber; low-pressure compressor

lpcw   long-pulse continuous wave

lpd   least perceptible difference

lpg   liquid propane gas

lph   lines per hour

lpi   lines per inch; low-power indicator

lpl   list-processing language

lpm lines per millimeter; lines per minute; liters per minute

lpo liquid phase oxidation

lps liters per second

lpw lumens per watt

lq linear quantifier; lowest quartile

lrd long-range data

lri long-range input

lrim long-range input monitor

lrm liquid radiation monitor

l/s lines per second; liters per second

lsa logistic support analysis

lsar local storage address register

lsb least significant bit

lsc least significant character

lsd last significant data; last significant digit; least significant difference; least significant digit

lsfa logistic system feasibility analysis

lsg list set generator

lsic large-scale integrated circuitry

lsp logical signal processor

lst large space telescope; liquid storage tank

lsw limit switch(ing)

lt line terminator; long ton; low temperature; low tension; low torque

lt/d long tons per day

ltm low thermal mass

ltu line terminating unit

lu logic unit

lub logical unit block

lv low viscosity; low voltage

lvhv low volume, high velocity

lvi low viscosity index

lvp low-voltage protection

lvr line voltage regulator

lw long wave

m mega (prefix: one million); meter; milli (prefix: one thousandth)

m² square meter

m³ cubic meter

M money (supply); thousand

ma milliampere

mA milliampere

mÅ milliangstrom

ma. ac. machine accessory

mab multibase arithmetic blocks

mac multiple-access computer

mad. mean absolute deviation

madre magnetic-drum receiving equipment

mae mean absolute error

maf minimum audible field

mag. magnetic

magloc magnetic logic computer

mag. mod. magnetic modulator

mai machine-aided indexing; mean annual increment

mamp milliampere

manop   manually operated; manual operation

manova   multivariate analysis of variance

map.   manifold absolute pressure; manifold air pressure; microassembly program

mar.   memory address register; minimal angle resolution

mart.   maintenance analysis and review technique

MART   Maintenance Analysis and Review Technique

mas   milliampere second

mass.   multiple-access sequential selection

mat.   machine-aided translation

mb   macrobiotic; megabyte; memory buffer; millibar

mbar   millibar

mbd   macroblock design

mb/d   million barrels per day

mbps   megabits per second; million bits per second

mbr   memory buffer register

mbs   magnetron beam switching

mb/s   megabits per second

mbt   mean body temperature

mbu   mobile tracking unit

mc   magnetic center; master control; megacycle; metric carat; millicycle

mcc   midcourse correction; multicomponent circuit

mccu   multiple communications control unit

MCDS   Management Control Data System

mcf   magnetic card file

mcg   microgram

mchan   multichannel

mc hr.   millicurie hour

mci   megacurie

mcp   main control panel; manual control panel; master control program; multiple chip package

mcps   megacycles per second

mcr   master control routine; modular circuit reliability

mcs   meridian control signal

mc/s   megacycles per second

mc/sec.   megacycles per second

mcu   microprocessor control unit; monitor control unit

mcvf   multichannel voice frequency

mcw   modulated continuous wave

m-d   modulator-demodulator

mde   matrix difference equation

mdf   main distributing frame

mdi   magnetic detection indicator

mdl   master design layout

mdn.   median

mdr   magnetic disk recorder; memory data register

mds   minimum discernible signal

mdt   mean down time

m/e   mechanical/electrical

mean max.   mean maximum

meco   main engine cutoff

mef   maximal expiratory flow

mei   marginal efficiency of investment

mend.   macroend

mep   mean effective pressure

mer   minimum energy requirements

mes   mutual energy support

mev   million electron volts

meV   megaelectronvolts

mf   medium frequency; millifarad

mF   millifarad

mfc   microfunction circuit

mfco   manual fuel cutoff

mfe   multiflow evaluator

mfso   main fuel shutoff

mftL   millifoot lamberts

mg   megagram; milligram

mG   milligauss

mgc   manual gain control

mg/d   million gallons per day

mgh   milligram hour

mg/l   milligrams per liter

mgn   micrograin

mgtrn   magnetron

mgw   maximum gross weight

mh   magnetic heading; millihenry

mH   millihenry

mhcp   mean horizontal candle power

mhf   medium high frequency

mhic   microware hybrid integrated circuit

mhr   maximum heat rate

mht   mean high tide

mhv   mean horizontal velocity

mhz   megahertz; millihertz

mHz   megahertz; millihertz

mi   myocardial infarction

mi.   mile

mi.^{2}   square mile

mi.^{3}   cubic mile

m of i   moment of inertia

mic   micrometer

mica.   macroinstruction compiler assembler

micr   magnetic ink character recognition

micromation   microfilm and automation

mif   migratory inhibitory factor

mifil   microwave filter

mig   metal inert gas

mi./gal.   miles per gallon

mi./h   miles per hour

mi./hr.   miles per hour

mike   micrometer; microphone

mil.   mileage; million

mil. m/t   million metric tons

mi./min.   miles per minute

min.   minute

min. trq.   minimum torque

min. wt.   minimum weight

mir   memory information register

MIS   Management Information System

mJ   megajoule; millijoule

mK   millikelvin

ml   machine language; millilambert; milliliter

mL millilambert

mlc machine level control; microelectric logic circuit

mlf media language format

mlr main line of resistance; multiple linear regression

mm megameter; millimeter; millimicron

mm² square millimeter

mm³ cubic millimeter

mma multiple module access

mmd mass median diameter

mmu millimass unit

mmx memory multiplexer

mnls modified new least squares

mo. month

moa minute of angle

mobl macro-oriented business language

moddem modulator-demodulator

moe measure of effectiveness

mof maximum observed frequency

mol machine-oriented language

mol. mole

mol./l molecules per liter

mol. wt. molecular weight

mot mean operating time

mΩ megaohm

mp manifold pressure; melting point

mpg miles per gallon

mph miles per hour

mpi mean point of impact

mpl   mathematical programming language

mpm   meters per minute

mpps   million pulses per second

mps   meters per second; microprocessor system

mpt   multipower transmission

mpu   microprocessor unit

mpx   multiplex

mq   memory quotient

mr   milliroentgen

mR   milliroentgen

mrad   megarad; millirad

mrdf   machine-readable data file

mre   mean radial error

mr/hr.   milliroentgens per hour

mrt   mean radiant temperature

mru   mobile radio unit

ms   mean square; metric system; millisecond

m/s   meters per second

msc   most significant character

msd   most significant digit

mse   mean square error

msg   monosodium glutamate

MSG   monosodium glutamate

mslp   mean sea level pressure

mst   mean solar time

msu   main storage unit; maximum-security unit; mo-dem-sharing unit

mt machine translation; maximum torque; mean time; megaton; metric ton

m/t manual transmission

mtcu magnetic-tape control unit

mtd mean temperature difference

mte maximum thermal energy

mtt magnetic tape terminal; mean transit time

multitran multiple translation

mux multiplex(er)

mv mean variation; megavolt; millivolt

mV megavolt; millivolt

mva mean vertical acceleration; megavolt ampere

mvc manual volume control

mw megawatt; milliwatt; molecular weight

mW megawatt; milliwatt

mwd megawatt day

mwe megawatts of electricity

mwh milliwatt hour

mWhr milliwatt hour

mwp maximum working pressure

mwr mean width ratio

mx multiplex

μ micro (prefix; one millionth)

μ**a** microampere

μ**bar** microbar

μ**F** microfarad

μ**g** microgram

μ**H** microhenry

μin   microinch

μm   micrometer

μm²   square micrometer

μm³   cubic micrometer

μs   microsecond

μv   microvolt

μV   microvolt

μw   microwatt

μW   microwatt

n   nano (prefix: one billionth)

N   newton

na   nanoampere; nucleic acid

NA   nucleic acid

nam   network access machine

nau   network addressable unit

nb   narrow band

n/b   narrow beam

N bal.   nitrogen balance

n-bomb   neutron bomb

N-bomb   neutron bomb; nuclear bomb

nbp   normal boiling point

nbw   noise bandwidth

nc   nitrocellulose; nuclear capability; numerical code; numerical control

NC   numerical control

nce   normal curve equivalent

ncp   network control program; normal circular pitch

ncr   natural circulation reactor

ncs   navigation control simulator

ncu   nitrogen control unit

nd   nuclear detonation

n/d   neutral density

ndb   nondirectional beacon

nde   nonlinear differential equation

ndl   network definition language

ndp   normal diametric pitch

ndro   nondestructive readout

ndu   nuclear data unit

ndw   net deadweight

nea   net energy analysis

ned   normal equivalent deviation

nef   noise-exposure forecast; nuclear energy factor

negatron   negative electron

nel   noise-exposure level

neo   near earth orbit

nep   noise equivalent power

net.   nuclear electronic transistor

neutron   neutral ion

news.   naval electronic warfare simulator

nF   nanofarad

n-fuel   nuclear fuel

N-fuel   nuclear fuel

ng   nitroglycerine

ngl   natural gas liquids

nhe   nitrogen heat exchange

nhp   nominal horsepower

nc   negative impedance converter

nid   network in dial

nida   numerically integrated differential analyzer

nipo   negative input-positive output

nl   new line

NL   new line

nlr   noise-load ratio

nls   new least squares; nonlinear system

nlt   new logic technology

nm   nanometer; neuromuscular; nuclear megaton

Nm   newton meter

Nm^2   newton per square meter

nme   noise-measuring equipment

nm/h   nautical miles per hour

nmi   nautical mile

nm/m   nautical miles per minute

nmph   nautical miles per hour

nmpm   nautical miles per minute

nmps   nautical miles per second

nmr   normal mode rejection; nuclear magnetic resonance

nnad   network nonaddressing device

nni   noise and number index

no op   no operation

NO OP   no operation

nop   normal operating procedure

notox   nontoxic

np neuropsychiatric; normal pressure

npl new processor line; new program language; noise-pollution level

N-pol. nuclear pollution

npr nuclear power reactor

n/p/r noise/power ratio

npt nominal pressure and temperature; normal pressure and temperature

nrl normal rated load

nrp normal rated power

nrt net registered tons; normal rated thrust

ns nanosecond; neuropsychiatric

nsd no significant deviation; noise suppression device

n/sec. neutrons per second

nsgn noise generator

nsi next sequential instruction

Ns/m^2 newton second per square meter

nsrt near surface reference temperature

nsu nitrogen supply unit

nt normal temperature

n/t net tonnage

ntc negative temperature coefficient

ntm net ton mile

ntp normal temperature and pressure

ntr noise-temperature ratio

nts not to scale

nt. wt. net weight

nuco numerical code

nul   no upper limit

nul.   null

NUL   null

num.   number(ed)(ing); numerical

nus   nuclear upper stage

nu-tec   nuclear detection

nv   needle valve; number of variables

n/v   nuclear vessel

nva   near visual acuity

nvg   null voltage generator

nvr   no voltage release

nvs   neutron velocity selector

nw   nanowatt

n/w   net weight

nW   nanowatt

nwg   national wire gauge

nwl   natural wavelength

nwt   net weight

nyr   nuclear yield requirement

nzf   near zero field

nzg   near zero gravity

nzt   nonzero test

oac   outer approach channel

oad   overall depth

oal   overall length

oapwl   overall power watt level

oat. outside air temperature

oaw overall width

ob output buffer

ob-gyn obstretrician-gynecologist

oc open circuit

ocb oil circuit breaker

ocg omnicardiogram

ocl operator control language

ocr optical character reader; optical character recognition

OCR optical character reader

octv open-circuit television

ocu operational conversion unit

ocv open-circuit voltage

od optical disc; outside diameter

odb output to display buffer

odt on-line debugging technique

od unit optical-density unit

oem optical electron microscope

o/f oxidizer to fuel (ratio)

oha outside helix angle

ohv overhead valve

olc on-line computer

olr overload relay

olrt on-line real time

ols ordinary least squares

omr optical mark reader; optical mark recognition

on. octane number

ool operator-oriented language

op operations; optical probe

o/p output

opa optoelectric pulse amplifier

op. amp. operational amplifier

opd optical path difference

opm operations per minute

opn. open; operation

OPN open

opr optical pattern recognition

opscan optical scanning

optoel optoelectronics

or. oxidation reduction

os oil solvent; operating system

OS operating system

osa oil-soluble acid

osd optical scanning device

osdp on-site data processing

osi open-system interconnection

outran output translator

ov observed velocity

o-w oil in water

o/w oil to water (ratio)

oz. ounce

oz. ap. apothecaries' ounce

oz. avd. avoirdupois ounce

ozd observed zenith distance

ozf ounce-force

oz.-f ounce-force

oz. t ounce troy

p pico (prefix: one trillionth); probability

pa paper advance; picoampere; power amplifier

Pa pascal

pabl problem analysis by logic

pabx private automatic branch exchange

PABX private automatic branch exchange

pac packaged assembly circuit; personal analog computer

par. parallax; perimeter acquisition radar; precision approach radar

param. parameter; parametric

paramp parametric amplifier

pardac parallel digital-to-analog converter

parsec parallax second

parsyn parametric synthesis

partan parallel tangents

pas power-assisted steering; public address system

p-a system public address system

pau programmer analysis unit

p/av. particular average

pave. position and velocity extraction

pax. private automatic exchange

PAX private automatic exchange

pb pulse beacon; pushbutton

p/b pushbutton

pbc   point of basal convergence

p/bhp   pounds per brake horsepower

pbw   parts by weight

pbx   personal business exchange; private branch exchange

PBX   private branch exchange

pc   percent; personal computer; pitch circle; point of curve; printed circuit; program counter; pulsating current

PC   personal computer

p/c   percent(age); processor controller; pulse counter

pcb   printed circuit board

pcc   program-controlled computer

pcd   pitch circle diameter

pce   pyrometric cone equivalent

pcg   phonocardiogram

pci   peripheral command indicator; process control interface

p-c lens   perspective-correction lens

pcm   pulse-code modulation; punch-card machine

pcmr   photochromic microreproduction

pcn   processing control number

pco   postcheckout operation

pcr   photoconductive relay; program control register

pcs   program counter storage; punched-card system

pct.   percent

pcu   power-control unit

pcur   pulsating current

pcv   packed-cell volume; pollution-control valve

pcx   periscope convex

pd   pitch diameter; pulse duration

p-d   prism diopter

pda   predicted drift angle; probability distribution analyzer

pdf   point detonating fuse; probability distribution function

pdm   pulse-delta modulation

pdn   public data network

pdp   power distribution panel

pdq   programmed data quantisizer

pdr   precision depth recorder

pdu   power distribution unit

pe   photoelectric; probable error; program element

pebd   pay entry base date

pec   photoelectric cell; position error correction

ped   personnel equipment data

pee.   photoelectric emission; pressure environment equipment

pei   precipitation-efficiency index

pem   photoelectromagnet; program element monitor

pencil.   pictorial encoding language

perp.   perpendicular

PERT   Program Evaluation and Review Technique

pes   photoelectric scanner

pet.   personal electronic translator; point of equal time; positive emission tomography

pf   performance factor; picofarad; pneumatic float; pulse frequency

pF   picofarad

pfd   personal flotation device

pfm   power factor meter; pulse frequency modulation

pfr   peak flow rate

p/ft.^{3}   pounds per cubic foot

pgh   pituitary growth hormone

pgr   precision graph recorder

pgs   predicted ground speed

pgt   per gross ton

ph   per hour

phm   phase meter

photr   photographic reconnaissance

phsp   phase splitter

pht   phototube

phv   phase velocity

phw   pressurized heavy water

pi   pig iron; point of interception; point of inversion; position indicator; programmed instruction

pia   peripheral interface adapter

pib   power ionosphere beacon

pic   positive-impedance converter; program-interrupt controller

pie.   plug-in electronics

pil   procedure-implementation language

pilp   parametric integer linear program

pin.   position indicator

p/in.^{2}   parts per square inch

p/in.^{3}   parts per cubic inch

pino   positive input-negative output

pio   precision-interrupt operation; programmable input/output

pip.   peripheral interchange package

pirid   passive infrared intrusion detector

piu   path information unit

piv   peak inverse voltage

pix   photographs; pictures

pk   psychokinesis

pk.   peck

pl   perception of light; phase line

p/l   payload

pla   plasma resin activity

plc   power-line carrier

pld.   payload

ple   primary loss expectancy

pm   primary memory; pulse modulation

p-m   permanent magnet; phase modulation

p/m   parts per million; pounds per minute

pmbx   private manual branch exchange

PMBX   private manual branch exchange

pme   performance measuring equipment

pmi   photographic microimage

pmm   pulse mode multiplex

pmr   pressure-modulated radiometer

p-m s   process-memory switch

pmu   performance monitor unit

pmx   private manual exchange

PMX   private manual exchange

p-n   positive-negative

po   power oscillator

poa   primary optical area

pod.   process-oriented design

pol   problem-oriented language

p on n   positive on negative

pop.   plasma osmotic pressure; postoperative

pos   product of sums

posistor   positive resistor

positron   positive electron

post-op   postoperative

post-sync   postsynchronization

pot.   point of tangency; potentiometer

p-p   peak to peak

ppa   photo-peak analysis

ppb   parts per billion

pph   pulses per hour

ppi   pages per inch

ppm   parts per million; pulse position modulation

ppo   polyphenylene oxide

pps   pulses per second

pr   percentile rank

prcu   power regulation and control unit

prd   pro-rata distribution

pre-op   preoperation(al)

prf   pulse recurrence frequency

pri photographic reconnaissance and interpretation; pulse recurrence interval

prm portable radiation monitor

procsim processor simulation

prodac programmed digital automatic control

prom programmable read-only memory

prp peak radiated power

prr pulse repetition rate

prt production-run tape

pru peripheral resistance unit

ps picosecond; pressure sensitive; pulmonary stenosis

pscu power-supply control unit

psdu power-switching distribution unit

pse psychological-stress evaluator

psec picosecond

psf point-spread function

psk phase shift keying

psn pulse-shaping network

psr pain-sensitivity range

pss packet-switching service

psu power supply unit

pt point of tangency

pt. pint

ptc positive temperature coefficient

ptm pulse-time modulation

ptr photoelectric tape reader

pts./hr. parts per hour

ptw per thousand words

pu   propulsion unit

pulsar   pulse and star

pup.   peripheral unit processor

pv   plasma valve; prime vertical

p/v   pressure vacuum; pressure valve

p&v   pressure and velocity

pw   packed weight; picowatt; pulse width

pW   picowatt

p-wave   pressure wave

pwl   power watt level

pwm   pulse width modulation

pwp   picowatt power

pwr   pressurized water reactor

pwt.   pennyweight

pzc   point of zero charge

qagc   quiet automatic gain control

qam   queued access method

qao   quality-assurance operation

qavc   quiet automatic volume control

qcb   queue control block

qcd   quality-control data

qcl   quality-control level

qco   quartz-crystal oscillator

qcrt   quick-change real time

qcu   quartz crystal unit

qcw   quadrant continuous wave

qds   quick-disconnect series

qem   quadrant electrometer

qev   quick exhaust valve

qfc   quantitative flight characteristics

qfe   quartz fiber electrometer

qfo   quartz frequency oscillator

ql   quintal

qpf   quantitative precipitation forecast

qrv   quick-release valve

qsam   queued sequential access method

qt.   quart

qta   quadrant transformer assembly

qtam   queued telecommunications access method

qwa   quarter-wave antenna

R   rankine; roentgen

r/a   radioactive

rac   relative address coding

rad   rapid-access disk

rad.   radian; radius

rad./s   radians per second

ram.   random-access memory

RAM   random-access memory

ras   reticular activating system

ratel   radiotelephone

rax   random access; remote access

rb   read buffer

rc   radio code; resistor-capacitor

rcc   remote communications complex

rd. rad

rd.^{2} square rod

read. real-time electronic access and display

recg radioelectrocardiograph

rem recognition memory

REM recognition memory

reo regenerated electrical output

rev./sec. revolutions per second

rf radio frequency

r/h relative humidity; roentgens per hour

r/hr. roentgens per hour

R/hr. roentgens per hour

ri random interval; retrograde inversion

riv radio influence voltage

rje remote job entry

rkg radiocardiogram

rkva reactive volt-ampere

r/m revolutions per minute

rmi radio magnetic indicator

r/min. revolutions per minute

rms root mean square

rmse root mean square error

Rn radon

rna ribonucleic acid

RNA ribonucleic acid

rom read-only memory

ROM read-only memory

rpc remote position control

rpe   range probable error

rps   revolutions per second

rri   range rate indicator

rs   response stimulus

r/s   revolutions per second

r-sq.   r-squared

r-s ratio   response-stimulus ratio

rss   root-sum square

rt   radio telephone; real time

rtn.   routine

RTN   routine

rtu   remote terminal unit

rtv   radio television

RTV   radio television

rtz   return to zero

rvm   reactive voltmeter

r/w   read/write

rwm   read-write memory

r/x   receiver

rz   return to zero

s   second

sa   semiautomatic

sam.   sequential-access method; serial access memory; synchronous amplitude modulation

SAM   sequential-access method

sa/v   surface area per volume

s/c   short circuit

scan. switched-circuit automatic network

scc single-channel controller

scn. scan

SCN scan

scp spherical candlepower

scr short-circuit radio

sctr. sector

SCTR sector

sd standard deviation

sdc signal data converter

sdt serial data transmission

se spherical equivalent; standard error

seb static error band

see. secondary electron emission

sel sound-exposure level

sem standard error of the mean

seu smallest executable unit

s/f shift forward; store and forward

s-ft. second-foot

sfa spatial frequency analyzer

sfv sight feed valve

she. standard hydrogen electrode

shf superhigh frequency

shp shaft horsepower

sh. tn. short ton

si shift in

SI shift in

sic semiconductor integrated circuit

simcon   simulated control

sip.   scientific information processing

sir.   selective information retrieval

slf   straight-line frequency

slt   solid-logic technology

s/m   sensory to motor (ratio)

smps   switched-mode power supply

smx   submultiplexer unit

s/n   signal to noise (ratio)

sni   sequence-number indicator

snr   signal to noise ratio

so.   shift out

SO   shift out

s/o   solvent to oil (ratio)

soa   speed of advance; speed of approach

soi   space-object identification

sop.   sum of products

sp   static pressure; summary plotter

s-p   sequential phase

span   signal-processing arithmetic unit

spg   specific gravity

spi   specific polarization index

spl   sound pressure level

spm   sequential processing machine; strokes per minute

sqc   statistical quality control

sqr   square root

sq. rt.   square root

ssa   solid-state amplifier

ssc   station-selection code

st   short ton

sta. mi.   statute miles

stp   standard temperature and pressure

str   synchronous transmitter receiver

stx   start of text

sw   shipper's weight

s-w   shortwave

s/w   standard weight

swt   short-wave transmission

syd   sum of the year's digits

sympac   symbolic program for automatic control

t   tonne (metric); troy

T   tera (prefix: one trillion)

t-a   toxin-antitoxin

tan.   tangent

tbp   true boiling point

tbsp.   tablespoon

t/c   temporary coefficient

tcl   transistor-coupled logic

tcr   temperature coefficient of resistance

tcu   tape-controlled unit

tcvr.   transceiver

t/d   tons per day

tgn.   tangent

t/hr.   tons per hour

thi   temperature-humidity index

thp   thrust horsepower

tm   standard mean temperature

t/min.   tons per minute

tmn.   transmission

TMN   transmission

tmv   true mean valve

tmw   thermal megawatts

ton   ton

tos   tape operating system

tp.   tape

TP   tape

t/p   test panel

tr   transmit-receive

t/r   transmit-receive

tsp.   teaspoon

tst.   test

TST   test

tu   thermal unit

tvc   thermal voltage converter; time-varying coefficient

twx   teletypewriter exchange

TWX   Teletypewriter Exchange (now Telex II)

tzd   true zenith distance

u   (unified) atomic mass unit

uai   universal azimuth indicator

ucl   upper control storage

uga   unity gain amplifier

uhf ultrahigh frequency

UHF ultrahigh frequency

u/i unit of issue

ul user language

ulf ultralow frequency

u/m unit of measure

unc. unconditional

UNC unconditional

unld. unload

UNLD unload

url user requirements language

us. unconditioned stimulus

USASCII USA Standard Code for Information Interchange

usw ultrashort wave

uv ultraviolet

u-v ultraviolet

v volt

V volt

va voltampere

v-a volt-ampere

VA voltampere

vcg vectorcardiogram

vco voltage-controlled oscillator

vcv variable compression ratio

vdi video-display input

vdt video-display terminal

VDT video display terminal

vf video frequency

vga variable-gain amplifier

vhf very high frequency

VHF very high frequency

vho very high output

vhs video home system

vi variable interval

vib./s vibrations per second

vla very low altiitude

vlo vertical lockout

vm voltmeter

v/m volts per meter

vof variable operating frequency

vox voice-operated transmission

vph variation per hour

vru voltage readout unit

vsi variable-speed indicator

vt vertical tabulation

vu voice unit

w watt

W watt

wal wide-angle lens

wba wide-band amplifier

w/d weight displacement (ratio)

wfl work-flow language

wg   wire gauge

wgt.   weight

wh   watt hour

Wh   watt hour

wo   write out

wp   word processor; word processing; working pressure

wpc   watts per candle

wpm   words per minute

wps   words per second

wrk.   work

WRK   work

ws   working space; working storage

wt.   weight

w/v   weight in volume

x   unknown quantity

xcvr   transceiver

xhf   extrahigh frequency

xmt   transmit

xya   x-y axis

xyv   x-y vector

ya   yaw axis

yd.   yard

yd.^{2}   square yard

yd.^{3}   cubic yard

z   zero

zai   zero address instruction

zf   zero frequency

zg   zero gravity

zn.   zenith

zrv   zero relative velocity

zs   zero shift

zwl   zero wavelength

zwv   zero wave velocity

ORGANIZATIONS

AA Addicts Anonymous; Alcoholics Anonymous

AAA American Academy of Advertising; American Anthropological Association; American Arbitration Association; American Automobile Association

AAAA American Association of Advertising Agencies

AAAL American Academy of Arts and Letters

AAAS American Academy of Arts and Sciences; American Association for the Advancement of Science

AACR American Association for Cancer Research

AAD American Academy of Dentists; American Academy of Dermatology

AADC Army Air Defense Command

AADS American Academy of Dental Science

AAG Association of American Geographers

AAHA American Animal Hospital Association; American Association of Handwriting Analysts; American Association of Homes for the Aging; American Association of Hospital Accountants

AAIA Association of American Indian Affairs

AAIE American Association of Industrial Editors; American Association of Industrial Engineers

AAN American Academy of Neurology; American Academy of Nutrition; American Association of Nurserymen

AARP American Association of Retired Persons

AAS Academy of Applied Science; American Antiquarian Society; American Astronautical Society; American Astronomical Society

AASM Association of American Steel Manufacturers

AASS Afro-American Students Society; American Association for Social Security

AASU Afro-American Student Union

AAUP American Association of University Presses; American Association of University Professors

AAUW American Association of University Women

ABA American Bankers Association; American Bar Association; American Booksellers Association

ABC American Broadcasting Company; Audit Bureau of Circulation

ABCA American Business Communications Association

ABJ Association of Broadcasting Journalists

ABLE Advocates for Border Law Enforcement

ABT American Ballet Theatre; American Board of Trade

ABWA American Business Women's Association

ACA American Civic Association; American Communications Association; American Composers Alliance

ACAE American Council for the Arts in Education

ACAP American Council on Alcohol Problems

ACBB American Council for Better Broadcasts

ACC   Air Control Center; Allied Control Commission

ACCESS   Association of Community Colleges for Excellence in Systems and Services

ACCF   American Committee for Cultural Freedom; American Council for Capital Formation; Association of Community College Facilities

ACDE   American Council for Drug Education

ACE   American Cinema Editors; American Council on Education; Army Corps of Engineers; Association for Community Education

ACEI   Association for Childhood Education International

ACEJ   American Council on Education for Journalism

ACES   Americans for the Competitive Enterprise System; Area Cooperative Educational Service

ACET   Advisory Committee on Electronics and Telecommunications

ACF   American Chess Foundation; American Choral Foundation; American Culinary Foundation; Anti-Crime Foundation

ACFA   American Cat Fanciers Association; Association of Commercial Finance Attorneys

ACFHE   Association of Colleges for Further and Higher Education

ACFL   Atlantic Coast Football League

ACHA   American Catholic Historical Association; American College Health Association; American College of Hospital Administrators

ACHR   American Council of Human Rights

ACJ   American Council for Judaism

ACJA   American Criminal Justice Association

ACLA   American Comparative Literature Association; Anti-Communist League of America

ACLI   American Council of Life Insurance

ACLO   Association of Cooperative Library Organizations

ACLU   American Civil Liberties Union; American College of Life Underwriters

ACM   American College of Musicians; Associated Colleges of the Midwest; Association for Computing Machinery

ACNHA   American College of Nursing Home Administrators

ACNS   American Council for Nationalities Service; Associated Correspondents News Service

ACOC   Air Command Operations Center

ACOCA   Army Communication Operations Center Agency

ACOG   American College of Obstetricians and Gynecologists

ACP   American College of Pharmacists; American College of Physicians

ACPE   Association for Continuing Professional Education

ACRL   Association of College and Research Libraries

ACRR   American Council on Race Relations

ACS   American Cancer Society; American Ceramic Society; American Chemical Society; American College of Surgeons; Association of Clinical Scientists

ACSA   Allied Communications Security Agency; American Cotton Shippers Association

ACSC   American Council on Schools and Colleges

ACSN   Association of Collegiate Schools of Nursing

ACSOC   Acoustical Society of America

ACSSN   Association of Colleges and Secondary Schools for Negroes

ACSW   Academy of Certified Social Workers

ACT   American Conservatory Theatre; Associated Community Theaters

ACTA   American Community Theatre Association

ACTFL   American Council on the Teaching of Foreign Languages

ACTI   Advisory Committee on Technology Innovation

ACTION   American Council to Improve Our Neighborhoods

ACTS   American Catholic Theological Society; American Christian Television System; Association of Career Training Schools

ACTSU   Association of Computer Time-Sharing Users

ACTU   Association of Catholic Trade Unionists

ACU   American Church Union; American Congregational Union; American Conservation Union; American Conservative Union

ACUG   Association of Computing User Groups

ACUI   Association of College Unions International

ACUP   Association of College and University Printers

ACUS   Atlantic Council of the United States

ACVC   Arms Control Verification Committee

ACWA   Amalgamated Clothing Workers of America

ADA   American Dairy Association; American Dental Association; American Dermatological Association; American Diabetes Association; American Dietetic Association; Americans for Democratic Action; Atomic Development Authority; Automobile Dealers Association

ADAA   American Dental Assistants Association; Art Dealers Association of America

ADBA   American Dog Breeders Association

ADC   Aerospace Defense Command; Agricultural Development Council; Air Defense Command

ADCC   Air Defense Control Center

ADCI   American Die Casting Institute

ADCIS   Association for the Development of Computer-Based Instruction Systems

ADC/NORAD   Air Defense Command/North American Air Defense

ADCOM   Aerospace Defense Command

ADD   Aerospace Defense Division

ADDIC   Alcoholic and Drug Dependency Intervention Council

ADDS   Alcohol and Drug Dependence Service

ADE   Association of Departments of English; Association for Documentary Editing

ADEA   American Driver Education Association

ADF   Air Defense Force; Air Development Force; Asian Development Fund

ADFL   Association of Departments of Foreign Languages

ADHA   American Dental Hygienists Association

ADI   American Documentation Institute

ADRA   Animal Diseases Research Association

ADRDE   Air Defense Research and Development Establishment

ADS   Alzheimer's Disease Society; American Daffodil Society; American Dahlia Society; American Dental Society; American Denture Society

ADTA   American Dental Trade Association

ADTC   Air Defense Technical Center; Air Defense Test Center; Armament Development Test Center

ADTI American Dinner Theatre Institute

ADTS Automatic Data and Telecommunications Service

ADWC Air Defense Weapons Center

AEA Actors' Equity Association; Adult Education Association; American Economic Association; American Education Association; Atomic Energy Authority

AEC Army Electronics Command; Atomic Energy Commission

AEDS Association of Educational Data Systems

AEF Americans for Economic Freedom; Artists Equity Fund

AEG Association of Engineering Geologists

AEI American Enterprise Institute

AEL Animal Education League

AELC Association of Evangelical Lutheran Churches

AEPI American Educational Publishers Institute

AERA American Educational Research Association

AERO Association of Electronic Reserve Officers

AES Aerospace Electrical Society; American Electrochemical Society; American Entomological Society; American Ethnological Society

AESC American Engineering Standards Committee

AETA American Educational Theatre Association

AFA Actors Fund of America; Advertising Federation of America; Air Force Association; American Forensic Association; American Forestry Association

AFB American Farm Bureau; American Foundation for the Blind

AFBF American Farm Bureau Federation

AFC American Football Conference

AFCC Air Force Communications Center

AFCR   American Federation for Clinical Research

AFD   Association of Food Distributors; Association of Footwear Distributors

AFFI   American Frozen Food Institute

AFFS   American Federation of Film Societies

AFGE   American Federation of Government Employees

AFH   American Foundation for Homeopathy

AFI   American Film Institute; American Friends of Israel; Armed Forces Institute; Association of Federal Investigators

AFIPS   American Federation of Information Processing Societies

AFIS   Air Force Intelligence Services; Armed Forces Information School

AFL   American Football League

AFL-CIO   American Federation of Labor and Congress of Industrial Organizations

AFM   American Federation of Musicians; Associated Fur Manufacturers

AFMH   American Foundation for Mental Hygiene

AFMR   American Foundation for Management Research

AFNC   Air Force Nurse Corps

AFNE   Americans for Nuclear Energy

AFO   Atlantic Fleet Organization

AFP   American Federation of Police

AFPC   American Food for Peace Council

AFPH   American Federation of the Physically Handicapped

AFRA   American Farm Research Association

AFRASEC   Afro-Asian Organization for Economic Cooperation

AFRTS Armed Forces Radio-Television Service

AFS American Fisheries Society; American Folklore Society; American Foundrymen's Society

AFSA American Federation of School Administrators; American Foreign Service Association; Armed Forces Security Agency

AFSB American Federation of Small Business

AFSC American Friends Service Committee

AFSM Association for Food Service Management

AFT American Federation of Teachers

AFTC American Fair Trade Council

AFTE American Federation of Technical Engineers

AFTRA American Federation of Television and Radio Artists

AFW Association for Family Welfare

AGA Adjutants General Association; American Gas Association; American Glassware Association; American Gold Association

AGAC American Guild of Authors and Composers

AGCA Associated General Contractors of America

AGDA American Gasoline Dealers Association; American Gun Dealers Association

AGI American Geographical Institute; American Geological Institute

AGM American Guild of Music

AGS American Association of Graduate Schools; American Gem Society; American Geographical Society; American Geriatrics Society; American Gynecological Society

AGSS American Geographical and Statistical Society

AGU American Geophysical Union

AHA American Heart Association; American Historical Association; American Humane Association; Animal Hospital Association

AHAM Association of Home Appliance Manufacturers

AHAUS Amateur Hockey Association of the United States

AHCA American Health Care Association

AHE Association for Higher Education

AHEA American Home Economics Association

AHF American Health Foundation; American Heritage Foundation

AHL American Hockey League

AHMA American Hardware Manufacturers Association; American Hotel and Motel Association

AHMS American Home Missionary Society

AHS American Hearing Society; American Horticultural Society; American Humane Society

AHSS Association of Home Study Schools

AI Amnesty International; Astrologers International

AIA Aerospace Industries Association; American Institute of Accountants; American Institute of Aeronautics; American Institute of Architects

AIAA Aerospace Industries Association of America; American Industrial Arts Association; American Institute of Aeronautics and Astronautics

AIB American Institute of Banking

AIBS American Institute of Biological Sciences

AIC American Institute of Chemists; Army Intelligence Center

AICPA American Institute of Certified Public Accountants

AICR American Institute for Cancer Research

AICS   Association of Independent Colleges and Schools

AICU   Association of International Colleges and Universities

AID   Agency for International Development; Association for International Development

AIDA   American Indian Development Association

AIDD   American Institute of Design and Drafting

AIEE   American Institute of Electrical Engineers

AIGA   American Institute of Graphic Arts

AIH   American Institute of Homeopathy

AIID   American Institute of Interior Designers

AIIE   American Institute of Industrial Engineers

AIIP   American Institute of Industrial Psychology

AILA   American Institute of Landscape Artists

AIME   American Institute of Mechanical Engineers

AIMU   American Institute of Marine Underwriters

AIN   American Institute of Nutrition

AIO   Americans for Indian Opportunity

AIP   American Independent Party; American Institute of Physics; American Institute of Planners; American Institute for Psychoanalysis

AIPO   American Institute of Public Opinion

AIR   American Institute of Research; Association for Immigration Reform

AIREA   Association of Independent Real Estate Appraisers

AITA   Air Industries and Transport Association

AJL   Association of Junior Leagues

AKC   American Kennel Club

ALA   American Legion Auxiliary; American Library Association; American Livestock Association; American Lung Association; Authors League of American

ALAL   Association of Legal Aid Lawyers

ALCOA   Aluminum Company of America

ALDA   American Land Development Association

ALEOA   American Law Enforcement Officers Association

ALF   American Life Federation; American Life Foundation; Animal Liberation Front; Arab Liberation Front

ALGU   Association of Land Grant Colleges and Universities

ALI   American Law Institute; American Liberties Institute

ALMA   Association of Literary Magazines of America

ALP   American Labor Party

ALPA   Air Line Pilots Association

ALRA   Abortion Law Reform Association

ALRB   Agricultural Labor Relations Board; Agricultural Labor Relations Bureau

ALSA   American Law Student Association

ALTA   American Land Title Association

AMA   Aircraft Manufacturers Association; American Machinery Association; American Management Association; American Maritime Association; American Marketing Association; American Medical Association; American Motel Association; American Municipal Association; Automobile Manufacturers Association

AMC   Air Materiel Command; American Mining Congress; American Motors Corporation; Army Materiel Command

AMCA   American Medical College Association

AMCO American Manufacturing Company

AMDB Agricultural Machinery Development Board

AMEME Association of Mining, Electrical, and Mechanical Engineers

AMF AIDS Medical Foundation; Arab Monetary Fund

AMF(A) Allied Mobile Force (Air)

AMF(L) Allied Mobile Force (Land)

AMFIS American Microfilm Information Society

AMI American Marine Institutes; American Military Institute

AMIA American Mutual Insurance Alliance

AML Applied Mathematics Lab

AMNH American Museum of Natural History

AMOCO American Oil Company

AMOP Association of Mail Order Publishers

AMP American Museum of Photography

AMPS Associated Music Publishers

AMPTP Association of Motion Picture and Television Producers

AMREX American Real Estate Exchange

AMS Administrative Management Society; American Mathematical Society; American Meteorological Society; American Musicological Society

AMU Associated Midwestern Universities; Association of Marine Underwriters

AMVETS American Veterans (World War II, Korea, Vietnam)

AMWA Americal Medical Women's Association; American Medical Writers' Association

ANA American Nature Association; American Neurological Association; American Newspaper Association; American Nurses' Association; Association of National Advertisers

ANARC Association of North American Radio Clubs

ANC African National Congress; American News Company; Arlington National Cemetery

ANCA Allied Naval Communications Agency; American National Cattlemen's Association

ANF American Nurses Foundation; Atlantic Nuclear Force

ANG Air National Guard; American Newspaper Guild

ANGUS Air National Guard of the United States

ANHA American Nursing Home Association

ANICO American National Insurance Company

ANL Argonne National Laboratory

ANMC American National Metric Council

ANP Associated Negro Press

ANPA American Newspaper Publishers Association

ANPO Aircraft Nuclear Propulsion Office

ANRC American National Red Cross

ANRPC Association of Natural Rubber Producing Countries

ANS American Nuclear Society; American Nutrition Society

ANSC American National Standards Committee

ANSI American National Standards Institute

ANTA American National Theatre and Academy

AOA American Oceanology Association; American Optometric Association; American Orthopedic Association; American Overseas Association

AOC Airport Operations Council; American Optical Company; Arabian Oil Company

AOLP Action Organization for the Liberation of Palestine

AOO American Oceanic Organization

AOPA Aircraft Owners and Pilots Association

AORN Association of Operating Room Nurses

AOS American Opera Society; American Ophthalmological Society; American Orchid Society; American Otological Society

AP Associated Press

APA Adult Parole Authority; Airline Passenger Association; American Pharmaceutical Association; American Philological Association; American Philosophical Association; American Pilots Association; American Planning Association; American Podiatry Association; American Press Association; American Psychiatric Association; American Psychological Association

APBPA Association of Professional Ball Players of America

APC American Philatelic Congress

APCA Air Pollution Control Association

APCB Air Pollution Control Board

APF Association of Protestant Faiths

APG Aberdeen Proving Ground

APHA American Public Health Association

APL Applied Physics Laboratory

APLA American Patent Law Association

APPA American Probation and Parole Association; American Pulp and Paper Association

APS Academy of Political Science; American Pediatric Society; American Philatelic Society; American Philosophical Society

APTA American Physical Therapy Association; American Public Transit Association

APTC Allied Printing Trades Council

APWA American Public Welfare Association; American Public Works Association

APWU American Postal Workers Union

AQAB Air Quality Advisory Board

ARA American Radio Association; American Railway Association; American Relief Association; American Rental Association; Area Redevelopment Administration

ARB Air Registration Board; Air Resources Board

ARBA American Road Builders Association

ARC Agricultural Relations Council; Agricultural Research Council; American Red Cross

ARCB Air Resources Control Board

ARCE American Record Collectors Exchange

ARCO Atlantic Richfield Company

ARCOS Anglo-Russian Cooperative Society

ARD Association of Research Directors

ARDA American Railway Development Association

ARDC Air Research and Development Command; American Racing Drivers Club

AREA American Railway Engineering Association

ARF Addiction Research Foundation; Advertising Research Foundation; African Research Foundation; American Rehabilitation Foundation; American Retail Foundation

ARIA Adult Reading Improvement Association

ARL Association of Research Libraries

AROCC Association for Research of Childhood Cancer

ARR American Right to Read

ARRS American-Russian Research Society

ARS Agricultural Research Service; Air Rescue Service; American Records Society; American Recreation Society; American Rescue Service; American Rose Society

ARTA Association of Retail Travel Agents

ARTCC Air Route Traffic Control Center

ARU American Railway Union

ASA Acoustical Society of America; African Studies Association; Amateur Softball Association; Amateur Swimming Association; American Society of Appraisers; American Society of Auctioneers; American Sociological Association; American Softball Association; American Standards Association; American Statistical Association; American Surgical Association; Atomic Security Agency

ASAB Association for the Study of Animal Behavior

ASAE American Society of Association Executives; American Society of Automotive Engineers

ASAIO American Society for Artificial Internal Organs

ASAS American Society of Animal Science

ASB Air Safety Board

ASBPE American Society of Business Press Editors

ASC American Security Council; American Society of Cinematographers; American Society of Criminology; American Society for Cybernetics

ASCA American School Counselor Association; American Senior Citizens Association; American Speech Correction Association

ASCAP American Society of Composers, Authors, and Publishers

ASCE American Society of Civil Engineers

ASCEF American Security Council Education Foundation

ASCHE American Society of Chemical Engineers

ASCI American Society for Clinical Investigation

ASCN American Society of Clinical Nutrition

ASCP American Society of Clinical Pathologists

ASDA American Safe Deposit Association; Atomic and Space Development Authority

ASDS American Society of Dental Surgeons

ASE American Stock Exchange

ASEE American Society of Electrical Engineers; American Society for Environmental Education

ASEI American Sports Education Institute

ASESA Armed Services Electro-Standards Agency

ASFA American Steel Foundrymen's Association

ASFFHF Association of Science Fiction, Fantasy, and Horror Films

ASFH Albert Schweitzer Friendship House

ASFP Association of Specialized Film Producers

ASFSA American School Food Service Association

ASG American Society of Genetics

ASGA Advertising Specialty Guild of America

ASGS American Scientific Glassblowers Society

ASHA American School Health Association; American Social Hygiene Association; American Speech and Hearing Association

ASHE American Society of Hospital Engineers; Association for the Study of Higher Education

ASHG American Society of Human Genetics

ASHP American Society of Hospital Pharmacists

ASI Aerospace Studies Institute; American Society of Indexers; American Statistics Institute

ASID American Society of Interior Designers

ASII American Science Information Institute

ASIL American Society of International Law

ASIM American Society of Insurance Management; American Society of Internal Medicine

ASIS American Society for Information Science

ASJA American Society of Journalists and Authors

ASLA American Savings and Loan Association; American Society of Landscape Architects

ASM American Society for Metals

ASME American Society of Magazine Editors; American Society of Mechanical Engineers

ASMH Association for Social and Moral Hygiene

ASMP American Society of Magazine Photographers

ASMPE American Society of Motion Picture Engineers

ASMT American Society of Medical Technologists

ASNE American Society of Newspaper Editors

ASNLH Association for the Study of Negro Life and History

ASNT American Society for Nondestructive Testing

ASO American School of Orthodontists; American Symphony Orchestra

ASOL American Symphony Orchestra League

ASOS American Society of Oral Surgeons

ASP Amalgamated Society of Printers

ASPA American Society for Public Administration

ASPCA American Society for the Prevention of Cruelty to Animals

ASPCC American Society for the Prevention of Cruelty to Children

ASPM American Society of Paramedics

ASPP American Society of Plant Physiologists

ASPR American Society of Psychical Research

ASPRS American Society of Plastic and Reconstructive Surgery

ASQC American Society for Quality Control

ASSE American Society of Safety Engineers; American Society of Sanitary Engineers

ASSOCHAM Associated Chambers of Commerce

ASSR American Society for the Study of Religion

ASSU American Sunday School Union

AST Alaska State Troopers; Association for Student Training

ASTA American Society of Travel Agents

ASTE American Society of Tool Engineers

ASTME American Society of Tool and Manufacturing Engineers

ASTRO Air-Space Travel Research Organization

ASTT American Society of Traffic and Transportation

ASU American Secular Union; American Student Union

ASUC American Society of University Composers

ASUSSR Academy of Sciences of the USSR

ASW Association of Social Workers

ASWRC Antisubmarine Warfare Research Center

ASWS Audubon Shrine and Wildlife Sanctuary

ASZ American Society of Zoologists

ASZD   American Society for Zero Defects

ATA   Advertising Typographers Association; Air Transport Association; American Taxicab Association; American Taxpayers Association; American Teachers Association; American Tennis Association; American Theatre Association; American Title Association; American Transit Association; American Trucking Association; Area Transportation Authority; Atlantic Treaty Association

ATAA   Advertising Typographers Association of America; Air Transport Association of America

ATAI   Air Transport Association International

ATAS   Academy of Television Arts and Sciences

ATB   Air Transportation Board

ATC   Air Transportation Corps; Army Training Center; Army Transportation Corps; Associated Travel Clubs; Athletic Training Council

ATCA   Air Traffic Control Association; American Theater Critics Association

ATCB   Air Traffic Control Board

ATE   Association of Teacher Educators

ATESL   Association of Teachers of English as a Second Language

ATF   American Type Founders

ATI   Air Technical Intelligence; American Television Institute

ATLA   American Trial Lawyers Association

ATMI   American Textile Manufacturers Institute

ATO   Academy of Teachers of Occupations

ATOS   Association of Temporary Office Services

ATPAS   Association of Teachers of Printing and Allied Subjects

ATPI   American Textbook Publishers Institute

ATRA   American Television and Radio Artists

ATS   American Theological Society; American Travel Service; Association of Theological Schools

ATSC   American Traffic Safety Council

ATSE   Alliance of Theatrical Stage Employees

ATSU   Association of Time-Sharing Users

AT&T   American Telephone & Telegraph

ATTI   Association of Teachers in Technical Institutions

ATU   Alliance of Telephone Unions; Amalgamated Transit Union; Anti-Terrorist Union

ATWE   Association of Technical Writers and Editors

AU   Atheists United

AUA   American Unitarian Association; American Urological Association; Associated Union of America

AUCOA   Association of United Contractors of America

AUCTU   All-Union Council of Trade Unions

AUEC   Association of University Evening Colleges

AUFL   Americans United for Life

AUPG   American University Publishers Group

AUS   Army of the United States

AUSA   Association of the United States Army

AUSCS   Americans United for Separation of Church and State

AUT   Association of University Teachers

AUU   Association of Urban Universities

AVA   American Vocational Association

AVC   American Veterans Committee

AVERA American Vocational Education Research Association

AVI Audio-Visual Institute

AVLA Audio-Visual Language Association

AVMA American Veterinary Medical Association

AVRA Audio-Visual Research Association

AWA American Watch Association; American Wine Association; American Women's Association; Aviation/ Space Writers Association

AWBA American World Boxing Association

AWCU Association of World Colleges and Universities

AWG Art Workers Guild

AWI Animal Welfare Institute

AWIS Association of Women in Science

AWIU Allied Workers International Union; Aluminum Workers International Union

AWL Animal Welfare League

AWMF Andrew W. Mellon Foundation

AWRA American Water Resources Association

AWRT American Women in Radio and Television

AWS American Weather Service; American Welding Society; Aviation Weather Service

AWU Aluminum Workers Union

AZA American Zionist Association

AZC American Zionist Council

AZF American Zionist Federation

AZI American Zinc Institute

BA Bank of America; Bureau of Accounts

BAA Bureau of African Affairs

BAC   Black Action Committee; Bureau of Air Commerce; Business Advisory Council

BAE   Bureau of Agricultural Economics; Bureau of American Ethnology

BAI   Bank Administration Institute; Bank of America International; Bureau of Animal Industry

BAPSA   Broadcast Advertising Producers Society of America

BAQC   Bureau of Air Quality Control

BAR   Bureau of Automotive Repair

BASE   Bank-Americard Service Exchange

BAT   Bureau of Apprenticeship and Training

BATF   Bureau of Alcohol, Tobacco, and Firearms

BATS   Business Air Transport Service

BAUA   Business Aircraft Users' Association

BAVA   Bureau of Audio-Visual Aids

BAVTE   Bureau of Adult, Vocational, and Technical Education

BB   Bureau of the Budget

BBA   Big Brothers of America

BBB   Better Business Bureau

BBHC   Buffalo Bill Historical Center

BBHF   B'nai B'rith Hillel Foundations

BBL   Big Brothers League

BBWAA   Baseball Writers' Association of America

BBYO   B'nai B'rith Youth Organization

BC   Bureau of the Census

BCA   Blue Cross Association; Bureau of Consular Affairs; Bureau of Consumer Affairs

BC/BS   Blue Cross/Blue Shield

BCCI   Bank of Credit and Commerce International

BCE   Board of Customs and Excise

BCES   Board of Cooperative Educational Services

BCI   Bureau of Criminal Identification

BCLA   Birth Control League of America

BD   Bureau of Drugs

BEH   Bureau of Education for the Handicapped

BEHC   Bio-Environmental Health Center

BEIA   Board of Education Inspectors' Association

BEMA   Business Equipment Manufacturers Association

BEMO   Base Equipment Management Office

BEP   Bureau of Engraving and Printing

BER   Bureau of Economic Regulation

BES   Bureau of Employment Security

BESE   Bureau of Elementary and Secondary Education

BESRL   Behavioral Science Research Laboratory

BETA   Business Equipment Trade Association

BEW   Board of Economic Welfare

BEWT   Bureau of East-West Trade

BFA   Broadcasting Foundation of America; Bureau of
  Financial Assistance

BFDC   Bureau of Foreign and Domestic Commerce

BFEA   Bureau of Far Eastern Affairs

BFI   Business Forms Institute

BFMA   Business Forms Management Association

BFO   Bureau of Field Operations

BFPPS   Bureau of Foods, Pesticides, and Product Safety

BFRS   Bio-Feedback Research Society

BFS   Board of Foreign Scholarships; Bureau of Family Services

BFSA   Black Faculty and Staff Association

BFUSA   Baseball Federation of the United States of America

BGA   Better Government Association

BGF   Banana Growers' Federation

BGFO   Bureau of Government Financial Operations

BH   Board of Health

BHE   Board of Higher Education

BHS   Burlesque Historical Society

BI   Bureau of Investigation

BIA   Braille Institute of America; Building Industry Association; Bureau of Indian Affairs

BIAA   Bureau of Inter-American Affairs

BIAC   Business and Industry Advisory Committee

BIB   Bureau of International Broadcasting

BIC   Bureau of International Commerce

BIE   Bureau of Industrial Economics

BIEPR   Bureau of International Economic Policy and Research

BIG   Basic Industries Group; Beneficial Insurance Group; Better Independent Grocers

BIL   Braille Institute Library

BILA   Bureau of International Labor Affairs

BIO   Broadcasting Information Office

BIOA   Bureau of International Organization Affairs

BIP   Board for International Broadcasting

BIR Board of Internal Revenue; Bureau of Intelligence and Research; Bureau of Internal Revenue

BIS Bank for International Settlements

BITB Building Industry Training Board

BJS Bureau of Justice Statistics

BLA Black Liberation Army

BLAST Black Legal Action for Soul in Television

BLE Brotherhood of Locomotive Engineers

BLEU Belgium-Luxembourg Economic Union

BLM Bureau of Land Management

BLS Bureau of Labor Statistics

BM Bureau of Medicine; Bureau of Mines; Bureau of the Mint

BMA Bank Marketing Association; Bicycle Manufacturers Association

BMB Ballistic Missile Branch

BMCS Bureau of Motor Carrier Safety

BMDCA Ballistic Missile Defense Communications Agency

BMI Book Manufacturers Institute

BMO Ballistic Missile Office

BMR Bureau of Mineral Resources

BN Bureau of Narcotics

BNA Bureau of National Affairs

BNDD Bureau of Narcotics and Dangerous Drugs

BNE Board of National Estimates

BNF Brand Name Foundation

BO Board of Ordnance; Bureau of Ordnance

BOA Boat Owners Association

BOAE   Bureau of Occupational and Adult Education

BOB   Bureau of the Budget

BOMA   Building Owners and Managers Association

BOMC   Book of the Month Club

BOT   Board of Trade

BP   Board of Parole; Bureau of Prisons

BPA   Beach Protection Authority; Book Publishers Association; Bureau of Public Assistance; Business Press Association

BPD   Bureau of the Public Debt

BPE   Bureau of Postsecondary Education

BPI   Bureau of Public Information

BPP   Black Panther Party

BPR   Bureau of Public Roads

BPS   Bureau of Product Safety

BPT   Bureau of Prison Terms

BPWA   Business and Professional Women's Association

BR   Bureau of Reclamation

BRA   Building Renovating Association

BRC   Broadcast Rating Council

BRI   Brain Research Institute; Bureau of Rehabilitation Inc.

BRIA   Biological Research Institute of America

BRL   Ballistic Research Laboratories

BRS   Bertrand Russell Society; Bureau of Railroad Safety; Buyers' Research Syndicate

BS   Bureau of Ships; Bureau of Standards

BSA   Bibliographical Society of America; Boy Scouts of America; Boy Scouts Association; Bureau of Supplies and Accounts

BSCA Bureau of Security and Consular Affairs

BSIA Better Speech Institute of America

BSIB Boy Scouts International Bureau

BSP Border Security Police

BSS Bureau of School Systems; Bureau of State Services

BSU Black Students Union

BSWB Boy Scouts World Bureau

BTA Board of Tax Appeals

BTAO Bureau of Technical Assistance Operations

BTC Board of Transport Commissioners; Building Trades Council

BTE Board of Teacher Education; Board of Transport Economics

BTG Building Trades Group

BTL Bell Telephone Laboratories

BTR Bureau of Trade Regulation

BU Board of Underwriters

BUDFIN Budget and Finance Division

BW *Business Week*

BWA Baptist World Alliance; Baseball Writers Association

BWL Biological War Laboratory

BWRC Biological Warfare Research Center

BZA Board of Zoning Adjustment

CAA Civil Aeronautics Administration; Civil Aeronautics Authority; Collectors of American Art; Community Action Agencies; Custom Agents Association

CAAA Composers, Authors, and Artists of America

CAAR Committee Against Academic Repression

CAAT Colleges of Applied Arts and Technology

CAB Circulation Audit Bureau; Civil Aeronautics Board; Consumer Affairs Bureau; Contract Appeals Board

CABA Charge Account Bankers Association

CAC Civic Administration Center; Civil Administration Commission; Consumer Advisory Council; Consumer Affairs Council

CAD Civil Air Defense

CAE Council on Anthropology and Education

CAEU Council of Arab Economic Unity

CAG Civil Air Guard; Composers-Authors Guild; Concert Artists Guild

CAGI Compressed Air and Gas Institute

CAI Cruelty to Animals Inspectorate; Culinary Arts Institute

CAJ Center for Administrative Justice

CAL Center for Applied Linguistics; Citizens Action League

CALM Citizens Against Legalized Murder

CAMA Civil Aerospace Medical Association

CAMDA Car and Motorcycle Drivers Association

CAMRC Child Abuse and Maltreatment Reporting Center

CAN Citizens Against Noise

CANA Clergy Against Nuclear Arms

CAP Civil Air Patrol; Combat Air Patrol; Consumer Action Panel

CAPES Collect Association for Public Events and Services

CAPMS Central Agency for Public Mobilization and Statistics

CAPS Clearinghouse on Counselling and Personnel Services; Creative Artists Public Service

CAR Civil Air Reserve

CARE Citizens Association for Racial Equality

CARG Corporate Accountability Research Group

CAS Center for Administrative Studies; Center for Auto Safety

CASB Cost-Accounting Standards Board

CASC Council for the Advancement of Small Colleges

CASD Center for Applied Studies in Development

CASE Coalition of Agencies Serving the Elderly; Committee on Academic Science and Engineering; Council for the Advancement of Secondary Education

CASMT Central Association of Science and Mathematics Teachers

CASRO Council of American Survey Research Organizations

CAST Center for Application of Sciences and Technology; Contemporary Artists Serving the Theater; Council for Agricultural Science and Technology

CASW Council for the Advancement of Science Writing

CAT Civil Air Transport

CATCC Carrier Air Traffic Control Center

CATIB Civil Air Transport Industry Training Board

CATRA Cutlery and Allied Trades Research Association

CATRALA Car and Truck Renting and Leasing Association

CAU Congress of American Unions; Consumer Affairs Union

CAUS   Colon Association of the United States

CAWP   Center for American Woman Politics

CAWU   Clerical and Administrative Workers' Union

CB   Census Bureau; Children's Bureau; Consultants Bureau

CBA   Christian Booksellers Association; Community Broadcasters Association; Consumer Bankers Association

CBBB   Council of Better Business Bureaus

CBE   Council for Basic Education; Council of Basic Education; Council of Biology Editors

CBEMA   Computer and Business Equipment Manufacturers Association

CBI   Central Bureau of Investigation; Council of the Building Industry

CBJO   Coordinating Board of Jewish Organizations

CBMM   Council of Building Materials Manufacturers

CBMS   Conference Board of Mathematical Sciences

CBO   Congressional Budget Office

CBOE   Chicago Board Options Exchange

CBOT   Chicago Board of Trade

CBRS   Citizen's Band Radio Service

CBS   Columbia Broadcasting System

CBT   Chicago Board of Trade

CCA   Camp and Cabin Association; Clearing Contractors Association; Community Concerts Association; Conservative Clubs of America; Consumers Cooperative Association

CCAS   Council of Colleges of Arts and Sciences

CCC Central Control Commission; Commercial Credit Corporation; Commodity Credit Corporation; Copyright Clearance Center; Crime and Correction Commission; Customs Cooperation Council

CCCA Classic Car Clubs of America; Conservative Christian Churches of America

CCCP Council on Cooperative College Projects

CCDN Central Council for District Nursing

CCF Citizens Council Forum; Congressional Clearinghouse on the Future

CCGEA Community College General Education Association

CCHE Central Council for Health Education; Coordinating Council for Higher Education

CCIA Consumer Credit Insurance Association

CCJ Center for Criminal Justice

CCJO Consultative Council of Jewish Organizations

CCL Council for Civil Liberties

CCLN Council for Computerized Library Networks

CCMA Community College Media Association

CCMS Committee on the Challenges of Modern Society

CCNR Citizens Committee on Natural Resources; Consultative Committee for Nuclear Research

CCP Chinese Communist Party

CCPO Central Civilian Personnel Office

CCR Commission on Civil Rights

CCRF City College Research Foundation

CCRKBA Citizens Committee for the Right to Keep and Bear Arms

CCS Council of Communication Societies

CCSA   Community College Service Association; Community College Student Association

CCSB   Credit Card Service Bureau

CCUN   Collegiate Council for the United Nations

CCUS   Chamber of Commerce of the United States

CDA   Catholic Daughters of America; Child Development Association

CDC   Centers for Disease Control; Citizens' Defense Corps; Civil Defense Council; Communicable Disease Center

CDF   Children's Defense Fund; Civil Defense Force; Community Development Foundation

CDI   Center for Defense Information

CDL   Citizens for Decency through Law; Citizens for Decent Literature; Country and Democratic League

CDMB   Civil Defense Mobilization Board

CDNS   Chicago Daily News Service

CDO   Civil Defense Organization

CDPA   Civil Defense Preparedness Agency

CDRI   Central Drug Research Institute

CDT   Council on Dental Therapeutics

CDU   Christian Democratic Union; Civil Disobedience Unit

CE   Church of England; Corps of Engineers

CEA   Childbirth Education Association; College English Association; Commodity Exchange Authority; Cooperative Education Association; Council of Economic Advisers

CEAA   Council of European-American Associations

CEANAR   Commission on Education in Agriculture and National Resources

CEARC Computer Education and Applied Research Center

CEB Central Electricity Board

CEC Civil Engineer Corps; Commodity Exchange Commission; Consolidated Edison Company; Consulting Engineers Council

CECH Citizenship Education Clearinghouse

CECR Center for Environmental Conflict Resolution

CEDR Committee for Economic Development and Research

CEE Center for Environmental Education

CEEB College Entrance Examination Board

CEEC Council for European Economic Cooperation

CEEED Council on Environment, Employment, Economy, and Development

CEF Children's Emergency Fund; Citizens for Educational Freedom

CEG Coalition for Economic Growth

CEI Council of Engineering Institutions

CEIE Committee on Excellence in Education

CEIF Council of European Industrial Federations

CEIP Carnegie Endowment for International Peace

CEMA Council for Economic Mutual Assistance; Council for Encouragement of Music and the Arts

CENA Coalition of Eastern Native Americans

CENTO Central Treaty Organization

CEOA Central European Operating Agency

CEP Council on Economic Priorities

CEPA Consumers Education and Protective Association

CEPB Civil Emergency Planning Bureau

CEPM Center for Educational Policy and Management

CEPR Center for Educational Policy Research

CEQ Council on Environmental Quality

CES Council for European Studies

CET Center for Employment Training; Council for Educational Technology

CETO Center for Educational Television Overseas

CF Conservation Foundation

CFA Consumer Federation of America; Correctional Facilities Association; Council for Foreign Affairs

CFAT Carnegie Foundation for the Advancement of Teaching

CFB Consumer Fraud Bureau

CFD Consumer Fraud Division

CFH Council on Family Health

CFM Council of Foreign Ministers

CFPTS Coalition for Peace through Strength

CFR Council on Foreign Relations

CFTC Commodity Futures Trading Commission

CGA Coast Guard Academy

CGS Coast and Geodetic Survey; Council of Graduate Schools

CH Carnegie Hall

CHA Catholic Hospital Association; Child Health Association; Community Health Association

CHANCE Complete Help and Assistance Necessary for College Education

CHL Central Hockey League

CHO Community Health Organization

CHR Commission on Human Rights

CHS Children's Home Society; Citizens for Highway Safety; Community Health Service

CI Carnegie Institute; Communist International; Consumers Institute

CIA Central Intelligence Agency; Commerce and Industry Association; Culinary Institute of America

CIAO Congress of Italian-American Organizations

CIB Central Intelligence Board; Criminal Investigation Bureau

CIC Consumer Information Center; Cooperative Insurance Corporation

CICP Committee to Investigate Copyright Problems

CICT Commission on International Commodity Trade

CICU Commission for Independent Colleges and Universities

CID Center for Industry Development; Central Institute for the Deaf

CIE Center for Independent Education

CIEP Council on International Economic Policy

CIL Center for Independent Living

CIME Council of Industry for Management Education

CIO Congress of Industrial Organizations

CIOMS Council for the International Organization of Medical Sciences

CIPA Committee for Independent Political Action

CIR Commission on Intergovernmental Relations

CIS Congressional Information Service

CISA Council for Independent School Aid

CIT Carnegie Institute of Technology; Central Institute of Technology

CLA   Commercial Law Association; Computer Law Association

CLAS   Computer Library Applications Service

CLC   Cost of Living Council

CLEO   Council on Legal Education Opportunity

CLGA   Composers and Lyricists Guild of America

CLIS   Central Library and Information Services; Clearinghouse for Library Information Sciences

CLR   Council on Library Research

CLRA   Consumer Law Reform Association

CLUSA   Cooperative League of the USA

CLW   Council for a Livable World

CM   Common Market

CMA   Central Monetary Authority; Chemical Manufacturers Association; Colleges of Mid-America

CMEA   Council for Mutual Economic Assistance

CMH   Council for the Mentally Handicapped

CMIA   Coal Mining Institute of America

CNAA   Council for National Academic Awards

CNS   Congress of Neurological Surgeons

COAS   Council of the Organization of American States

COE   Corps of Engineers; Council for Occupational Education

COHA   Council on Hemispheric Affairs

COHO   Council of Health Organizations

COLC   Cost of Living Council

COLPA   Commission on Law and Public Affairs

COLT   Council on Library Technology

Comintern   Communist International

CONEA Confederation of National Educational Associations

COPL Council of Planning Librarians

CORE Congress of Racial Equality

CORT Council on Radio and Television

COSI Center of Science and Industry

COSR Committee on Space Research

COST Congressional Office of Science and Technology

COSW Citizen's Organization for a Sane World

CPA Consumer Protection Agency; Council of Professional Associations

CPB Consumer Protection Bureau; Corporation for Public Broadcasting

CPC City Planning Commission; Communist Party of China

CPD Committee on the Present Danger

CPEA Confederation of Professional and Executive Associations

CPGB Communist Party of Great Britain

CPH Corps of Public Health

CPJ Communist Party of Japan

CPRA Council for the Preservation of Rural America

CPS College Press Service; Consumer Purchasing Service

CPSC Consumer Product Safety Commission

CPSU Communist Party of the Soviet Union

CPTS Council of Professional Technological Societies

CPY Communist Party of Yugosolavia

CRA Community Redevelopment Agency

CRB Civilian Review Board

CRC Civil Rights Commission

CRD Crop Research Division

CRE Commission for Racial Equality

CRF Cancer Research Foundation; Citizens Research Foundation

CRI Communications Research Institute

CRIB Computerized Resources Information Bank

CRL Center for Research Libraries

CRS Coast Radio Service; Community Relations Service; Congressional Research Service

CSA Community Services Administration; Confederate States of America

CSC Central Security Council; Civil Service Commission

CSD Community Service for the Disabled

CSIR Council of Scientific and Industrial Research

CSO Community Services Organization; Community Standards Organization

CSTA Correspondence School Teachers Association

CSWE Council on Social Work Education

CTA Commerical Travellers Association

CTB Cable Television Bureau

CTIC Cable Television Information Center

CUA Council on Urban Affairs

CURE Citizens United for Racial Equality

CURF Citizens Union Research Foundation

CWA Civil Works Administration; Communication Workers of America; Crime Writers Association

CWL Catholic Women's League

CWLA Child Welfare League of America

CWP   Communist Workers Party

CYL   Chinese Youth League

CYMA   Catholic Young Men's Association

CYO   Catholic Youth Organization

CZA   Canal Zone Authority; Coastal Zone Authority

DA   Daughters of America; Department of Agriculture; Department of the Army

DAA   Dental Assistants Association

DAP   Democratic Action Party; Division of Air Pollution

DAWN   Drug Abuse Warning Network

DBC   Drum and Bugle Corps

DBP   Division of Beaches and Parks

DC   Department of Commerce; Diners Club

DCA   Department of Civil Aviation; Department of Consumer Affairs; Digital Computers Association; Division of Consumer Affairs; Drug Control Agency

DCATA   Drug, Chemical, and Allied Trades Association

DCC   Disease Control Center

DCI   Department of Citizenship and Immigration

DCJ   Department of Criminal Justice

DCN   Defense Communication Network

DCP   Department of Consumer Protection

DDA   Diemakers and Diecutters Association; Disabled Drivers Association

DDEM   Dwight D. Eisenhower Museum.

DE   Department of Education; Department of Employment; Department of Energy; Department of the Environment

DEA   Drug Enforcement Administration

DEB   Dental Examining Board

DEC   Developmental Education Center; Digital Equipment Corporation

DECUS   Digital Equipment Computer Users Society

DEHS   Division of Emergency Health Services

DEIR   Department of Employment and Industrial Relations

DEQ   Department of Environmental Quality

DER   Department of Environmental Resources

DES   Department of Education and Science

DEU   Data Exchange Union

DFA   Dairy Farmers Association; Department of Foreign Affairs

DFG   Department of Fish and Game

DFLP   Democratic Front for the Liberation of Palestine

DGA   Directors Guild of America

DGTA   Dry Goods Trade Association

DH   Department of Health

DHC   Department of Housing and Construction

DHHS   Department of Health and Human Services

DHI   Dental Health International

DHUD   Department of Housing and Urban Development

DI   Department of the Interior

DIB   Department of Information and Broadcasting

DIE   Division of International Education

DIS   Dow Industrial Service

DISI   Dairy Industries International

DITC Disability Insurance Training Council

DJ Department of Justice

DKP Democratic Korea Party

DL Department of Labor

DLP Democratic Labor Party

DMA Direct Mail Association

DMAA Direct Mail Advertising Association

DMMA Direct Mail/Marketing Association

DMR Department of Main Roads

DN Department of the Navy

DNA Defense Nuclear Agency

DNC Democratic National Committee

DND Division of Narcotic Drugs

DNR Department of Natural Resources

DO Department of Oceanography

DOA Department of Agriculture; Department of the Army

DOC Department of Commerce; Department of Correction

DOD Department of Defense

DOE Department of Education; Department of Energy

DoEd Department of Education

DoEn Department of Energy

DOI Department of Industry; Department of the Interior

DoInt Department of the Interior

DOJ Department of Justice

DOL Department of Labor

DON Department of the Navy

DOS Department of State

DOT Department of Tourism; Department of Transportation

DOW Dow Chemical Company

DPA Data Processing Agency; Division of Public Affairs

DPH Department of Public Health; Department of Public Highways

DPI Department of Public Information; Department of Public Instruction

DPS Department of Public Safety

DPW Department of Public Works

DRC Drug Rehabilitation Center; Dynamics Research Corporation

DRDO Defense Research and Development Organization

DS Delta Society; Department of Sanitation; Department of State

DSA Department of Substance Abuse

DSC Document Service Center

DSF Daughters of St. Francis of Assisi

DSI Dairy Society International

DSNA Dictionary Society of North America

DSP Democratic Socialist Party

DSS Department of Supply and Services

DSW Department of Social Welfare

DT Department of Tourism; Department of Transportation; Department of the Treasury

DTA Defense Transportation Administration

DTC Department of Trade and Commerce

DTF Domestic Textiles Federation

DURD Department of Urban and Regional Development

DVA Department of Veterans Affairs

DVH Division for the Visually Handicapped

DVS Division of Vital Statistics

DWP Department of Water and Power

DYF Democratic Youth Front

DYS Department of Youth Services; Division of Youth Services

DZ Department of Zoology

EAA Electric Appliance Association; Experimental Aircraft Association; Export Advertising Association

EAB Ethnic Affairs Bureau

EAEC East African Economic Community; European Atomic Energy Community

EAES European Atomic Energy Society

EAIC East African Industrial Council

EATA East Asia Travel Association

EAW Electrical Association for Women

EBC Educational Broadcasting Corporation

EBS Emergency Broadcast System

EC European Community; Executive Committee; Executive Council

ECA Economic Commission for Africa; Economic Control Agency; Economic Cooperation Administration

ECAB Employees' Compensation Appeals Board

ECC Emergency Conservation Committee; Employees Compensation Commission; European Cultural Center

ECCI Executive Committee Communist International

ECDU   European Christian Democratic Union

ECE   Economic Commission for Europe

ECEO   Economic Crime Enforcement Office

ECF   Edgar Cayce Foundation

ECM   European Common Market

ECME   Economic Commission for the Middle East

ECO   European Coal Organization

ECS   Employment Counseling Service

ECSC   European Coal and Steel Community

ECWA   Economic Commission for Western Asia

EDA   Environmental Development Administration; Environmental Development Agency

EDB   Economic Development Board; Energy Development Board

EDC   Educational Development Council; Export Development Committee; Export Development Corporation

EDDS   Electronic Devices Data Service

EDF   Environmental Defense Fund; European Development Fund; Everyman Defense Fund

EDI   Economic Development Institute

EDLNA   Exotique Dancers League of North America

EDPC   Electric Data Processing Center

EDS   Electric Devices Society; English Dialect Society; Environmental Data Services

EDU   European Democratic Union

EEA   Electronic Engineering Association

EEC   European Economic Community

EEOC   Economic Employment Opportunity Committee; Equal Employment Opportunity Commission

EEUA Engineering Equipment Users Association

EF Educational Foundation; Engineering Foundation

EFA Epilepsy Foundation of America; Evangelical Friends Alliance

EFLA Educational Film Library Association

EFPA Educational Film Producers Association

EFTA European Free Trade Association

EHA Environmental Health Association

EHL Eastern Hockey League

EHS Environmental Health Service

EIA Electronics Industries Association; Energy Information Administration; Engineering Institute of America

EIC Education Information Center; Energy Information Center

EK Eastman Kodak

ELEC European League for Economic Cooperation

EMA Electronics Manufacturers Association; European Marketing Association; Evaporated Milk Association

EMS Emergency Medical Service; Export Marketing Service

EMTA Electro-Mechanical Trade Association

EMU Economic and Monetary Union

ENA English Newspaper Association

ENEA European Nuclear Energy Association

EOA Economic Oil Association

EOC Economic Opportunity Commission; Equal Opportunity Commission

EOP Executive Office of the President

EPA Economic Planning Agency; Environmental Protection Agency; Evangelical Press Association

EPAA   Educational Press Association of America; Employing Printers Association of America

EPC   Economic and Planning Council; Economic Policy Council; Educational Publishers' Council; European Planning Council

EPEA   Electrical Power Engineers Association

EPI   Environmental Policy Institute

EPO   Emergency Planning Office

EPSA   Energy Products and Services Administration

EQB   Environmental Quality Board

EQC   Environmental Quality Council

ERA   Engineering Research Association

ERB   Environmental Review Board; Equipment Review Board

ERC   Economic Research Council; Educational Resources Center; Enlisted Reserve Corps

ERCA   Educational Research Council of America

ERIC   Educational Resources Information Center

ERL   Environmental Research Laboratories

ERTA   Energy Research and Technology Administration

ES   Electrochemical Society; Entomological Society; Ethnological Society; Etymological Society; Extension Service

ESA   Ecological Society of America; Economic Stabilization Agency; Employment Standards Administration; Engineers and Scientists of America; European Space Agency

ESC   Economic and Social Council; Executive Service Corps

ESCO   Educational, Scientific, and Cultural Organization

ESTEC   European Space Technology Center

ETA English Teachers Association; European Teachers Association

ETC European Travel Commission

ETI Equipment and Tool Institute

ETO Energy Technology Office

ETS Educational Television Station

ETUC European Trade Union Confederation

EWA East and West Association; Education Writers Association

EXIMBANK Export-Import Bank

EYOA Economic and Youth Opportunities Agency

FAA Federal Aviation Agency; Film Artists' Association

FAC Federal Aviation Commission; Finance Affairs Commission

FAO Fleet Air Defense

FAO Food and Agriculture Organization

FAPC Food and Agricultural Planning Committee

FARI Foreign Affairs Research Institute

FARR Feminist Alliance Against Rape

FAS Farm Advisory Service; Federal Agricultural Service

FASB Financial Accounting Standards Board

FAT Folk Arts Theater

F&AUA Fire and Accident Underwriters Association

FBI Federal Bureau of Investigation; Food Business Institute

FBLA Future Business Leaders of America

FBN Federal Bureau of Narcotics

FCA   Farm Credit Administration; Financial Corporation of America; Foster Care Association

FCB   Flight Certification Board

FCC   Federal Communications Commission; Federal Council of Churches

FCDA   Federal Civil Defense Administration

FCI   Federal Correctional Institution; Foreign Credit Insurance Association

FCIC   Farm Crop Insurance Corporation

FCST   Federal Council for Science and Technology

FD   Foundation for the Disabled

FDA   Food and Drug Administration

FDAA   Federal Disaster Assistance Administration

FDEA   Federal Drug Enforcement Administration

FDIC   Federal Deposit Insurance Corporation

FECB   Foreign Exchange Control Board

FEI   Free Enterprise Institute

FEMA   Farm Equipment Manufacturers Association; Federal Emergency Management Agency; Fire Equipment Manufacturers Association; Foundry Equipment Manufacturers Association

FENSA   Film Entertainment National Service Association

FEO   Federal Energy Office; Federal Executive Office; Federation of Economic Organizations

FEPC   Fair Employment Practices Commission

FERA   Federal Emergency Relief Administration

FERC   Federal Energy Regulatory Commission

FETS   Far East Trade Service

FFA   Fire Fighters Association; Future Farmers of America

FFC   Farmers Federation Cooperative

FFCB   Federal Farm Credit Board

FFF   Frozen Food Foundation

FFI   Frozen Foods Institute

FFLA   Federal Farm Loan Association

FFMC   Federal Farm Mortgage Corporation

FFRF   Freedom from Religion Foundation

FFU   Fire Fighters Union

FGA   Freer Gallery of Art

FHA   Farmers Home Administration; Federal Highway Administration; Federal Housing Administration; Future Homemakers of America

FHAA   Field Hockey Association of America

FHLB   Federal Home Loan Bank

FIA   Factory Insurance Association; Federal Insurance Administration; Federal Intelligence Agency

FIB   Fishing Industry Board

FIC   Foundation for International Cooperation

FIDA   Federal Industrial Development Authority

FIG   Farmers Insurance Group

FIRA   Federal Investment Review Agency

FIRB   Foreign Investment Review Board

FIS   Flight Information Service

FISC   Financial Industries Service Corporation

FIT   Fashion Institute of Technology

FJA   Future Journalists of America

FLA   Federal Loan Administration; Federal Loan Agency

FLB   Federal Land Bank

FLC   Federal Library Committee

FLGB   Federal Loan Guarantee Board

FLIC   Film Library Information Council

FLRA   Federal Labor Relations Authority

FMA   Federal Maritime Administration; Financial Management Association

FMC   Federal Maritime Commission; Federated Motor (ing) Club; Federated Mountain Club; Ford Motor Company

FMFIC   Federation of Mutual Fire Insurance Companies

FOL   Federation of Labor; Friends of the Land

FOR   Foundation for Ocean Research

FOS   Fisheries Organization Society

FOTM   Friends of Old-Time Music

FPA   Family Planning Association; Foreign Policy Association

FPC   Federal Power Commission; Food Packaging Council; Friends Peace Committee

FPWA   Federation of Professional Writers of America

FQS   Federal Quarantine Service

FRA   Federal Railroad Administration; Food Retailers Association

FRB   Federal Reserve Bank; Federal Reserve Board

FRC   Federal Radio Commission; Foreign Relations Council

FREB   Federal Real Estate Board

FRS   Financial Relations Society; Foundation Research Service

FS   Foreign Service; Forest Service; Friends Society

FSA Farm Security Administration; Federal Security Administration; Federal Security Agency; Federation of South Arabia; Freethinkers Society of America; Future Scientists of America

FSAA Family Service Agency of America; Family Service Association of America

FSC Family Services Bureau; Federal Safety Council; Food Standards Committee

FSI Foreign Service Institute

FSIC Federal Savings Insurance Corporation

FSLA Federal Savings and Loan Association

FSLIC Federal Savings and Loan Insurance Corporation

FSR Foreign Service Reserve

FSS Federal Supply Service

FSSC Foreign Student Service Council

FSU Friends of the Soviet Union

FSWA Federation of Sewage Works Associations

FTA Free Trade Association; Future Teachers of America

FTB Franchise Tax Board

FTC Fair Trade Commission; Federal Trade Commission

FTL Federal Telecommunications Laboratory

FTMA Federation of Textile Manufacturers Associations

FTU Federation of Trade Unions

FUA Farm Underwriters Association

FUP Friends United Press

FUW Federation of University Women

FWA Family Welfare Association; Farm Workers Association; Federal Works Agency

FWAA   Football Writers Association of America

FWHF   Federation of World Health Foundations

FWL   Foundation for World Literacy

FWPCA   Federal Water Pollution Control Administration

FWQA   Federal Water Quality Association

FWRC   Federal Water Resources Council

FWU   Food Workers Union

GA   Gamblers Anonymous; Geographical Association; Geologists Association

GAA   Gay Activists Alliance; General Aviation Association

GAFD   Guild of American Funeral Directors

GAI   Government Affairs Institute

GALA   Gay Atheist League of America

GAMA   Gas Appliance Manufacturers Association; General Aviation Manufacturers Association

GAMAA   Guitar and Accessories Manufacturers Association of America

GAO   General Accounting Office; General Auditing Office; Government Accounting Office

GA S&L   Great American Savings and Loan

GASP   Group Against Smog and Pollution

GATA   Graphic Arts Technical Association

GAU   Gay Academic Union

GBF   Great Books Foundation

GBMA   Golf Ball Manufacturers Association

GCA   Girls' Clubs of America; Greeting Card Association

GD   General Dynamics

GDPS Government Document Publishing Service

GDU Guide Dog Users

GEA Gravure Engravers Association

GEB Grain Elevators Board

GEC General Electric Company

GEICO Government Employees Insurance Company

GES Government Economic Service

GFTU General Federation of Trade Unions

GFWC General Federation of Women's Clubs

GHI Good Housekeeping Institute

GI Gimbel Brothers

GIA Goodwill Industries of America

GID General Intelligence Division

GIO Government Information Organization; Government Insurance Office

GIS Geoscience Information Society

GIT Georgia Institute of Technology

GLAD Gay and Lesbian Advocates and Defenders

GLC Great Lakes Commission

GMA Gallery of Modern Art; Grocery Manufacturers of America

GMC General Motors Corporation; Gulf Maritime Company

GMI General Motors Institute

GMWU General and Municipal Workers Union

GP Gallop Poll

GPA Gas Processors Association

GPL General Precision Laboratory

GPO Government Printing Office

GPU   General Postal Union

GRA   Governmental Research Association

GRC   Gale Research Company; Government Research Corporation; Gulf Research Corporation

GRO   Greenwich Royal Observatory

GS   Geochemical Society; Geological Survey; Gerontological Society; Girl Scouts

GSA   General Services Administration; Geological Society of America; Girl Scouts of America

GSB   Government Savings Bank

GTA   Government Telecommunications Agency

GTC   Government Training Center; Guild of Television Cameramen

GTU   Graduate Theological Union

GWI   Ground Water Institute

HAC   Hughes Aircraft Company

HAF   Hebrew Arts Foundation

HARC   Human Affairs Research Center

HARM   Humans Against Rape and Molestation

HAWE   Honorary Association for Women in Education

HBA   Hollywood Bowl Association; Hospital Benefit Association; Housing Builders Association

HBJ   Harcourt Brace Jovanovich

HBS   Harvard Business School

HC   House of Commons

HCA   Hospital Corporation of America; Hotel Corporation of America

HCFA   Health Care Financing Administration

HCVA   Historic Commercial Vehicle Association

HEA   Home Economics Association

HEC   Hydro-Electric Commission

HEF   Hospital Employees Federation

HEPC   Hydro-Electric Power Commission

HEW   Health, Education, and Welfare (Department of)

HF   Hall of Fame

HFGA   Hall of Fame for Great Americans

HFM   Henry Ford Museum

HHFA   Housing and Home Finance Agency

HIA   Hospital Industries Association; Housing Improvement Association

HIAA   Health Insurance Association of America

HKU   Hong Kong University

HL   House of Lords

HLB   Hotel Licensing Board

HLF   Human Life Foundation

HLS   Harvard Law School

HMA   Home Manufacturers Association

HMO   Health Maintenance Organization

HMSO   His (Her) Majesty's Stationery Office

HMTA   Hotel-Motel Association

HNC   Human Nutrition Council

HOA   Home Owners Association

HOLC   Home Owners Loan Corporation

HOLUA   Home Office Life Underwriters Association

HOPE   Help Organize Peace Everywhere

HP   House of Parliament

HR   House of Representatives

HRA   Hardware Retailers Association; Human Resources Administration

HRB   Housing and Redevelopment Board

HRC   Human Rights Commission

HRDA   Human Resources Development Agency

HRL   Human Resources Laboratory

HSA   Health Services Administration; Hispanic Society of America; Hospital Savings Association

HSRI   Highway Safety Research Institute

HSUS   Humane Society of the United States

HTSA   Highway Traffic Safety Administration

HU   Harvard University

HUA   Housing and Urban Affairs

HUAC   House Un-American Activities Committee

HUD   Housing and Urban Development (Department of)

HUDC   Housing and Urban Development Corporation

HUP   Harvard University Press

IAB   Industry Advisory Board; Inter-American Bank

IAC   Industry Advisory Commission

IACA   Independent Air Carriers Association

IACB   International Association of Convention Bureaus

IAEA   International Atomic Energy Agency

IAF   Inter-American Foundation; International Association of Firefighters

IAG   International Association of Gerontology

IAIA   Institute of American Indian Arts

IAL International Arbitration League

IAM Institute of Appliance Manufacturers; International Academy of Medicine; International Association of Machinists; International Association of Meteorology

IAMC Inter-American Music Council

IAPA Inter-American Police Academy; Inter-American Press Association

IAS Institute for Advanced Study; International Accountants Society

IASP International Association for Suicide Prevention

IAT Institute for Applied Technology

IATA International Air Transport Association

IAW International Alliance of Women

IBA Independent Bankers Association; Independent Broadcasting Association; International Bar Association; Investment Bankers Association

IBC International Broadcasting Corporation

IBEW International Brotherhood of Electrical Workers

IBFI International Business Farms Industries

IBSA International Bible Student Association

IBU International Broadcasting Union

IBWM International Bureau of Weights and Measures

ICA Industry Communication Association; Institute of Chartered Accountants; International Communications Agency; International Cooperative Administration

ICAA International Council on Alcohol and Addictions

ICBO Interracial Council for Business Opportunities

ICC Indian Claims Commission; International Chamber of Commerce; International Control Commission; Interstate Commerce Commission

ICG Industries Consultative Group

ICIA International Credit Insurance Association

ICM Institute of Computer Management

ICMA International City Managers' Association

ICND International Commission on Narcotic Drugs

ICR Institute of Cancer Research; Institute for Cooperative Research

ICRC International Committee of the Red Cross

ICS Indian Civil Service; Institution of Computer Sciences; International College of Surgeons

ICSE International Committee for Sexual Equality

ICSS International Council for the Social Studies

ICST Institute for Computer Sciences and Technology

ICW International Council of Women

ICWU International Chemical Workers Union

ID Interior Department

IDA Industrial Development Agency

IDB Industrial Development Board

IDEA International Drug Enforcement Association

IDO International Disarmament Organization

IDR Institute for Dream Research

IDS Interior Designers Society

IEE Institute of Electrical Engineers; Institute of Electronic Engineering

IEEE Institute of Electrical and Electronic Engineers

IEP Institute of Experimental Psychology

IES Indian Educational Service; Information Exchange Service

IFA   Industrial Forestry Association; Industry Film Association; International Federation of Actors

IFAD   International Fund for Agricultural Development

IFAW   International Fund for Animal Welfare

IFC   Inland Fisheries Commission; International Fisheries Commission

IFF   Institute for the Future

IFRC   International Fusion Research Council

IFS   International Foundation for Science

IFTU   International Federation of Trade Unions

IGA   Independent Grocers Alliance

IGC   Intergovernmental Copyright Committee

IIE   Institute of Industrial Engineers

IIW   International Institute of Welding

ILA   International Laundry Association; International Law Association; International Longshoremen's Association

ILAA   International Legal Aid Association

ILC   International Law Commission

ILHR   International League of Human Rights

ILO   International Labor Organization

ILP   Independent Labour Party

IMA   Industrial Marketing Association; International Management Association

IMC   International Maritime Committee; International Monetary Conference

IMF   International Monetary Fund

IMRA   Industrial Marketing Research Association

IMS   Industrial Management Society

IMU   International Mailers Union

INA Iraqi News Agency; Israeli News Agency

INC Indian National Congress; International Narcotics Control

INCREF International Children's Rescue Fund

INF International Naturist Federation; International Nudist Federation

INFOTERM International Information Center for Terminology

INGA Interstate Natural Gas Association

INLA Irish National Liberation Army

INP International News Photos

INPA International Newspaper Promotion Association

INPO Institute of Nuclear Power Operations

INS Immigration and Naturalization Service; International News Service

INSTAAR Institute of Arctic and Alpine Research

INSURV Inspection and Survey (Board of)

INTECOM International Council for Technical Communication

INTELSAT International Telecommunications Satellite Organization

INTERPOL International Criminal Police Organization

INTERTELL International Intelligence Legion

INTUC Indian National Trades Union Congress

IOB Intelligence Oversight Board

IOBB Independent Order of B'nai B'rith

IOC International Olympic Committee

IOCU International Organization of Consumer Unions

IOGP Independent Oil and Gas Producers

IOS Investors Overseas Services

IPA Independent Publishers Association; International Press Association

IPB International Peace Bureau

IPCA Industrial Pest Control Association

IPI International Patent Institute

IPO International Projects Office

IPPA International Planned Parenthood Association

IPRA International Professional Rodeo Association; International Public Relations Association

IPRO International Patent Research Office

IPS Information Processing Society

IRA Intercollegiate Rowing Association; International Racquetball Association; International Reading Association; International Recreation Association; Irish Republican Army

IRAB Institute for Research in Animal Behavior

IRAC Industrial Relations Advisory Committee

IRB Industrial Relations Bureau; Industrial Review Board; Insurance Rating Board

IRC Industrial Relations Council; International Red Cross

IRI Industrial Research Institute

IRLA Independent Research Library Association

IRN Independent Radio News

IRO International Refugee Organization; International Relief Organization

IRR Institute of Race Relations

IRRA Industrial Relations Research Association

IRS Internal Revenue Service; International Rorschach Society

IRTS   International Radio and Television Society

IRTU   International Railway Temperance Union; International Road Transport Union

ISA   Instrument Society of America; International Standards Association; International Student Association

ISAB   Institute for the Study of Animal Behavior

ISAC   International Security Affairs Committee

ISAR   International Society for Astrological Research

ISAS   Institute of Space and Aeronautical Science

ISC   Industrial Security Commission; Interstate Sanitation Commission

ISES   International Solar Energy Society

ISF   International Science Foundation; International Shipping Federation; International Softball Federation

ISO   International Standards Organization

ISPA   International Society for the Protection of Animals

ISR   Institute for Sex Research; International Society of Radiology

ISRD   International Society for the Rehabilitation of the Disabled

ISSS   International Society for the Study of Symbols

ISTA   Institute of Science and Technology

ISTB   Interstate Tariff Bureau

ISW   Institute for Solid Wastes

ISWA   International Science Writers Association

ITA   Independent Teachers Association; International Trade Administration

ITAB   Industrial Technical Advisory Board

ITB Industrial Training Board

ITC Industrial Training Council; International Trade Commission

ITF International Television Federation; International Trade Federation

ITN International Television Network

ITNA Independent Television News Association

ITO International Trade Organization

ITS International Thespian Society; International Trade Secretariat

ITSC International Telecommunications Satellite Consortium

IT&T International Telephone and Telegraph

ITTA International Table Tennis Association

ITU International Telecommunications Union; International Typographical Union

IUW Industrial Union of Workers

IVA International Volleyball Association

IWA Institute of World Affairs; Insurance Workers of America

IWC International Whaling Commission

IWL Institute of World Leadership

IWPO International Word Processing Organization

IWW Industrial Workers of the World

IYF International Youth Federation

IZTO Interzonal Trade Office

JAMA Japan Automobile Manufacturers Association

JBC Jamaica Broadcasting Corporation; Japan Broadcasting Corporation

JBS John Birch Society

JBT Jewelers Board of Trade

JC Juvenile Corps

JCA Joint Commission on Accreditation; Joint Communications Agency

JCAE Joint Committee on Atomic Energy

JCB Joint Consultative Board

JCC Job Corps Center; Junior Chamber of Commerce

JCEE Joint Council on Economic Education

JCP Japan Communist Party; J. C. Penney

JCRR Joint Commission on Rural Reconstruction

JD Justice Department

JDC Juvenile Detention Center

JDS John Dewey Society; Joint Defense Staff

JEA Journalism Education Association

JEC Joint Economic Committee

JF Jewish Federation

JFP Jobs for Progress

JGS Joint General Staff

JHC John Hancock Center

JHH Johns Hopkins Hospital

JIC Joint Industry Council; Joint Intelligence Center; Joint Intelligence Committee

JLS Junior Literary Society

JMC Joint Maritime Commission; Joint Maritime Congress

JNN Japan News Network

JOBS Job Opportunities in the Business Sector

JPB Joint Planning Board

JPC   Joint Planning Council

JPGM   J. Paul Getty Museum

JPS   Juvenile Probation Service

JRC   Junior Red Cross

JRN   Japan Radio Network

JSC   Johnson Space Center

JSP   Japan Socialist Party

JTC   Junior Training Corps

JTS   Jewish Theological Seminary

KACIA   Korean-American Commerce and Industry Association

KBS   Korean Broadcasting System

KC   Knights of Columbus

KCA   Kitchen Cabinet Association

KCNA   Korean Central News Agency

KCPA   Kennedy Center for the Performing Arts

KFC   Kentucky Fried Chicken

KGB   Committee of State Security; Soviet Secret Police (Russian *Komitet Gossudarrstvennoi Bezopastnosti*)

KI   Kiwanis International

KKK   Ku Klux Klan

KWP   Korean Workers Party

LA   Licensing Authority

LAB   Liquor Administration Board

LAC   League of Arab Countries

LACL   Latin America Citizens League

LACM   Latin America Common Market

LADIES   Life After Divorce Is Eventually Sane

LADO   Latin America Defense Organization; Latin American Development Organization

LAFTA   Latin America Free Trade Association

LAM   London Academy of Music

LAMA   Library Administration and Management Association

LARC   League Against Religious Coercion

LAS   League of Arab States; Lebanese-American Society; Legal Aid Society

LATUF   Latin America Trade Union Federation

LAW   League of American Writers

LBI   Lloyds Bank International

LBJL   Lyndon Baines Johnson Library

LBS   Libyan Broadcasting Service

LC   Library of Congress

LCA   Learning Corporation of America; Library Club of America

LCRT   Lincoln Center Repertory Theater

LCSA   Lewis and Clark Society of America

LCY   League of Communists of Yugoslavia

LDF   Legal Defense Fund

LDP   Liberal Democratic Party

LEA   Locomotive Engineers Association; Lutheran Education Association

LEAA   Law Enforcement Assistance Administration

LEC   Law Enforcement Center; Livestock Equipment Council

LEDC   League for Emotionally Disturbed Children

LEEA   Law Enforcement Education Agency

LEPA   Law Enforcement Planning Agency

LEY   Liberal European Youth

LGPA   Livestock and Grain Producers Association

LGU   Ladies Golf Union

LHW   League of Hispanic Women

LI   Lions International

LIA   Laser Institute of America; Lead Industries Association; Leather Industries of America

LIAA   Life Insurance Association of America

LIC   Liquor Industry Council

LIFE   Ladies Involved for Education; League for International Food Education

LIMRA   Life Insurance Marketing and Research Association

LIO   Lions International Organization; Livestock Improvement Organization

LIRS   Lutheran Immigration and Refugee Service

LITA   Library and Information Technology Association

LITINT   Literary International

LIUNA   Laborers International Union of North America

LL   Little League

LLA   Lend-Lease Administration; Luther League of America

LLC   Libertarian Law Council

LLL   Lawrence Livermore Laboratories

LLUU   Laymen's League-Unitarian Universalist

LMA   League for Mutual Aid

LMDC   Lawyers Military Defense Committee

LMPA   Library and Museum of the Performing Arts

LMSA   Labor Management Services Administration

LMVUS   League of Men Voters of the United States

LN   League of Nations

LNA   Libyan News Agency

L-NCP   Liberal-National Country Party

LNS   Liberation News Service

LNU   League of Nations Union

LO   Lowell Observatory

LOOS   League of Older Students

LOYA   League of Young Adventurers

LP   Labour Party; Liberal Party; Libertarian Party

LPA   Labor Party Association; Little People of America

LPE   London Press Exchange

LPGA   Ladies Professional Golf Association

LPI   Lightning Protection Institute

LPNA   Licensed Practical Nurses Association

LPSA   Liberal Party of South Africa

LRA   Labor Research Association; Libertarian Republican Alliance

LRB   Labor Research Bureau; Legislative Reference Bureau; Loyalty Review Board

LRC   Law Reform Commission

LRCS   League of Red Cross Societies

LRL   Lawrence Radiation Laboratory; Lunar Receiving Laboratory

LRY   Liberal Religious Youth

LSA   Labor Services Agency; Land Settlement Association; Leukemia Society of America; Linguistic Society of America

LSF   Lloyd Shaw Foundation

LSI   Lunar Science Institute

LSNR   League of Struggle for Negro Rights

LSWY   League of Socialist Working Youth

LTA   Lawn Tennis Association

LUA   Life Underwriters Association

LUAC   Land Use Advisory Council

LUC   Land Use Commission

LULAC   League of United Latin-America Citizens

LVA   Literary Volunteers of America

LVUSA   Legion of Valor of the USA

LWF   Lutheran World Federation

LWU   Leather Workers Union

LWV   League of Women Voters

LWVUS   League of Women Voters of the United States

LZOA   Labor Zionist Organization of America

MA   Manpower Administration; Maritime Administration; Metric Association; Mountaineering Association

MAA   Mathematical Association of America; Motel Association of America; Mutual Aid Association

MAAH   Museum of African-American History

MAC   Middle Atlantic Conference; Municipal Assistance Corporation

MACA   Maritime Air Control Authority

MADD   Mothers Against Drunk Drivers; Mothers Against Drunk Driving

MAES   Mexican American Engineering Society

MAF   Middle Atlantic Fisheries

MAI Museum of the American Indian

MANFED Manufacturers Federation

MANWA Mexican-American National Women's Association

MAOF Mexican-American Opportunity Foundation

MAPI Machinery and Allied Products Institute

MARAD Maritime Administration

MARI Middle American Research Institute

MARIS Maritime Research Information Service

MAS Marine Acoustical Services; Military Agency for Standardization

MASA Mail Advertising Service Association

MASCA Middle Atlantic States Correctional Association

MASH Mobile Army Surgical Hospital

MASUA Mid-America State Universities Association

MATA Motorcycle and Allied Trades Association

MAUS Metric Association of the United States

MAYA Mexican-American Youth Association

MAYO Mexican American Youth Organization

MB Marketing Board; Munitions Board; Music for the Blind

MBA Marine Biological Association; Master Builders Association; Men's Basketball Association; Mortgage Bankers of America; Mortgage Brokers Association

MBAA Master Brewers Association of America

MBCA Motor Boat Club of America

MBCC Migratory Bird Conservation Commission

MBS Motor Business Society; Music Broadcasting Society; Mutual Broadcasting System

MBSA Municipal Board Standards Association

MC Manpower Commission; Maritime Commission

MCA Music Corporation of America; Music Critics Association

MCAA Military Civil Affairs Administration

MCAT Midwest Council on Airborne Television

MCB Metric Conversion Board; Metric Conversion Bureau

MCBA Master Car Builders' Association

MCC Missile Control Center; Mission Control Center

MCDA Manpower and Career Development Agency

MCL Marine Corps League

MCLA Marine Corps League Auxiliary

MCP Malaysian Communist Party

MCROA Marine Corps Reserve Officers Association

MCSB Motor Carriers Service Bureau

MCTA Motor Carriers Traffic Association

MDA Mutual Defense Agency

MDAA Muscular Dystrophy Association of America

MDC Metropolitan District Commission

MDNA Machinery Dealers National Association

MEA Maritime Employers Association; Municipal Employees Association; Music Educators Association; Musical Educators Association

MEC Monetary and Economic Council

MECU Municipal Employees Credit Union

MEDIA Manufacturers Educational Drug Information Association

MEDICO Medical International Corporation

MEDRC Medical Reserve Corps

MEDRESCO Medical Research Council

MEL Music Education League

MEPC Maritime Environment Protection Committee

MERC Music Education Research Council

MERIT Medical Relief International

MESA Mechanics Educational Society of America; Mining Enforcement and Safety Administration

METCO Metropolitan Countil for Educational Opportunity

METO Middle East Treaty Organization

MEWA Motor and Equipment Wholesalers Association

MFA Master Fencers Association; Museum of Fine Arts

MFPB Mineral Fiber Products Bureau

MFSA Master Floor Sanders Association; Metal Finishing Suppliers' Association

MFTB Motor Freight Traffic Bureau

MFW Maritime Federation of the World

MGA Military Government Association; Mushroom Growers Association

MGC Machine Gun Corps; Marriage Guidance Council

MGIC Mortgage Guarantee Insurance Corporation

MGM Metro-Goldwyn-Mayer

MHA Marine Historical Association; Mental Health Administration; Mental Health Association; Mental Health Authority; Multiple Handicapped Association

MHMA Mobile Homes Manufacturers Association

MHQ Maritime Headquarters

MHRA Modern Humanities Research Association

MHT Museum of History and Technology

MIA Marble Institute of America; Mica Industry Association; Millinery Institute of America

MIAC Manufacturing Industries Advisory Council

MIB Management Improvement Board; Maritime Index Bureau

MIC Motorcycle Industry Council; Music Industry Council

MICS Museum of the International College of Surgeons

MIF Milk Industry Foundation; Miners International Federation

MIO Metric Information Office

MIP Manufacturers of Illumination Products

MIPTC Men's International Professional Tennis Council

MIRA Motor Industry's Research Association

MIS Management Information Service; Minstrel Instruction Service

MISO Military Intelligence Service Organization

MIT Massachusetts Institute of Technology

MLA Marine Librarians Association; Master Locksmiths Association; Medical Library Association; Modern Language Association; Music Library Association

MLAA Modern Language Association of America

MLB Marginal Lands Board; Maritime Labor Board; Multiple Listing Bureau

MLBPA Major League Baseball Players Association

MLC Meat and Livestock Commission

MLL Music Lovers League

MLRB Mutual Loss Research Bureau

MLS Multiple Listing Service

MM Moral Majority

MMA   Metropolitan Museum of Art; Minute Men of America; Music Masters Association; Music of Modern Art

MMB   Milk Marketing Board

MMCB   Midwest Motor Carriers Bureau

MMRB   Master Material Review Board

MMSA   Mining and Metallurgical Society of America

MNH   Museum of Natural History

MNLL   Malaysian National Liberation League

MNP   Malay National Party

MNPL   Machinist Non-Partisan Political League

MOA   Metropolitan Opera Association; Music Operators of America

MOCA   Museum of Contemporary Art

MOG   Metropolitan Opera Guild

MOMA   Museum of Modern Art

MOMS   Mothers for Moral Stability

MOTAT   Museum of Transport and Technology

MOWW   Military Order of the World Wars

MPA   Magazine Publishers Association; Medical Procurement Agency; Mobile Press Association; Modern Poetry Association; Motion Picture Alliance; Music Publishers Association

MPAA   Motion Picture Association of America; Musical Performing Arts Association

MPAUS   Music Publishers Association of the United States

MPB   Missing Persons Bureau

MPC   Manpower and Personnel Council; Military Pioneer Corps; Military Police Corps

MPDA   Motion Picture Distributors Association

MPMI Magazine and Paperback Marketing Institute

MPRP Mongolian Peoples Revolutionary Party; Muslim Peoples Republican Party

MPU Medical Practitioners Union

MRA Master Retailers Association

MRB Material Review Board; Mutual Reinsurance Bureau

MRC Market Research Council; Medical Reserve Corps; Men's Republican Club; Motor Racing Club

MRCA Market Research Corporation of America

MRCP Maoist Revolutionary Communist Party

MRDC Military Research and Development Center

MRF Mayo Research Foundation; Music Research Foundation

MRP Mobile Repair Party

MRS Market Research Society

MRUA Mobile Radio Users' Association

MS Manuscript Society; Metallurgical Society; Meteoritical Society

MSA Marine Safety Agency; Maritime Safety Agency; Middle States Association; Mineralogical Society of America; Mutual Security Agency; Mutual Society of Arts

MSC Manned Spacecraft Center; Maple Syrup Council; Medical Service Corps

MSFC Marshall Space Flight Center

MSG Madison Square Garden

MSMA Master Sign Makers' Association

MSPB Merit Systems Protection Board

MSRA Multiple Shoe Retailers' Association

MSS Movement Shorthand Society; Multiple Sclerosis Society

MSSA Maintenance Supply Services Agency

MTA Manpower Training Association; Market Technicians Association; Metropolitan Transit Authority; Motor Trade Association; Music Teachers Association

MTB Materials Transportation Bureau

MTBA Machine Tool Builders' Association

MTC Missile Test Center; Motor Transport Corps

MTCB Metropolitan Taxicab Board

MTDB Metropolitan Transit Development Board

MTEA Metal Trades Employers Association

MTF Metal Trades Federation

MTIA Metal Trades Industry Association

MTIRA Machine Tool Industry Research Association

MTMA Modern Teaching Methods Association

MTN Medical Television Network

MTNA Music Teachers National Association

MTRF Mark Twain Research Foundation

MTTA Machine Tool Trades' Association

MU Musicians Union

MUA Machinery Users' Association; Monotype Users' Association

MVMA Motor Vehicle Manufacturers Association

MVPCB Motor Vehicle Pollution Control Board

MWA Mystery Writers of America

MWAI Mystery Writers of America, Incorporated

MWF Medical Women's Federation

MWIA Medical Women's International Association

MWL   Mutual Welfare League

MWO   Mount Wilson Observatory

MZ   Museum of Zoology

NA   Narcotics Anonymous; National Archives; Neurotics Anonymous

NAA   National Aeronautic Association; National Association of Accountants; National Auctioneers Association; National Automobile Association

NAAA   National Alliance of Athletic Associations; National Association of American Academicians; National Auto Auction Association

NAAB   National Architectural Accrediting Board

NAABC   National Association of American Business Clubs

NAAC   National Agricultural Advisory Commission

NAACP   National Association for the Advancement of Colored People

NAADC   North America Area Defense Command

NAAN   National Advertising Agency Network

NAAS   National Agricultural Advisory Service

NAAUS   National Archery Association of the United States

NAB   National Alliance of Businessmen; National Association of Broadcasters; National Association of Businessmen; Newspaper Advertising Bureau

NABA   North American Benefit Association

NABB   National Association for Better Broadcasting

NABC   National Association of Boys' Clubs

NABE   National Association of Book Editors; National Association of Business Economists

NABET   National Association of Broadcast Employees and Technicians

NABP   National Association of Book Publishers

NABRT   National Association for Better Radio and Television

NABS   National Association of Barber Schools; National Association of Black Students

NABT   National Association of Blind Teachers

NAC   National Arts Club; National Association of Chiropodists; North Atlantic Council; Northeast Air Command

NACA   National Air Carrier Association; National Armored Car Association

NACB   National Association of Convention Bureaus

NACCD   National Advisory Commission on Civil Disorders

NACD   National Association for Community Development; National Association of Corporate Directors

NACEEO   National Advisory Council on Equality of Educational Opportunity

NACH   National Advisory Council for the Handicapped

NACOA   National Advisory Committee on Oceans and Atmosphere

NACSE   National Association of Civil Service Employees

NACW   National Advisory Committee on Women

NADA   National Association of Drug Addiction; National Automobile Dealers Association

NADF   National Alzheimer's Disease Foundation

NAE   National Academy of Education; National Academy of Engineering

NAEA   National Art Education Association

NAESP National Association of Elementary School Principals

NAF National Abortion Foundation; National Amputation Foundation; National Arts Foundation

NAFC National Association of Food Chains

NAFD National Association of Funeral Directors

NAFM National Association of Furniture Manufacturers

NAFMB National Association of FM Broadcasters

NAG Negro Actors Guild

NAGC National Association for Gifted Children

NAGE National Association of Government Employees

NAHB National Association of Home Builders

NAHC National Advisory Health Council; National Anti-Hunger Coalition

NAIA National Association of Insurance Agents; National Association of Intercollegiate Athletics

NAIB National Association of Insurance Brokers

NAICU National Association of Independent Colleges and Universities

NAJ National Association for Justice

NAL New American Library

NALC National Association of Letter Carriers

NALS National Association of Legal Secretaries

NAM National Air Museum; National Association of Manufacturers

NAME National Association of Marine Engineers; National Association of Media Educators; National Association of Medical Examiners

NAMSB National Association of Mutual Savings Banks

NANA North America Newspaper Alliance

NANM   National Association of Negro Musicians

NAP   National Association of Parliamentarians; National Association of Postmasters; National Association of Publishers

NAPA   National Association of Performing Artists; National Association of Purchasing Agents

NAPO   National Association of Probation Officers; National Association of Property Owners

NAR   National Association of Realtors

NARAL   National Abortion Rights Action League; National Association for the Repeal of Abortion Laws

NARAS   National Academy of Recording Arts and Sciences

NARC   National Association for Retarded Children

NARCO   United Nations Narcotics Commission

NARD   National Association of Retail Druggists

NARM   National Association of Retail Merchants

NARP   National Association of Railroad Passengers

NARS   National Archives and Records Service

NARTB   National·Association of Radio and Television Broadcasters

NAS   National Academy of Sciences; National Agricultural Society; National Audubon Society

NASA   National Aeronautics and Space Administration; National Appliance Service Association; North American Sailing Association

NASC   National Aeronautics and Space Council; National Aircraft Standards Committee; National Alliance of Senior Citizens; National Association of Student Councils; North America Supply Council; Northwest Association of Schools and Colleges

NASD   National Association of Securities Dealers

NASL   North America Soccer League

NASM   National Air and Space Museum; National Association of Schools of Music

NASPA   National Society of Public Accountants

NASRC   National Association of State Racing Commissioners

NASS   National Association of School Superintendents

NASSP   National Association of Secondary-School Principals

NASTL   National Anti-Steel-Trap League

NASU   National Adult School Union

NASULGC   National Association of State Universities and Land-Grant Colleges

NASW   National Association of Science Writers; National Association of Social Workers

NATA   National Association of Tax Accountants; National Association of Tax Administrators; North Atlantic Treaty Alliance

NATAS   National Academy of Television Arts and Sciences

NATIE   National Association of Trade and Industrial Education

NATO   National Association of Taxicab Owners; National Association of Theater Owners; National Association of Trailer Owners; National Association of Travel Organizations; North Atlantic Treaty Organization

NAVH   National Association for the Visually Handicapped

NAVS   North American Vegetarian Society

NAW   National Association of Wholesalers; National Association for Women

NAWA   National Association of Women Artists

NAWF National Aborigine Welfare Fund; North America Wildlife Foundation

NAWM National Association of Wool Manufacturers

NAWPA North American Water and Power Alliance

NAYC National Association of Youth Clubs

NBA National Band Association; National Bankers Association; National Bar Association; National Basketball Association; National Boat Association; National Bowling Association; National Boxing Association; National Button Association

NBBB National Better Business Bureau

NBBS New British Broadcasting Station

NBC National Basketball Congress; National Book Committee; National Broadcasting Commission; National Broadcasting Company; Nigerian Broadcasting Corporation

NBCA National Baseball Congress of America; National Beagle Club of America

NBCC National Book Critics Circle

NBEA National Business Education Association

NBL National Basketball League; National Book League

NBME National Board of Medical Examiners

NBO Navy Bureau of Ordnance

NBPA National Bark Producers Association; National Basketball Players Association; National Black Police Association

NBPC National Border Patrol Council

NBS National Broadcasting Service; National Bureau of Standards

NBST National Board for Science and Technology

NBTA National Business Teachers Association

NCA National Chiropractic Association; National Civic Association; National Council on the Aging; National Council on Alcoholism; National Council on the Arts; National Credit Association

NCAA National Collegiate Athletic Association

NCAAA National Center of Afro-American Artists

NCAC National Copyright Advisory Committee

NCAI National Congress of American Indians; National Council on Alcoholism, Inc.

NCANH National Council for the Accreditation of Nursing Homes

NCAPC National Center for Air Pollution Control

NCASF National Council of American-Soviet Friendship

NCAW National Council for Animal Welfare

NCC National Cadet Corps; National Computer Center; National Computer Council

NCCD National Council on Crime and Delinquency

NCCH National Council to Control Handguns

NCCY National Council of Catholic Youth

NCDA National Center for Drug Analysis; National Council on Drug Abuse

NCDC National Centers for Disease Control; National Communicable Disease Center

NCF National Consumer Federation

NCFA National Commission of Fine Arts; National Consumer Finance Association

NCFDA National Council on Federal Disaster Assistance

NCI National Cancer Institute

NCL National Consumers League

NCM National Congress for Men

NCMC National Center on Missing Children

NCMDA National Commission on Marijuana and Drug Abuse

NCNA New China News Agency

NCNW National Council of Negro Women

NCOA National Council on the Aging

NCOC National Commission on Organized Crime; National Council on Organized Crime

NCR National Cash Register

NCS National Cartoonists Society; Numerical Control Society

NCTA National Cable Television Association

NCUA National Credit Union Administration; National Credit Union Association

NCUC National Commission on Unemployment Compensation

NCUF National Computer Users Forum

NCW National Council of Women

NDA National Dairy Association; National Dairymen's Association; National Dental Association

NDAC National Defense Advisory Commission; National Defense Advisory Committee; Nuclear Defense Affairs Committee

NDC National Dairy Council; National Defense Corps

NDP National Democratic Party; New Democratic Party

NEA National Editorial Association; National Education Association; National Electrification Administration; National Endowment for the Arts; Nuclear Energy Agency

NEATO Northeast Asian Treaty Organization

NEC National Economic Council

NECM New England Conservatory of Music

NEGRO National Economic Growth and Reconstruction Organization

NEH National Endowment for the Humanities

NEIC National Earthquake Information Center; National Energy Information Center

NERA National Emergency Relief Administration

NET National Educational Television

NETRC National Educational Television and Radio Center

NEWS New England Wildflower Society

NFA National Faculty Association; National Food Administration; New Farmers of America; Northwest Fisheries Association

NFAC National Food and Agricultural Council

NFAH National Foundation for the Arts and Humanities

NFAL National Foundation of Arts and Letters

NFBF National Farm Bureau Federation

NFBPWC National Federation of Business and Professional Women's Clubs

NFC National Football Conference

NFDA National Food Distributors Association

NFIE National Foundation for the Improvement of Education

NFL National Film Library; National Football League; National Forensic League; National Foresters League

NFLSV National Front for the Liberation of South Vietnam

NFMD National Foundation for the March of Dimes

NFO   National Farmers Organization

NFP   National Federation Party

NFPA   National Fire Protection Association; National Fluid Power Association; National Forest Products Association

NFS   National Fire Service

NFT   National Film Theatre

NFTC   National Foreign Trade Council

NFU   National Farmers Union

NG   National Guard

NGA   National Gallery of Art; National Governors Association

NGAUS   National Guard Association of the United States

NGC   National Gambling Commission

NGF   National Genetics Foundation; National Golf Foundation

NGI   National Garden Institute

NGPA   Natural Gas Processors Association

NGS   National Geodetic Survey; National Geographic Society

NHA   National Health Association; National Hockey Association; National Housing Administration; New Homemakers of America

NHC   National Health Council

NHF   National Health Foundation; National Heart Foundation

NHI   National Health Institute

NHIC   National Home Improvement Council

NHL   National Hockey League

NHO   National Hospice Organization

NHS   National Health Service; National Historical Society; National Honor Society

NHSA   National Head-Start Association; Negro Historical Society of America

NHSB   National Highway Safety Bureau

NHSC   National Highway Safety Council; National Home Study Council

NIA   National Institute on Aging; National Irrigation Administration; Neighborhood Improvement Association

NIAA   National Institute on Alcohol Abuse and Alcoholism

NIAL   National Institute of Arts and Letters

NIB   National Information Bureau

NIC   National Industrial Council

NICB   National Industrial Conference Board

NIH   National Institutes of Health

NIJ   National Institute of Justice

NIMH   National Institute of Mental Health

NIPH   National Institute of Public Health

NIS   National Institute of Science; National Intelligence Service

NISC   National Industrial Safety Committee

NIST   National Institute of Science and Technology

NITA   National Industrial Television Association

NITV   National Iranian Television

NIWU   National Industrial Workers Union

NIYC   National Indian Youth Council

NJAC   National Joint Advisory Council

NKF   National Kidney Foundation

NKVD People's Commissariat for Internal Affairs (Russian *Narodnyi Kommissariat Vnutrennikh Del*)

NLA National Leukemia Association

NLAA National Legal Aid Association

NLRB National Labor Relations Board

NLTA National Lawn Tennis Association

NMA National Management Association; Northwest Mining Association

NMB National Maritime Board; National Mediation Board

NMCB National Metric Conversion Board

NMHA National Mental Health Association

NML National Measurement Laboratory; National Music League

NMPA National Music Publishers Association

NMTA National Metal Trades Association

NMTBA National Machine Tool Builders' Association

NNC National News Council

NNPA National Negro Press Association; National Newspaper Promotion Association; National Newspaper Publishers Association

NNS National Newspaper Syndicate

NOA National Opera Association; National Optical Association; National Orchestral Association

NOC National Oceanographic Council: National Olympic Committee

NOMA National Office Management Association

NON National Office Management Association

NOPWC National Old People's Welfare Council

NORAD North American Air Defense

NORML National Organization for the Reform of Marijuana Laws; National Organization for the Reinforcement of Marijuana Laws; National Organization for the Repeal of Marijuana Laws

NORWEB Northwestern Electricity Board

NOS NATO Office of Security

NOSA National Occupational Safety Association

NOSTA National Ocean Science and Technology Agency

NOW National Organization for Women

NOWAPA North American Water and Power Alliance

NPA National Parenthood Association; National Parks Association; National Pet Association; National Petroleum Association; National Pharmaceutical Association; National Pilots Association; National Planning Association; Newspaper Publishers Association

NPABC National Public Affairs Broadcast Center

NPACT National Public Affairs Center for Television

NPB National Park Board; National Productivity Board

NPC National Patent Council; National Peoples Congress; National Press club

NPF National Park Foundation; National Parkinson Foundation; National Piano Foundation; National Poetry Foundation

NPPA National Press Photographers Association

NPPR Nationalist Party of Puerto Rico

NPR National Public Radio

NPRA National Parks and Recreation Association

NPS Narcotics Prevention Service; National Park Service

NRA National Racing Authority; National Recovery Administration; National Recreation Association; National Rehabilitation Association; National Restaurant Association; National Rifle Association; Naval Reserve Association

NRAA   National Rifle Association of America

NRAC   National Research Advisory Council; National Rural Advisory Council

NRB   National Religious Broadcasters; National Research Bureau; National Roads Board; National Rubber Bureau

NRC   National Racquetball Club; National Republican Club; National Research Council; Nuclear Regulatory Commission; Nuclear Research Council

NRCA   National Resources Council of America; National Retail Credit Association

NRECA   National Rural Electric Cooperative Association

NRFA   National Retail Furniture Association

NRFL   National Rugby Football League

NRLC   National Right to Life Committee

NRP   National Republican Party

NRPA   National Recreation and Park Association

NRPB   National Research and Planning Board

NRPC   National Railroad Passenger Corporation

NRTA   National Retired Teachers Association

NRWC   National Right to Work Committee

NSA   National Safety Association; National Secretaries Association; National Security Agency; National Standards Association; National Students Association; Neurological Society of America; Nuclear Science Association

NSB   National Science Board

NSC   National Safety Council; National Security Council; National Standards Commission

NSCC   National Society for Crippled Children

NSCDRF   National Sickle Cell Disease Research Foundation

NSF   National Science Foundation

NSID   National Society of Interior Designers

NSL   National Standards Laboratory

NSLF   National Socialist Liberation Front

NSMR   National Society for Medical Research

NSNA   National Student Nurses Association

NSPA   National Scholastic Press Association; National Society of Public Accountants

NSPCC   National Society for the Prevention of Cruelty to Children

NSRA   National Shoe Retailers Association; National Shorthand Reporters Association

NSRP   National States Rights Party

NSSC   National Society for the Study of Communication

NSTA   National Science Teachers Association

NSWPP   National Socialist White People's Party

NTA   National Tax Association; National Tennis Association; National Tourist Association; National Tuberculosis Association

NTDPMA   National Tool, Die, and Precision Machining Association

NTIS   National Technical Information Service

NTL   National Tennis League; National Training Laboratories

NTO   National Tenants Organization

NTUC   National Trades Union Congress

NUL   National Union for Liberation; National Urban League

NUP Negro Universities Press

NUWA National Unemployed Workers Association

NVGA National Vocabulary Guidance Association

NVMA National Veterinary Medical Association

NWA National Wrestling Alliance

NWAA National Wheelchair Athletic Association

NWAC National Women's Advisory Council

NWBA National Wheelchair Basketball Association

NWC National War College; National Water Commission; National Writers Club

NWF National Wildlife Federation

NWLF New World Liberation Front

NWR National Wildlife Refuge

NWRLF New World Radical Liberation Front

NWRO National Welfare Rights Organization

NWS National Weather Service

NWU National Workers Union; National Writers Union

NYA National Youth Administration

NYC National Yacht Club; Neighborhood Youth Corps

NYR National Young Republicans

NYSE New York Stock Exchange

OAAA Outdoor Advertising Association of America

OAAU Organization of Afro-American Unity

OAS Organization of American States

OAU Organization for African Unity

OBE Office of Business Economics

OBRA Overseas Broadcasting Representatives' Association

OCA Office of Consumer Affairs

OCAS Organization of Central American States

OCD Office of Civil Defense

ODC Overseas Development Corporation; Overseas Development Council

ODM Office of Defense Mobilization

ODSE Open-Door Student Exchange

OEA Office of Economic Adjustment; Office Education Association; Outdoor Education Association; Overseas Education Association

OEC Office of Energy Conservation

OECD Organization for Economic Cooperation and Development

OECS Organization of East Caribbean States

OEEC Organization for European Economic Cooperation

OEEO Office of Equal Educational Opportunities

OEMA Office Equipment Manufacturers Association

OEO Office of Economic Opportunity

OEP Office of Emergency Preparedness; Office of Energy Planning

OEQC Office of Environmental Quality Control

OFC Overseas Food Corporation

OGE Office of Government Ethics

OHIA Oil Heat Institute of America

OHS Office of Highway Safety; Oral Hygiene Society

OIAA Office of Inter-American Affairs

OICD Office of International Cooperation and Development

OIE   Office of Indian Education

OLEP   Office of Law Enforcement and Planning

OMA   Ocean Mining Administration

OMAT   Office of Manpower, Automation, and Training

OME   Office of Manpower Economics; Office of Minerals Exploration

OMEF   Office Machines and Equipment Federation

OMF   Office of Management and Finance

OMPER   Office of Manpower Policy Evaluation and Research

OMSF   Office of Manned Space Flight

ONA   Overseas News Agency

OPA   Office of Population Affairs; Office of Price Administration; Office of Public Affairs

OPBE   Office of Planning, Budgeting, and Evaluation

OPC   Overseas Press Club

OPEC   Oil Producers' Economic Cartel; Organization of Petroleum Exporting Countries

OPMA   Office Products Manufacturers Association

OPS   Office of Price Stabilization

OPU   Unemployed Peoples Union

ORA   Oil Refiners Association

ORC   Officers Reserve Corps; Offshore Racing Council; Opinion Research Corporation

ORI   Ocean Research Institute; Ocean Resources Institute; Office Research Institute

ORT   Order of Railroad Telegraphers; Organization for Rehabilitation through Training

OS   Optical Society

OSA   Optical Society of America

OSBM Office of Space Biology and Medicine

OSCA Office of Senior Citizens Affairs

OSS Office of Space Science; Office of Strategic Services

OST Office of Science and Technology

OTA Occupational Therapists Association; Office of Technology Assessment

OTBA Owners, Traders, Breeders Association

OTC Organization for Trade Cooperation; Overseas Telecommunications Commission

OUA Order of United Americans

OUP Oxford University Press

OVA Office of Veterans Affairs

OWAA Outdoor Writers' Association of America

OWAEC Organization for West African Economic Cooperation

OWHA Oliver Wendell Holmes Association

OWM Office of Weights and Measures

PA Parents Anonymous

PAA Photographers Association of America; Purchasing Agents Association

PAAC Public Arts Advisory Council

PAB Price Adjustment Board

PAC Pan-Africanist Congress; Pan-American Congress; Political Action Committee

PACE Professional Association of Consulting Engineers

PAD People Against Displacement

PAL Police Athletic League

PANA Pan-African News Agency; Pan-Asian Newspaper Alliance

Pan Am   Pan American World Airways

PANANEWS   Pan-Asian Newspaper Alliance

PARMA   Public Agency Risk Managers Association

PARS   Prisoners Aid and Rehabilitation Society

PASC   Pan-American Standards Committee

PASF   Photographic Art and Science Foundation

PATA   Pacific Area Travel Association

PATO   Pacific-Asian Treaty Organization

PAU   Pan American Union

PAW   People for the American Way

PAWA   Pan-American Women's Association; Pan American World Airways

PAWO   Pan-African Women's Organization

PBA   Professional Bookmen of America; Professional Bowlers Association

PBAA   Periodical and Book Association of America

PBI   Pitney-Bowes, Incorporated

PBS   Philippine Broadcasting Service; Public Broadcasting Service

PC   Peace Corps

PCA   Pest Control Association; Pollution Control Agency

PCC   Price Control Council

PCMA   Post Card Manufacturers Association; Professional Convention Management Association

PCP   Progressive Conservative Party

PCPF   President's Council on Physical Fitness

PDF   Parkinson's Disease Foundation

PEA   Plastic Engineers Association; Public Education Association

PEACE People Emerging Against Corrupt Establishments

PECUSA Presidential Ethics Commission

PEN Poets, Playwrights, Editors, Essayists, and Novelists

PEO Protect Each Other

PEPA Petroleum Electric Power Association

PERA Production Engineering Research Association

PERB Public Employment Relations Board

PERC Peace on Earth Research Center

PERO President's Emergency Relief Organization

PES Philosophy of Education Society

PETA People for the Ethical Treatment of Animals

PFI Pet Food Institute; Police Foundation Institute

PFLO Popular Front for the Liberation of Oman

PFLP Popular Front for the Liberation of Palestine

PFP Progressive Federal Party

PG Proctor & Gamble

PGA Professional Golfers Association

PGMA Private Grocers' Merchandising Association

PGWA Pottery and Glass Wholesalers' Association

PH Philharmonic Hall

PHA Public Housing Administration

PHO Public Hazards Office

PHRI Public Health Research Institute

PHS Public Health Service

PI Plastics Institute

PIA Plastics Institute of America; Printing Industries of America

PIC Private Industry Council

PIE Pacific Intercultural Exchange

PIEA Petroleum Industry Electrical Association

PIF Paper Industry Federation

PIMA Paper Industry Management Association

PIOSA Pan Indian Ocean Science Association

PIPA Pacific Industrial Property Association

PIRA Paper Industries Research Association; Printing Industry Research Association

PIRF Petroleum Industry Research Foundation

PLA Palestine Liberation Army; Pedestrian's League of America; People's Liberation Army; Philatelic Literature Association; Public Library Association

PLAV Polish Legion of American Veterans

PLO Palestine Liberation Organization; Peoples Liberation Organization; Presidential Libraries Office

PLP Parliamentary Labour Party; Partners for Liveable Places; Progressive Labor Party

PMA Pacific Maritime Association; Pencil Makers Association; Pharmaceutical Manufacturers Association

PMEA Powder Metallurgy Equipment Association

PMEL Precision Measuring Equipment Laboratory

PMNH Peabody Museum of Natural History

PMO Provost Marshal's Office

PMSA Pacific Merchant Shipping Association

PMTB Pacific Motor Tariff Bureau

PMU Pattern Makers Union

PNA Philippines News Agency

PNAC President's National Advisory Committee

PNCC   President's National Crime Commission

PNEU   Parents' National Education Union

PNITC   Pacific Northwest International Trade Council

PNLA   Pacific Northwest Library Association

PNS   Philippine News Service

POA   Police Officers Association; Prison Officers Association

POAU   Protestants and Other Americans for Separation of Church and State

POETS   Phooey on Everything—Tomorrow's Saturday

POPA   Property Owners Protection Association

POPS   People Opposed to Pornography in Schools

PORA   Police Officers Research Association

POS   Patent Office Society

POUNC   Post Office Users' National Council

POWER   Professionals Organized for Women's Equal Rights

PPA   Pakistan Press Association; People for Prison Alternatives; Periodical Publishers Association; Professional Photographers of America; Proletarian Party of America; Public Personnel Association

PPC   Policy Planning Council

PPFA   Planned Parenthood Federation of America

PPIC   Plumbing and Piping Industry Council

PPL   Police Protective League

PPNW   Physicians for the Prevention of Nuclear War

PPP   Peoples Party of Pakistan

PPSAWA   Pan Pacific and Southeast Asia Women's Association

PPSB   Periodical Publishers' Service Bureau

PPU   Peace Pledge Union

PRA   Psychological Research Association; Public Roads Administration; Puerto Rico Association

PRC   Postal Rate Commission

PRD   Pesticides Regulation Division

PREDA   Puerto Rico Economic Development Administration

PRF   Public Relations Foundation

PRI   Plastics and Rubber Institute

PRINCE   Parts, Reliability, and Information Center

PRODAC   Production Advisers Consortium

PRP   People's Revolutionary Party

PRRWO   Puerto Rican Revolutionary Workers Organization

PRSA   Public Relations Society of America

PRSP   Puerto Rican Socialist Party

PRSSA   Public Relations Student Society of America

PRU   Polish-Russian Union

PS   Paleontological Society; Pharmaceutical Society

PSA   Photographic Society of America; Poetry Society of America; Public Service Administration; Public Service Association

PSAL   Public School Athletic League

PSB   Public Service Board

PSC   Product Safety Commission; Public Service Commission

PSEA   Physical Security Equipment Agency

PSI   Professional Secretaries International

PSM   People for Self Management

PSMA Power Saw Manufacturers Association; Pressure-Sensitive Manufacturers Association

PSNA Phytochemical Society of North America

PSRF Profit Sharing Research Foundation

PSRO Professional Services Review Organization; Professional Standards Review Organization

PSSC Public Service Satellite Consortium

PSTA Public Safety and Training Association

PSWO Picture and Sound World Organization

PTA Parent-Teacher Association; Protestant Teachers Association

PTC Power Transmission Council

PTO Patent and Trademark Office

PTU Plumbing Trade Union

PUB Public Utilities Board

PUC Public Utilities Commission

PUFF People United to Fight Frustrations

PUP People's United Party; Princeton University Press

PUSH People United to Save Humanity

PVA Paralyzed Veterans of America; Prison Visitors' Association

PWA Prison Wardens Association; Professional Writers of America; Psychic Workers Association; Public Works Administration

PWC Parents Who Care

PWD Public Works Department

PWHS Public Works Historical Society

PWM Partnership for World Mission

PWP Parents Without Partners

QAB Quality Assurance Board

QBAA Quality Brands Associates of America

QBAC Quality Bakers of America Cooperative

QCI Quota Club International

QCSR Quaker Committee on Social Rehabilitation

QRPA Quartermaster Radiation Planning Agency

QS Queensland Society

RAA Royal Academy Association

RAAA Relocation Assistance Association of America

RAB Radio Advertising Bureau

RAC Research Advisory Council; Rubber Allocation Committee

RACA Recovered Alcoholic Clergy Association

RADIC Research and Development Information Center

RAF Royal Air Force

RAFO Reserve of Air Force Officers

RAPRA Rubber and Plastics Research Association

RARO Regular Army Reserve of Officers

RAUS Retired Association for the Uniformed Services

RAWA Renaissance Artists and Writers Association

RBA Roadside Business Association

RBO Russian Brotherhood Organization

RCA Radio Corporation of America; Radio Council of America; Rodeo Cowboys Association

RCAR Religious Coalition for Abortion Rights

RCB Retail Credit Bureau

RCC   Rape Crisis Center; Rescue Control Center

RCIA   Retail Clerks International Association; Retail Credit Institute of America

RCOA   Radio Club of America; Record Club of America

RCP   Revolutionary Communist Party

RDA   Railway Development Association

RDS   Rural Development Society

REA   Railway Express Agency; Rural Education Association; Rural Electrification Administration

REACH   Rape Emergency Aid and Counseling for Her

R&EC   Research and Engineering Council

REIC   Radiation Effects Information Center; Rare Earth Information Center

REMA   Refrigeration Equipment Manufacturers Association

REPC   Regional Economic Planning Council

RESA   Research Society of America

RETMA   Radio-Electronics-Television Manufacturers Association

RETRA   Radio, Electrical, and Television Retailers Association

RFC   Reconstruction Finance Corporation

RFFS   River and Flood Forecasting Service

RFL   Rugby Football League

RFU   Rugby Football Union

RGA   Republican Governors Association; Rubber Growers' Association

RHA   Rural Housing Alliance

RHK   Radio Hong Kong

RIA Railroad Insurance Association; Research Institute of America; Robot Institute of America

RIAA Record Industry Association of America; Recording Industry Association of America

RIDA Rural and Industrial Development Authority

RIMR Rockefeller Institute for Medical Research

RIND Research Institute of National Defense

RINS Research Institute for the Natural Sciences

RIT Rochester Institute of Technology

RJA Retail Jewelers of America

RLA Religious Liberty Association

RLCA Rural Letter Carriers' Association

RMA Radio Manufacturers Association; Regional Manpower Administration; Rubber Manufacturers Association

RMOGA Rocky Mountain Oil and Gas Association

RNA Romantic Novelists' Association

RNC Republican National Committee

RNWMP Royal Northwest Mounted Police

RNZ Radio New Zealand

ROA Reserve Officers Association; Retired Officers Association

ROTC Reserve Officers Training Corps

RPA Rationalist Press Association; Regional Planning Association

RPEA Regional Planning and Evaluation Agency

RPL Rocket Propulsion Laboratory

RPO Royal Philharmonic Orchestra

RR Remington Rand

RRB Railroad Retirement Board

RRC Regional Resource Center

RREA Rural/Regional Education Association

RRF Reading Reform Foundation

RRI Rubber Research Institute

RRS Radiation Research Society

RSA Railway Supervisors Association; Railway Supply Association; Regional Science Association

RSL Revolutionary Socialist League

RSMA Railway Systems and Management Association

RSNA Radiological Society of North America

RSROAA Roller Skating Rink Operators Association of America

RSS Remote Sensing Society; Rural Sociological Society

RTA Refrigeration Trade Association

RTC Reserve Training Corps

RTEB Radio Trades Examination Board

RTES Radio and Television Executives Society

RTMA Radio and Television Manufacturers Association

RTNA Radio and Television News Association

RTRA Radio and Television Retailers' Association

RTS Rubber Traders Society

RU Readers Union; Rugby Union

RVA Regular Veterans Association

RVC Rifle Volunteer Corps

RVIA Recreation Vehicle Industry Association

RVN Republic of Vietnam

RWA   Railway Wheel Association; Regional Water Authority

RWEMA   Ralph Waldo Emerson Memorial Association

RWG   Radio Writers' Guild

RWS   Regional Weather Service

RYA   Railroad Yardmasters of America

SA   Salvation Army; Society of Actuaries; Sugar Association

SAA   Shakespeare Association of America; Society for Academic Achievement; Society for American Archeology; Society of American Archivists; Speech Association of America; Swedish-American Association

SAAA   Salvation Army Association of America

SAAS   Society of African and Afro-American Students

SAAT   Society of Architects and Allied Technicians

SAB   Scientific Advisory Board; Society of American Bacteriologists

SABE   Society for Automation in Business Education

SABW   Society of American Business Writers

SACEM   Society of Authors, Composers, and Editors of Music (Société des Auteurs, Compositeurs et Éditeurs de la Musique)

SACEUR   Supreme Allied Command, Europe

SACO   Sino-American Cooperative Organization

SACP   South African Communist Party

SACSEA   Supreme Allied Command, South-East Asia

SADD   Students Against Drunk Drivers

SAE   Society for the Advancement of Education; Society of American Etchers; Society of Automotive Engineers

SAF Society of American Florists; Society of American Foresters

SAG Screen Actors Guild

SAGA Society of American Graphic Artists

SAGGA Scout and Guide Graduate Association

SAH Society of American Historians; Society of Automotive Historians

SAHAND Society Against Have a Nice Day

SAI Schizophrenics Anonymous International

SALT Society for Applied Learning Technology

SAM Society for the Advancement of Management; Society of Aerospace Medicine; Society of American Magicians

SAMA Student American Medical Association

SAME Society of American Military Engineers

SANTA Souvenir and Novelty Trade Association

SAODAP Special Action Office for Drug Abuse Prevention

SAPM Society for the Aid of Psychological Minorities

SAR Sons of the American Revolution

SASI Society of Air Safety Investigators

SAST Society for the Advancement of Space Travel

SATO South American Travel Organization; Southern African Treaty Organization

SATW Society of American Travel Writers

SAWA Screen Advertising World Association; Soil and Water Management Association

SBA Small Business Administration; Small Businesses Association

SBC Small Business Council

SBFA Small Business Foundation of America

SBME Society of Business Magazine Editors; State Board of Medical Examiners

SC Security Council

SCA Science Clubs of America; Screen Composers Association; Senior Citizens of America; Shipbuilders Council of America; Society of Consumer Affairs; Speech Communication Association; Synagogue Council of America

SCAPA Society for Checking the Abuses of Public Advertising

SCBW Society of Children's Book Writers

SCC Sea Cadet Corps

SCCA Society of Company and Commercial Accountants

SCE Society for Clinical Ecology

SCF Save the Children Federation

SCG Society of the Classic Guitar

SCI Society of Chemical Industries; Society of the Chemical Industry

SCIA Signal Corps Intelligence Agency

SCIRP Select Commission on Immigration and Refugee Policy

SCORE Service Corps of Retired Executives

SCOTUS Supreme Court of the United States

SCP Social Credit Party

SCR Signal Corps Radio

SCS Society of Civil Servants; Society for a Clinical Surgery; Society for Computer Simulation; Soil Conversation Service

SCSA Soil Conservation Society of America

SCT   Society of Commercial Teachers

SCUP   Society for College and University Planning

SCUS   Supreme Court of the United States

SCV   Sons of Confederate Veterans

SDA   Social Democratic Alliance; Students for Democratic Action

SDCE   Society of Die Casting Engineers

SDLP   Social Democratic and Labour Party

SDP   Social Democratic Party; Socialist Democratic Party

SDS   Students for a Democratic Society

SEA   Safety Equipment Association; Science and Education Administration; Students for Ecological Action

SEAAC   South-East Asian Air Command

SEATO   Southeast Asia Treaty Organization

SEC   Securities and Exchange Commission

SEE   Society of Environmental Engineers

SEFT   Society for Education in Film and Television

SEG   Screen Extras Guild; Society of Economic Geologists

SEIA   Security Equipment Industry Association; Solar Energy Industries Association; Solar Energy Institute of America

SEIU   Service Employees International Union

SENI   Society for the Encouragement of National Industry

SEP   Society of Engineering Psychologists

SER   Society for Educational Reconstruction

SERI   Solar Energy Research Institute

SES   Society of Engineering Science; Soil Erosion Service

SESA Social and Economic Statistics Administration; Solar Energy Society of America

SETP Society of Experimental Test Pilots

SFA Saks Fifth Avenue; Scientific Film Association; Soroptimist Federation of the Americas; Speech Foundation of America; Symphony Foundation of America

SFE Society of Fire Engineers

SFO Space Flight Operations

SFRA Science Fiction Research Association

SFTA Society of Film and Television Arts

SFWA Science Fiction Writers of America

SGO Surgeon General's Office

SGS Society of General Surgeons

SH Symphony Hall

SHAME Save, Help Animals Man Exploits; Society to Humiliate, Aggravate, Mortify, and Embarrass Smokers

SHF Soil and Health Foundation

SHHV Society for Health and Human Values

SHT Society for the History of Technology

SI Society of Illustrators

SIA Sanitary Institute of America; Securities Industries Association; Soroptimist International Association

SIB Society of Insurance Brokers

SID Society for International Development

SIE Society of Industrial Engineers

SIF Society for Individual Freedom

SIL Society for Individual Liberty

SIM Society for Industrial Microbiology

SIN Society for International Numismatics

SIR Society for Individual Responsibility; Society of Industrial Realtors

SIRA Scientific Instrument Research Association

SIRS School Information and Research Service

SIS Shut-In Society

SITU Society for the Investigation of the Unexplained

S-K Sloan-Kettering

SKCC Sloan-Kettering Cancer Center

SLA Showmen's League of America; Sleep-Learning Association; Standard Life Association

SLAM Society's League Against Molestation

SLL Socialist Labor League

SLRP Society for Long-Range Planning

SLTC Society of Leather Trades Chemists

SM Society of Medalists

SMA Steel Manufacturers Association

SMIS Society for Management Information Systems

SMMA Small Motor Manufacturers Association

SMPTE Society of Motion Picture and Television Engineers

SMW Society of Magazine Writers

SNAP Society of National Association Publishers; Society of National Publications

SNCC Student Non-Violent Coordinating Committee

SNPO Space Nuclear Propulsion Office

SNW Symphony of the New World

SOAR Save Our American Resources; Society of Authors' Representatives

SOC Save Our Children

SOCAP   Society of Consumer Affairs Professionals

SOHO   Save Our Heritage Organization

SOLIT   Society of Library and Information Technicians

SOM   Society of Occupational Medicine

SOS   Save Our School(s); Save Our Shore; Stamp Out Smog

SOTAA   State of the Art Association

SOUR   Stamp Out Urban Renewal

SOW   Sunflower Ordnance Works

SP   Socialist Party

SPA   Salt Producers Association; Society for Personnel Administration; State Principals Association

SPAB   Society for the Protection of Ancient Buildings

SPAI   Screen Printing Association International

SPAR   Society of Photographer and Artists Representatives

SPARS   Women's Coast Guard Reserve

SPBF   Scientific Peace Builders Foundation

SPC   Society for the Prevention of Crime; South Pacific Commission

SPCA   Society for the Prevention of Cruelty to Animals

SPCC   Society for the Prevention of Cruelty to Children

SPCH   Society for the Prevention of Cruelty to Homosexuals

SPCW   Society for the Prevention of Cruelty to Women

SPE   Society of Petroleum Engineers; Society of Plastics Engineers

SPEAK   Society for Preserving and Encouraging Arts and Knowledge

SPEC   Society for Pollution and Environmental Control

SPI Society of Photographic Illustrators; Society of the Plastics Industry; Society of Professional Investigators

SPIE Society of Photographic and Instrumentation Engineers

SPIL Society for the Promotion and Improvement of Libraries

SPJ Society of Professional Journalists

SPMA Sewage Plant Manufacturers Association

SPNM Society for the Promotion of New Music

SPR Society for Pediatric Research; Society for Psychical Research

SPS Society of Plastic Surgeons

SPSA Senate Press Secretaries Association

SPV Society for the Prevention of Vice

SPVA Self-Propelled Vehicles Association

SRA Science Research Association; Spelling Reform Association

SRC Science Research Council; Signal Reserve Corps

SRCD Society for Research in Child Development

SRI Scientific Research Institute; Space Research Institute

SRNA Shipbuilders and Repairers National Association

SRS Scoliosis Research Society

SRSA Scientific Research Society of America

SSA Seismological Society of America; Social Security Administration

SSAC Soldier's, Sailor's, and Airmen's Club

SSAR Society for the Study of Amphibians and Reptiles

SSB   Selective Service Board; Space Science Board

SSDA   Self-Service Development Association

SSFC   Severe Storms Forecast Center

SSMA   School Science and Mathematics Association; Stainless Steel Manufacturers Association

SSP   Society for Scholarly Publishing; Society of St. Paul

SSRS   Society for Social Responsibility in Science

SSSA   Simplified Spelling Society of America; Soil Science Society of America

STA   Society of Typographic Arts

STASH   Student Association for the Study of Hallucinogens

STC   Satellite Television Corporation; Satellite Tracking Committee; Society for Technical Communication

STI   Service Tools Institute; Space Technology Institute

STOPP   Society of Teachers Opposed to Physical Punishment

STR   Society for Theatre Research

STRAC   Strategic Army Corps

STRC   Science and Technology Research Center; Scientific, Technical, and Research Commission

STSD   Society of Teachers of Speech and Drama

STW   Society of Technical Writers

STWE   Society of Technical Writers and Editors

SUNOCO   Sun Oil Company

SUP   Socialist Unity Party

SUSA   Scouting USA

SUVCW   Sons of Union Veterans of the Civil War

SWE Society of Wine Educators; Society of Women Engineers

SWF Stockholders for World Freedom

SWMA Steel World Manufacturers Association

SWPA Surplus War Property Administration

SWWJ Society of Women Writers and Journalists

SZA Student Zionist Association

SZO Student Zionist Organization

TA Trans-America Corporation

TAA Technical Assistance Administration; Transportation Association of America

TAALS The American Association of Language Specialists

TAG The Association for the Gifted

TAGA Technical Association of the Graphic Arts

TALMA Truck and Ladder Manufacturers Association

TAMA Training Aids Management Agency

TAMIS Technical Meetings Information Service

TAPPI Technical Association of the Pulp and Paper Industry

TAS Traveler's Aid Society

TASO Training Aids Service Office

TBA Television Bureau of Advertising

TBC Trinidad Broadcasting Company

TBMA Timber Building Manufacturers Association

TBS Tokyo Broadcasting System

TC   Tariff Commission

TCA   Tanners Council of America; Technical Cooperation Administration; Television Corporation of America

TCFB   Transcontinental Freight Bureau

TCMA   Tabulating Card Manufacturers Association

TCPA   Town and Country Planning Association

TCUS   Tax Court of the United States

TD   Treasury Department

TDA   Timber Development Association; Train Dispatchers Association

TDB   Trade Development Bank; Trade and Development Board

TDU   Teamsters for a Democratic Union

TEB   Tax Exemption Board

TEC   Technical Education Council

TEMA   Telecommunications Engineering and Manufacturing Association

TERA   The Electrical Research Association

TESA   Television and Electronic Service Association

TFA   Task Force on Alcoholism; Textile Fabrics Association

TGWU   Transport and General Workers' Union

TIA   Tax Institute of America

TIAA   Teachers Insurance and Annuity Association of America

TICA   Technical Information Center Administration

TIMS   The Institute of Management Sciences

TIU   Telecommunications International Union

TLA Theatre Library Association; Trial Lawyers Association

TLS The Law Society

TLTB Trunk Line Tariff Bureau

TMA Theatrical Mutual Association; Tile Manufacturers Association; Tobacco Merchants Association; Toiletry Merchandisers Association; Toy Manufacturers Association

TMF The Menninger Foundation

TMIC Toxic Materials Information Center

TMIF Three-Mile Island Facility

TMSA Technical Marketing Society of America

TMUS Toy Manufacturers of the United States

TNA The National Archives

TNG The National Grange; The Newspaper Guild

TOA Theatre Owners of America; The Orchestral Association

TPA Travelers' Protective Association

TPBA Transit Patrolmen's Benevolent Association

TPC The Peace Corps

TPF Thomas Paine Foundation

TPNHS Thomas Paine National Historical Society

TPS Technical Publishing Society

TRA Textile Refinishers Association; Trade Relations Association; Travel Research Association

TRADA Timber Research and Development Association

TRAUS Thoroughbred Racing Association of the U.S.

TRCS Trade Relations Council of the United States

TRF Transportation Research Foundation; Tuna Research Foundation; Turf Research Foundation

TRI The Rockefeller Institute

TROA The Retired Officers Association

TSA Tourist Savings Association; Transportation Standardization Agency

TSBA Trustee Savings Banks Association

TSWG Television and Screen Writers' Guild

TTF Timber Trade Federation

TTMA Truck-Trailer Manufacturers Association

TU Typographical Union

TUI Trade Union International

TVA Tennessee Valley Authority

TWA Textile Waste Association; Toy Wholesalers Association; Trans World Airlines

TWP True Whig Party

TWU Transport Workers Union

TWUA Textile Workers Union of America; Transport Workers Union of America

UAB Unemployment Assistance Board

UAC Urban Affairs Council

UAI Urban America Incorporated

UAP Union of American Physicians; Union of Associated Professors

UAU Universities Athletic Union

UBA United Business Associates

UBSA   United Business Schools Association

UCA   United Consumers of America

UCIW   Union of Commercial and Industrial Workers

UCLA   University of California at Los Angeles

UCP   United Cerebral Palsy

UDC   United Daughters of the Confederacy

UDP   United Democratic Party

UFON   Unidentified Flying Objects Network

UFS   University Film Society

UGW   United Garment Workers

UHAB   Urban Housing Assistance Board

UIP   United Irish Party

UL   Universal League

ULA   United Labor Agency

ULL   Unitarian Laymen's League

UMTA   Urban Mass Transportation Administration

UN   United Nations

UNA   United Nations Assembly; United Nations Association; United Natives Association

UNACC   United Nations Administrative Committee on Coordination

UNARCO   United Nations Narcotics Commission

UNCF   United Nations Children's Fund; United Negro College Fund

UNCTAD   United Nations Conference on Trade and Development

UNDRO   United Nations Disaster Relief Office

UNEDA United Nations Economic Development Association

UNESCO United Nations Educational, Scientific, and Cultural Organization

UNFAO United Nations Food and Agricultural Organization

UNIDO United Nations Industrial Development Organization

UNIP United Independent Party

UNRRA United Nations Relief and Rehabilitation Administration

UNSC United Nations Security Council

UNTC United Nations Trusteeship Council

UPA United Productions of America

UPAA University Photographers Association of America

UPOW Union of Post Office Workers

UPS United Parcel Service

UPSW Union of Postal Service Workers

UPWA United Public Workers of America

URA Urban Redevelopment Authority; Urban Renewal Administration

URC Urban Renewal Commission

URP United Revolutionary Party

USA United States of America; United States Army; United Steelworkers of America

USAAF United States Army Air Force

USACE U.S. Army Corps of Engineers

USAEC United States Atomic Energy Commission

USAF United States Air Force

USAFR   U.S. Air Force Reserve

USAID   United States Aid for International Development

USAR   U.S. Army Reserve

USBC   United States Bureau of the Census; United States Bureau of Customs

USBLS   United States Bureau of Labor Statistics

USBP   United States Border Patrol; United States Bureau of Prisons

USBS   United States Bureau of Standards

USBTA   United States Board of Tax Appeals

USC   United States Congress

USCC   United States Chamber of Commerce

USCG   United States Coast Guard

USCGR   U.S. Coast Guard Reserve

USCRC   United States Civil Rights Commission

USCS   United States Civil Service; United States Customs Service

USCSC   United States Civil Service Commission

USDA   United States Department of Agriculture

USDC   United States Department of Commerce

USDE   United States Department of Education; United States Department of Energy

USDEA   United States Drug Enforcement Agency

USDHEW   United States Department of Health, Education, and Welfare

USDHUD   United States Department of Housing and Urban Development

USDI   United States Department of the Interior

USDJ United States Department of Justice

USDL United States Department of Labor

USDT United States Department of Transportation

USERC United States Environment and Resources Council

USES United States Employment Service

USFL United States Football League

USFSA United States Figure Skating Association

USFWS United States Fish and Wildlife Service

USGA United States Golf Association

USGPO United States Government Printing Office

USGS United States Geological Survey

USHHFA United States Housing and Home Finance Agency

USIA United States Information Agency

USI&NS United States Immigration and Nautralization Service

USIS United States Information Service

USITC United States International Trade Commission

USLP U.S. Labor Party

USM United States Mint

USMA United States Maritime Administration; United States Metric Association; United States Military Academy

USMC United States Marine Corps; United States Maritime Commission

USMCR U.S. Marine Corps Reserve

USNA United States Naval Academy

USNARS   United States National Archives and Records Service

USNG   United States National Guard

USNR   U.S. Naval Reserve

USO   United Service Organization

USOC   United States Olympic Committee

USOEO   United States Office of Economic Opportunity

USPHS   United States Public Health Service

USPS   United States Postal Service

USRA   United States Railway Association

USS   United States Senate

USSFA   United States Soccer Football Association

USSSA   United States Social Security Administration

USTA   United States Tennis Association; United States Trademark Association

USTC   United States Tariff Commission

USWA   United Steel Workers of America

USWAC   United States Women's Army Corps

USWB   United States Weather Bureau

UTA   Urban Transportation Administration

UTWA   United Textile Workers of America

UWP   Up with People

VA   Veterans Administration

VES   Veterans Employment Service

VESC   Vehicle Equipment Safety Commission

VFW   Veterans of Foreign Wars

VIA   Vision Institute of America

VISTA   Volunteers in Service to America

VNA   Visiting Nurses Association

VOA   Voice of America

VWW I   Veterans of World War I

WAA   Women's Auxiliary Association

WAB   Wage Adjustment Board

WACL   World Anti-Communist League

WAF   Women in the Air Force

WAP   Women Against Pornography

WATA   World Association of Travel Agencies

WAVES   Women Accepted for Volunteer Emergency Service

WBA   World Boxing Association

WBC   World Boxing Commission

WBF   World Bridge Federation

WBT   World Board of Trade

WCB   Workmen's Compensation Board

WEAL   Women's Equity Action League

WFA   World Federalists Association; World Friendship Association

WFAW   World Federation of Agricultural Workers

WFC   World Food Council

WFL   World Football League

WFTU   World Federation of Trade Unions

WGA   Writers' Guild of America

WHA World Hockey Association

WHO World Health Organization

WLF Women's Liberation Front

WMAC Waste Management Advisory Council

WMB War Mobilization Board

WMO World Meteorological Organization

WPA Works Progress Administration; World Psychiatric Association

WPB War Production Board

WPBL Women's Professional Basketball League

WPC World Peace Council

WPF World Peace Foundation

WPS Wildlife Preservation Society

WTA Women's Tennis Association; World Tennis Association

WVA World Veterinary Association

WWI Weight Watchers International

WWNFF Woodrow Wilson National Fellowship Foundation

WWSA Walt Whitman Society of America

YAA Yachtsmen's Association of America

YCI Young Communist International

YEO Youth Employment Office

YMCA Young Men's Christian Association

YMHA Young Men's Hebrew Association

YOC Youth Opportunity Corps

YPSL Young People's Socialist League

YWCA Young Women's Christian Association

YWHA Young Women's Hebrew Association

ZOA Zionist Organization of America

ZS Zoological Society

ZSS Zero-Sum Society

ACADEMIC DEGREES

A.A. associate in accounting; associate in arts

A.A.Ag. associate of arts in agriculture

A.A.A.S. associate in arts and science

A.Ae.E. associate in aeronautical engineering

A.A.F.A. associate in arts in fine arts

A.Agric. associate in agriculture

A.A.H.E. associate in arts in home economics

A.B. bachelor of arts

A.C.Ed. associate in commercial education

A.C.S. associate in commercial science

A.E. associate in education; associate in engineering

A.Ed. associate in education

AE.E. associate in engineering

A.En. associate in English

A.Eng. associate in engineering

A.F.A. associate in fine arts

A.G.E.   associate in general education

A.H.E.   associate in home economics

A.L.M.   master of liberal arts (Latin *Artium Liberalium Magister*)

A.M.   master of arts

A.M.E.   advanced master of education

A.M.L.S.   master of arts in library science

A.M.R.   master of arts in research

A.M.T.   associate in mechanical technology; associate in medical technology; master of arts-teaching

A.Mus.   associate in music

A.N.   associate in nursing

A.R.E.   associate in religious education

A.Sc.   associate in science

A.S.S.   associate in secretarial science/secretarial studies

A.Tech.   associate in technology

B.A.   bachelor of arts (Latin *Baccalaureus Artium*)

B.A.A.   bachelor of applied arts

B.A.E.   bachelor of aeronautical engineering; bachelor of agricultural engineering; bachelor of architectural engineering; bachelor of art education; bachelor of arts in education

B.A.Econ.   bachelor of arts in economics

B.A.Ed.   bachelor of arts in education

B.Ae.E.   bachelor of aeronautical engineering

B.Ag.   bachelor of agriculture

B.Agr.   bachelor of agriculture

B.Agr.Eco.   bachelor of agricultural economics

B.Agric.   bachelor of agriculture

B.Ag.Sc.   bachelor of agricultural science

B.A.I.   bachelor of engineering (Latin *Baccalureus in Arte Ingeniaria*)

B.A.Mus.   bachelor of arts in music

B.A.O.   bachelor of the art of obstetrics; bachelor of arts in oratory

B.A.P.E.   bachelor of arts in physical education

B.App.Arts   bachelor of applied arts

B.App.Sci.   bachelor of applied science

B.Ar.   bachelor of architecture

B.Arch.   bachelor of architecture

B.Arch.E.   bachelor of architectural engineering

B.Arch, & T.P.   bachelor of architecture and town planning

B.A.S.   bachelor of agricultural science; bachelor of applied science

B.A.S.S.   bachelor of arts in social science

B.B.A.   bachelor of business administration

B.B.S.   bachelor of business science

B.C.   bachelor of chemistry; bachelor of commerce

B.C.E.   bachelor of chemical engineering; bachelor of civil engineering

B.C.L.   bachelor of civil law

B.C.S.   bachelor of criminal science

B.D.   bachelor of divinity

B.D.S.   bachelor of dental surgery

B.E.   bachelor of education; bachelor of engineering

B.E.E.   bachelor of electrical engineering

B.Elec.&Tel.Eng.   bachelor of electronics and telecommunications engineering

B.E.M.   bachelor of engineering

B.Eng.Sci.   bachelor of engineering science

B.Eng.Tech.   bachelor of engineering technology

B.E.P.   bachelor of engineering physics

B.E.S.   bachelor of engineering science

B.F.   bachelor of finance; bachelor of forestry

B.F.A.   bachelor of fine arts

B.For. Sci.   bachelor of forestry science

B.F.S.   bachelor of foreign service

B.F.T.   bachelor of foreign trade

B.G.E.   bachelor of geological engineering

B.Gen.Ed.   bachelor of general education

B.H.Adm.   bachelor of hospital administration

B.H.E.   bachelor of home economics

B.Hort.   bachelor of horticulture

B.Hort.Sci.   bachelor of horticultural science

B.H.Sci.   bachelor of household science

B.Hyg.   bachelor of hygiene

B.I.E.   bachelor of industrial engineering

B.I.M.   bachelor of Indian medicine

B.L.   bachelor of letters

B.L.A.   bachelor of landscape architecture; bachelor of liberal arts

B.L.I.   bachelor of literary interpretation

B.Lib.S.   bachelor of library science

B.Lib.Sci.   bachelor of library science

B.Lit(t). bachelor of letters (Latin *Baccalaureus Literarum*); bachelor of literature

B.L.M. bachelor of land management

B.L.S. bachelor of library science; bachelor of library service

B.M. bachelor of medicine; bachelor of music

B.Mar.E. bachelor of marine engineering

B.Mar.Eng. bachelor of marine engineering

B.Math. bachelor of mathematics

B.M.E. bachelor of mechanical engineering; bachelor of mining engineering; bachelor of music education

B.Med. bachelor of medicine

B.M.Ed. bachelor of music education

B.Med.Biol. bachelor of medical biology

B.Med.Sc. bachelor of medical science

B.Met. bachelor of metallurgy

B.Met.E. bachelor of metallurgical engineering

B.Mgt.Eng. bachelor of management engineering

B.Mic. bachelor of microbiology

B.Min.E. bachelor of mining engineering

B.M.L. bachelor of modern languages

B.M.S. bachelor of marine science; bachelor of medical science

B.M.T. bachelor of medical technology

B.Mus. bachelor of music

B.N. bachelor of nursing

B.Nav. bachelor of navigation

B.N.S. bachelor of natural science; bachelor of naval science

B.N.Sc. bachelor of nursing science

B.P. bachelor of pharmacy; bachelor of philosophy

B.P.A. bachelor of professional arts

B.Paed. bachelor of paediatrics

B.Pd. bachelor of pedagogy

B.Pe. bachelor of pedagogy

B.P.E. bachelor of physical education

B.Pet.E. bachelor of petroleum engineering

B.P.H. bachelor of public health

B.Pharm. bachelor of pharmacy

B.P.H.E. bachelor of physical and health education

B.Phil. bachelor of philosophy

B.Phys. bachelor of physics

B.Phys.Ed. bachelor of physical education

B.Phys.Thy. bachelor of physical therapy

B.Ps. bachelor in psychology

B.Psych. bachelor of psychology

B.P.T. bachelor of physiotherapy

B.R.E. bachelor of religious education

B.Ru.Eng. bachelor of rural engineering

B.Ru.Sci. bachelor of rural science

B.S. bachelor of science

B.S.A. bachelor of agricultural science

B.S.A.A. bachelor of science in applied arts

B.S.Adv. bachelor of science in advertising

B.S.A.E. bachelor of science in aeronautical engineering; bachelor of science in architectural engineering

B.S.Agr. bachelor of science in agriculture

B.S.Arch. bachelor of science in architecture

B.S.Arch.Eng. bachelor of science in architectural engineering

B.S.Art Ed. bachelor of science in art education

B.S.Bus. bachelor of science in business

B.Sc. bachelor of science

B.S.C. bachelor of science in commerce

B.Sc.Acc. bachelor of science in accounting

B.Sc.Ag.&A.H. bachelor of science in agriculture and animal husbandry

B.Sc.Agr.Bio. bachelor of science in agricultural biology

B.Sc.Agr.Eco. bachelor of science in agricultural economics

B.Sc.Agr.Eng. bachelor of science in agricultural engineering

B.Sc.Ag(ri)(c). bachelor of science in agriculture

B.Sc.Arch. bachelor of science in architecture

B.Sc.B.A. bachelor of science in business administration

B.Sc.C.E. bachelor of science in civil engineering

B.Sc.Chem.E. bachelor of science in chemical engineering

B.Sc.Dent. bachelor of science in dentistry

B.Sc.Dom.Sc. bachelor of science in domestic science

B.S.C.E. bachelor of science in civil engineering

B.S.Ch. bachelor of science in chemistry

B.S.Chm. bachelor of science in chemistry

B.Sc.Nurs. bachelor of science in nursing

B.Sc.S.S. bachelor of science in secretarial studies

B.Sc.Vet.Sc. bachelor of science in veterinary science

B.S.Dent. bachelor of science in dentistry

B.S.D.H.   bachelor of science in dental hygiene

B.S.E.   bachelor of sanitary engineering; bachelor of science education; bachelor of science engineering

B.S.Ec.   bachelor of science in economics

B.S.Ed.   bachelor of science in education

B.S.E.E.   bachelor of science in electrical engineering

B.S.El.E.   bachelor of science in electronic engineering

B.S.Eng.   bachelor of science in engineering

B.S.F.   bachelor of science in forestry

B.S.Fin.   bachelor of science in finance

B.S.For.   bachelor of science in forestry

B.S.F.S.   bachelor of science in foreign service

B.S.G.E.   bachelor of geological engineering; bachelor of science in general engineering

B.S.Gen.Nur.   bachelor of science in general nursing

B.S.Geog.   bachelor of science in geography

B.S.Geol.   bachelor of science in geology

B.S.Geol.Eng.   bachelor of science in geological engineering

B.S.H.A.   bachelor of science in hospital administration

B.S.H.E.   bachelor of science in home economics

B.S.H.Eco.   bachelor of science in home economics

B.S.H.Ed.   bachelor of science in health education

B.S.Ind.Art   bachelor of science in industrial art

B.S.Ind.Chem.   bachelor of science in industrial chemistry

B.S.Ind.Ed.   bachelor of science in industrial education

B.S.Ind.Eng.   bachelor of science in industrial engineering

B.S.I.R.   bachelor of science in industrial relations

B.S.J.   bachelor of science in journalism

B.S.Jr.   bachelor of science in journalism

B.S.Lab.Rel.   bachelor of science in labor relations

B.S.L.S.   bachelor of library science; bachelor of science in library science

B.S.Mar.Eng.   bachelor of science in marine engineering

B.S.M.E.   bachelor of science in mechanical engineering; bachelor of science in mining engineering; bachelor of science in music education

B.S.Med.   bachelor of science in medicine

B.S.Med.Rec.   bachelor of science in medical records

B.S.Med.Rec.Lib.   bachelor of science in medical records librarianship

B.S.Med.Tech.   bachelor of science in medical technology

B.S.Met.   bachelor of science in metallurgy

B.S.Met.Eng.   bachelor of science in metallurgical engineering

B.S.Mgt.Sci.   bachelor of science in management science

B.S.Min.   bachelor of science in mineralogy; bachelor of science in mining

B.S.Min.Eng.   bachelor of science in mining engineering

B.S.Mus.Ed.   bachelor of science in music education

B.S.N.   bachelor of science in nursing

B.S.N.A.   bachelor of science in nursing administration

B.S.Nat.Hist.   bachelor of science in natural history

B.S.N.I.T.   bachelor of science in nautical industrial technology

B.S.Nurs.   bachelor of science in nursing

B.S.Nurs.Ed.   bachelor of science in nursing education

B.S.Occ.Ther.   bachelor of science in occupational therapy

B.Soc.Sci.   bachelor of social science

B.Soc.St.   bachelor of social studies

B.Soc.Wk.   bachelor of social work

B.S.Opt.   bachelor of science in optometry

B.S.O.T.   bachelor of science in occupational therapy

B.S.P.   bachelor of science in pharmacy

B.S.P.A.   bachelor of science in public administration

B.S.P.E.   bachelor of science in physical education

B.S.Per.&Pub.Rel.   bachelor of science in personnel and public relations

B.S.Pet.   bachelor of science in petroleum

B.S.Pet.Eng.   bachelor of science in petroleum engineering

B.S.P.H.   bachelor of science in public health

B.S.Phar.   bachelor of science in pharmacy

B.S.Pharm.   bachelor of science in pharmacy

B.S.P.H.N.   bachelor of science in public health nursing

B.S.Phys.Ed.   bachelor of science in physical education

B.S.Phys.Edu.   bachelor of science in physical education

B.S.Phys.Ther.   bachelor of science in physical therapy

B.S.P.T.   bachelor of science in physical therapy

B.Sp.Thy.   bachelor of speech therapy

B.S.R.   bachelor of science in rehabilitation

B.S.Rec.   bachelor of science in recreation

B.S.Ret.   bachelor of science in retailing

B.S.R.T.   bachelor of science in radiological technology

B.S.S.   bachelor of sanitary science; bachelor of science in science; bachelor of secretarial science; bachelor of social science

B.S.S.A.   bachelor of science in secretarial administration

B.S.Sc.   bachelor of sanitary science

B.S.Sc.Eng.   bachelor of science in science engineering

B.S.Sec.Ed.   bachelor of science in secondary education

B.S.Sec.Sci.   bachelor of science in secretarial science

B.S.Soc.Serv.   bachelor of science in social service

B.S.Soc.St.   bachelor of science in social studies

B.S.Soc.Wk.   bachelor of science in social work

B.S.S.S.   bachelor of science in secretarial studies; bachelor of science in social science

B.S.S.Sc.   bachelor of science in social science

B.S.Struc.Eng.   bachelor of science in structural engineering

B.S.Text.   bachelor of science in textiles

B.S.Trans.   bachelor of science in transportation

B.Sur.   bachelor of surgery

B.Surv.   bachelor of surveying

B.S.Voc.Ed.   bachelor of science in vocational education

B.S.W.   bachelor of social work

B.T.   bachelor of theology

B.Th.   bachelor of theology

B.T.P.   bachelor of town planning

B.T.R.P.   bachelor of town and regional planning

B.V.E.   bachelor of vocational education

B.Vet.Med.   bachelor of veterinary medicine

B.Vet.Sci.   bachelor of veterinary science

B.Vet.Sur.   bachelor of veterinary surgery

B.V.M.   bachelor of veterinary medicine

B.V.M.S.   bachelor of veterinary medicine and surgery

B.V.S.   bachelor of veterinary science; bachelor of veterinary surgery

B.V.Sc.   bachelor of veterinary science

B.V.Sc.&A.H.   bachelor of veterinary science and animal husbandry

C.A.S.   certificate of advanced studies

C.B.   bachelor of surgery (Latin *Chirurgiae Baccalaureus*)

Ch.D.   doctor of chemistry

Chir.Doc.   doctor of surgery (Latin *Chirurgiae Doctor*)

Ch.M.   master of surgery (Latin *Chirurgiae Magister*)

C.M.   master of surgery (Latin *Chirurgiae Magister*)

C.S.B.   bachelor of Christian science

D.Adm.   doctor of administration

D.Ae.   doctor of aeronautics

D.A.E.   diploma in advanced engineering

D.Ae.Eng.   doctor of aeronautical engineering

D.Ae.Sc.   doctor of aeronautical science

D.Ag.   doctor of agriculture

D.Agr.   doctor of agriculture

D.Agr.Eng.   doctor of agricultural engineering

D.Agr.Sc.   doctor of agricultural science

D.Av.Med.   diploma in aviation medicine

D.Bi.Chem.   doctor of biological chemistry

D.Bi.Eng.   doctor of biological engineering

D.Bi.Phy.   doctor of biological physics

D.Bi.Sc.   doctor of biological sciences

D.B.M.   diploma in business management

D.C.   doctor of chiropractic

D.C.D.   diploma in chest diseases

D.C.E.   doctor of civil engineering

D.C.E.P.   diploma of child and educational psychology

D.Ch.   doctor of surgery (Latin *Doctor Chirugiae*)

D.Ch.E.   doctor of chemical engineering

D.Civ.L.   doctor of civil law

D.C.L.   doctor of canon law; doctor of civil law

D.Cl.Sci.   doctor of clinical science

D.C.M.   doctor of comparative medicine

D.Cn.L.   doctor of canon law

D.Com.   doctor of commerce

D.Com.L.   doctor of commercial law

D.Comp.L.   doctor of comparative law

D.C.S.   doctor of Christian science; doctor of commercial science

D.D.   doctor of divinity

D.D.O.   diploma in dental orthopedics

D.D.R.   diploma in diagnostic radiology

D.D.S.   doctor of dental science; doctor of dental surgery

D.D.Sc.   doctor of dental science

D.E.   doctor of economics

D.Ed.   doctor of education

D.Elo.   doctor of elocution

D.En.   doctor of English

D.Eng.   doctor of engineering

D.Eng.Sc.   doctor of engineering science

D.Ent.   doctor of entomology

D.F.A.   doctor of fine arts

D.F.Sc.   doctor of financial science

D.G.C.   diploma in guidance and counseling

D.H.L.   doctor of Hebrew letters; doctor of Hebrew literature

D.Hor.   doctor of horticulture

D.H.S.   doctor of health science(s)

D.Hum.L.   doctor of humane letters

D.Hy.   doctor of hygiene

D.Ing.   doctor of engineering (Latin *Doctor Ingeniariae*)

Dip.A.D.   diploma in art and design

Dip.Agr.   diploma in agriculture

Dip.A.Ling.   diploma in applied linguistics

Dip.A.M.   diploma in applied mechanics

Dip.Amer.Bd.P.&N.   diplomate of the American Board of Psychiatry and Neurology

Dip.Anth.   diploma in anthropology

Dip.App.Sci.   diploma in applied science

Dip.Arch.   diploma in architecture

Dip.Ars.   diploma in arts

Dip.Bac.   diploma in bacteriology

Dip.B.M.S.   diploma in basic medical science

Dip.C.A.M.   diploma in communications, advertising, and marketing

Dip.Card.   diploma in cardiology

Dip.Com.   diploma in commerce

Dip.D.P. diploma in drawing and painting

Dip.D.S. diploma in dental surgery

Dip.Eco. diploma in economics

Dip.Ed. diploma in education

Dip.Eng. diploma in engineering

Dip.F.A. diploma in fine arts

Dip.For. diploma in forestry

Dip.G.&O. diploma in gynaecology and obstetrics

Dip.G.T. diploma in glass technology

Dip.H.A. diploma in hospital administration

Dip.H.E. diploma in highway engineering

Dip.Hus. diploma in husbandry

Dip.J. diploma in journalism

Dip.L. diploma in language

Dip.Lib. diploma in librarianship

Dip.Lib.Sci. diploma in library science

Dip.M.E. diploma in mechanical engineering

Dip.M.F.O.S. diploma in maxial, facial, and oral surgery

Dip.Mgmnt. diploma of management

Dip.Micro. diploma in microbiology

Dip.Mus.Edu. diploma in musical education

Dip.N.A.&A.C. diploma in numerical analysis and automatic computing

Dip.N.S.Edu. diploma in nursery school education

Dip.O.L. diploma in oriental learning

Dip.Phar. diploma in pharmacology

Dip.Phys.Edu. diploma in physical education

Dip.P.&O.T.   diploma in physical and occupational therapy

Dip.Pub.Adm.   diploma in public administration

Dip.S.W.   diploma in social work

Dip.T.   teachers diploma

Dip.T.&C.P.   diploma in town and country planning

Dip.Tec.   diploma in technology

Dip.The.   diploma in theology

Dip.T.P.   diploma in town planning

Dip.V.F.M.   diploma in valuation and farm management

D.Ir.Eng.   doctor of irrigation engineering

D.J.   doctor of law (Latin *Doctor Juris*)

D.L.O.   diploma in laryngology and otology

D.L.S.   doctor of library science; doctor of library service

D.L.Sc.   doctor of library science

D.M.   doctor of mathematics; doctor of medicine; doctor of music; doctor of musicology

D.Math.   doctor of mathematics

D.M.D.   doctor of dental medicine (Latin *Dentariae Medicinae Doctor*)

D.Mec.E.   doctor of mechanical engineering

D.Mech.   doctor of mechanics

D.Med.   doctor of medicine

D.M.Ed.   doctor of musical education

D.Met.   doctor of metallurgy

D.Met.Eng.   doctor of metallurgical engineering

D.Meteor.   doctor of meteorology

D.Mi.Eng.   doctor of mining engineering

D.Mil.S.   doctor of military science

D.M.L.   doctor of modern languages

D.M.S.   doctor of medical science

D.M.Sc.   doctor of medical science

D.Mus.   doctor of music

D.Mus.A.   doctor of musical arts

D.Mus.Ed.   doctor of musical education

D.M.V.   doctor of veterinary medicine

D.N.   diploma in nursing; diploma in nutrition

D.N.Arch.   doctor of naval architecture

D.N.Ed.   doctor of nursing education

D.N.Eng.   doctor of naval engineering

D.N.Sc.   doctor of nursing science

D.O.   doctor of optometry; doctor of osteopathy

Doc.Eng.   doctor of engineering

D.Oph.   doctor of ophthalmology

D.Ophth.   doctor of ophthalmology

D.Opt.   doctor of optometry

D.Or.   doctor of oratory

D.O.S.   doctor of ocular science; doctor of optical science; doctor of optometric science

D.O.T.   diploma in occupational therapy

D.P.   doctor of pharmacy; doctor of podiatry

D.P.A.   doctor of public administration

D.P.E.   doctor of physical education

D.Ped.   doctor of pedagogy

D.Ph.   doctor of philosophy (Latin *Doctor Philosophiae*)

D.P.H.   doctor of public health

D.Pharm.   doctor of pharmacy

D.Phil. doctor of philosophy

D.Ph.Sc. doctor of physical science

D.Phys.Med. diploma in physical medicine

D.P.M. doctor of pediatric medicine

D.Pol.Eco. doctor of political economy

D.Pol.Sci. doctor of political science

D.Psych. doctor of psychology

D.Psy.Sci. doctor of psychological science

D.Ae.Sc. doctor of aeronautical science

Dr.Agr. doctor of agriculture

Dr.Bi.Chem. doctor of biological chemistry

Dr.Bus.Adm. doctor of business administration

Dr.Chem. doctor of chemistry

D.R.E. doctor of religious education

Dr.Ec. doctor of economics

Dr.Eng. doctor of engineering

Dr.Ent. doctor of entomology

Dr.Hor. doctor of horticulture

Dr.Hy. doctor of hygiene

Dr.J.Sc. doctor of judicial science

Dr.Jur. doctor of law (Latin *Doctor Juris*)

Dr.Lit. doctor of literature

Dr.Med. doctor of medicine (Latin *Doctor Medicinae*)

Dr.Mus. doctor of music

Dr.Nat.Sci. doctor of natural science

Dr.P.H. doctor of public health

Dr.Pol.Sc. doctor of political science(s)

Dr.Ra.Eng. doctor of radio engineering

Dr.Rec.   doctor of recreation

Dr.Re.Eng.   doctor of refrigeration engineering

Dr.Sc.   doctor of science

Dr.Sci.   doctor of science

Dr.Tech.   doctor of technology

Dr.Theol.   doctor of theology

D.Ru.Eng.   doctor of rural engineering

D.Rur.Sci.   doctor of rural science

D.S.   doctor of science

D.Sc.   doctor of science

D.S.C.   doctor of Christian science; doctor of commercial science; doctor of surgical chiropody

D.Sc.   doctor of science

D.Sc.Com.   doctor of science in commerce

D.Sc.Eco.   doctor of science in economics

D.Sc.Eng.   doctor of science in engineering

D.Sch.Mus.   doctor of school music

D.Sc.Hyg.   doctor of science in hygiene

D.Sc.I.   doctor of science in industry

D.Sc.Jur.   doctor of the science of jurisprudence

D.Sc.L.   doctor of the science of law

D.Scn.   doctor of scientology

D.Sc.Os.   doctor of the science of osteopathy

D.Sc.Pol.   doctor of political science(s)

D.S.E.   doctor of science in economics

D.S.Met.Eng.   doctor of science in metallurgical engineering

D.S.O.   doctor of the science of oratory

D.Soc.Sci.   doctor of social science

D.So.Se.   doctor of social service

D.S.S.   doctor of sacred scripture; doctor of social sciences

D.S.T.   doctor of sacred theology

D.St.Eng.   doctor of structural engineering

D.Sur.   doctor of surgery

D.S.W.   doctor of social welfare

D.T.   doctor of theology

D.T.Chem.   doctor of technical chemistry

D.Tech.   doctor of technology

D.T.Eng.   doctor of textile engineering

D.Th.   doctor of theology

D.Theol.   doctor of theology

D.T.M.   doctor of tropical medicine

D.V.A.   doctor of visual aids

D.V.M.   doctor of veterinary medicine

D.V.M.S.   doctor of veterinary medicine and science

D.V.R.   doctor of veterinary radiology

D.V.S.   doctor of veterinary surgery

D.V.Sc.   doctor of veterinary science

D.Z.   doctor of zoology

D.Zool.   doctor of zoology

Ed.B.   bachelor of education

Ed.D.   doctor of education

Ed.M.   master of education

Eng.D.   doctor of engineering

Eng.Sc.D.   doctor of engineering science

J.C.D.   doctor of canon law; doctor of civil law

J.D.   doctor of jurisprudence; doctor of law(s) (Latin *Juris* or *Jurim Doctor*)

L.A.M.   master of liberal arts (Latin *Liberalium Artium Magister*)

L.B.   bachelor of letters (Latin *Baccalaureus Litterarum*)

L.H.D.   doctor of humane letters (Latin *Litterarum Humaniorum Doctor*)

Litt.B.   bachelor of letters (Latin *Litterarum Baccalaureus*)

Litt.D.   doctor of letters (Latin *Litterarum Doctor*)

LL.B.   bachelor of laws (Latin *Legum Baccalaureus*)

LL.D.   doctor of laws (Latin *Legum Doctor*)

LL.M.   master of laws (Latin *Legum Magister*)

L.S.D.   doctor of library science

M.A.   master of arts (Latin *Magister Artium*)

M.A.Arch.   master of arts in architecture

M.A.B.E.   master of agricultural business and economics

M.Ac.   master of accountancy

M.A.C.E.   master of air-conditioning education; master of air-conditioning engineering

M.Agr.   master of agriculture

M.A.L.D.   master of arts in law and diplomacy

M.A.L.S.   master of arts in liberal studies; master of arts in library science; master of arts in library service

M.Ar.   master of architecture

M.Ar.Sci.   master of arts and sciences

M.A.S.   master of applied science

M.A.Sc.   master of applied science

M.A.Soc.Stud.   master of arts in social studies

Math.D.   doctor of mathematics

M.A.Theol.   master of arts in theology

M.B.   bachelor of medicine

M.B.A.   master of business administration

M.B.Ed.   master of business education

M.Bi.Chem.   master of biological chemistry

M.Bi.Eng.   master of biological engineering

M.Bi.Phy.   master of biological physics

M.Bi.S.   master of biological science

M.B.M.   master of business management

M.Bus.Ed.   master of business education

M.C.   master of surgery (Latin *Magister Chirurgiae*)

M.C.B.   master of clinical biochemistry

M.C.D.   doctor of comparative medicine; master of civic design

M.C.Eng.   master of civil engineering

M.Ch.D.   master of dental surgery (Latin *Magister Chirurgiae Dentalis*)

M.Ch.E.   master of chemical engineering

M.Chem.E.   master of chemical engineering

M.Chir.   master of surgery (Latin *Magister Chirurgiae*)

M.Ch.Orth.   master of orthopedic surgery (Latin *Magister Chirurgiae Orthopaedicae*)

M.Ch.Otol.   master of otorhinolaryngological surgery

M.Chrom.   master of chromatics

M.C.J.   master of comparative jurisprudence

M.C.L.   master of civil law

M.Clin.Psychol.   master of clinical psychology

M.Cl.Sc.   master of clinical science

M.Com.Adm.   master of commercial administration

M.Comm.H.   master of community health

M.Comp.Law   master of comparative law

M.Com.Sc.   master of commercial science

M.C.P.   master of city planning

M.C.R.   master of comparative religion

M.C.S.   master of commercial science

M.D.   doctor of medicine

M.D.E.   master of domestic economy

M.Des.   master of design

M.Did.   master of didactics

M.Di.Eng.   master of diesel engineering

M.Dip.   master of diplomacy

M.Div.   master of divinity

M.D.S.   master of dental surgery

M.D.Sc.   master of dental science

M.D.V.   doctor of veterinary medicine

M.E.   master of education

M.E.A.   master of engineering administration

M.Ec.   master of economics

M.E.C.   master of engineering chemistry

M.Econ.   master of economics

M.Ed.   master of education

M.E.D.   master of elementary didactics

M.Ed.L.Sc.   master of education in library science

M.E.E.   master of electrical engineering

M.E.Eng.   master of electrical engineering

M.E.L.   master of English literature

M.Elo.   master of elocution

M.Eng.   master of engineering

M.Eng.P.A.   master of engineering and public administration

M.Ent.   master of entomology

M.E.P.   master of engineering physics

M.E.P.A.   master of engineering and public administration

M.E.P.H.   master of public health engineering

M.E.Sc.   master of engineering science

M.F.   master of forestry

M.F.A.   master of fine arts

M.F.A.Mus.   master of fine arts in music

M.F.Eng.   master of forest engineering

M.For.   master of forestry

M.F.S.   master of food science; master of foreign service; master of foreign study

M.F.T.   master of foreign trade

M.G.E.   master of geological engineering

M.Geol.Eng.   master of geological engineering

M.H.E.   master of home economics

M.H.E.E. master of home economics education

M.H.E.Ed. master of home economics education

M.H.E. master of highway engineering

M.Hi.Eng. master of highway engineering

M.H.L. master of Hebrew literature

M.Hor. master of horticulture

M.Ho.Sc. master of household science

M.Hy. master of hygiene

M.Hyg. master of hygiene

M.I.A. master of internal affairs

M.I.E. master of industrial engineering

M.I.H. master of industrial health

M.I.L.R. master of industrial and labor relations

M.Int.Med. master of international medicine

M.I.S. master of international service

M.J. master of journalism

M.L. Licentiate in medicine (Latin *Medicinae Licentiatus*)

M.L.A. master of landscape architecture

M.L.Des. master of landscape design

M.L.Eng. master of landscape engineering

M.Lib. master of librarianship

M.Lib.Sci. master of library science

M.Lit. master of letters; master of literature

M.L.S. master of library science

M.M. master of music

M.M.E. master of mechanical engineering; master of music education

M.Mech.Eng. master of mechanical engineering

M.Med.   master of medicine

M.Met.   master of metallurgy

M.Met.E.   master of metallurgical engineering

M.Mgt.Eng.   master of management engineering

M.Mic.   master of microbiology

M.Mi.Eng.   master of mining engineering

M.M.S.   master of management studies; master of medical science

M.Mus.   master of music

M.N.   master of nursing

M.N.A.   master of nursing administration

M.N.Arch.   master of naval architecture

M.N.E.   master of nuclear engineering

M.N.Eng.   master of naval engineering

M.N.S.   master of nutritional science

M.N.Sc.   master of nursing science

M.Nurs.   master of nursing

M.O.G.   master of obstetrics and gynaecology

M.O.I.G.   master of occupational information and guidance

M.O.L.   master of oriental languages

M.Opt.   master of optometry

M.P.A.   master of professional accounting; master of public administration; master of public works

M.Pd.   master of pedagogy

M.P.E.   master of physical education

M.Pe.Eng.   master of petroleum engineering

M.Ph.   master of philosophy

M.P.H. master of public health

M.Phar. master of pharmacy

M.Ph.Ed. master of public health

M.P.H.Eng. master of public health engineering

M.Phil. master of philosophy

M.Pho. master of photography

M.Ph.Sc. master of physical science

M.P.H.T.M. master of public health and tropical medicine

M.Phy. master of physics

M.P.L. master of patent law

M.Pol.Econ. master of political economy

M.P.P. master of physical planning

M.Prof.Acc. master of professional accountancy

M.Ps. master of psychology

M.Ps.O. master of psychology orientation

M.P.S.W. master of psychiatric social work

M.Psych. master of psychology

M.Psy.Med. master of psychological medicine

M.Rad. master of radiology

M.Ra.Eng. master of radio engineering

M.R.E. master of religious education

M.Ref.Eng. master of refrigeration engineering

M.R.P. master in regional planning

M.R.Sc. master of rural science

M.S. master of science; master of surgery

M.S.Agr.Eng. master of science in agricultural engineering

M.S.B.A.   master of science in business administration

M.S.Bus.   master of science in business

M.Sc.   master of science

M.S.C.E.   master of science in civil engineering

M.S.Ch.E.   master of science in chemical engineering

M.Sc.L.   master of science of law

M.S.D.   master of scientific didactics

M.S.Dent.   master of science in dentistry

M.S.Derm.   master of science in dermatology

M.S.E.   master of sanitary engineering; master of science in education; master of science in engineering

M.S.Ed.   master of science in education

M.S.E.E.   master of science in electrical engineering

M.S.E.M.   master of science in engineering mechanics

M.S.Eng.   master of science in engineering

M.S.G.E.   master of science in geological engineering

M.S.H.   master of science in horticulture; master of science in hygiene

M.S.H.A.   master of science in hospital administration

M.S.H.E.   master of science in home economics

M.S.Hort.   master of science in horticulture

M.S.Hyg.   master of science in hygiene

M.S.Ind.Eng.   master of science in industrial engineering

M.S.J.   master of science in journalism

M.S.L.   master of science in linguistics

M.S.L.S.   master of science in library science

M.S.M.   master of science in music

M.S.M.E.   master of science in mechanical engineering

M.S.Med.   master of medical science

M.S.Mus.   master of science in music

M.S.Mus.Ed.   master of science in music education

M.S.N.   master of science in nursing

M.S.N.Ed.   master of science in nursing education

M.S.Nucl.Eng.   master of science in nuclear engineering

M.Soc.Sci.   master of social science

M.Soc.Wk.   master of social work

M.S.Ophthal.   master of ophthalmological surgery

M.S.Ortho.   master of orthopedic surgery

M.S.P.   master of science in pharmacy

M.S.Pet.Eng.   master of science in petroleum engineering

M.S.P.H.   master of science in public health

M.S.Pharm.   master of science in pharmacy

M.S.P.H.E.   master of science in public health engineering

M.S.P.H.Ed.   master of science in public health education

M.S.Rec.   master of science in recreation

M.S.Ret.   master of science in retailing

M.S.S.   master of social science

M.S.Sc.   master of sanitary science; master of social science

M.S.S.E.   master of science in sanitary engineering

M.S.S.Eng.   master of science in sanitary engineering

M.S.S.S.   master of science in social service

M.S.St.Eng.   master of science in structural engineering

M.S.S.W.   master of science in social work

M.S.T.   master of science in teaching

M.Stat.   master of statistics

M.S.T.Ed.   master of science in teacher education

M.S.Trans.   master of science in transportation

M.S.Trans.E.   master of science in transportation engineering

M.Surgery   master of surgery

M.Surv.   master of surveying

M.S.W.   master of social welfare; master of social work

M.T.C.   master of textile chemistry

M.Tech.   master in technology

M.Tel.Eng.   master of telecommunications engineering

M.Text.   master of textiles

M.Th.   master of theology

M.T.P.   master of town planning

M.T.R.P.   master of town and regional planning

M.U.P.   master of urban planning

Mus.Bac.   bachelor of music

Mus.D.   doctor of music

Mus.Ed.B.   bachelor of music education

Mus.Ed.D.   doctor of music education

Mus.Ed.M.   master of music education

Mus.M.   master of music

M.V.E.   master of vocational education

M.Vet.Med.   master of veterinary medicine

M.Vet.Sci.   master of veterinary science

M.V.Sc.   master of veterinary science

M.Z.Sc.   master of zoological science

Pd.B. bachelor of pedagogy (Latin *Pedagogiae Baccalaureus*)

Pd.D. doctor of pedagogy (Latin *Pedagogiae Doctor*)

Pd.M. master of pedagogy (Latin *Pedagogiae Magister*)

Phar.B. bachelor of pharmacy

Phar.D. doctor of pharmacy

Phar.M. master of pharmacy (Latin *Pharmaciae Magister*)

Pharm.D. doctor of pharmacy (Latin *Pharmaciae Doctor*)

Ph.B bachelor of philosophy (Latin *Philosophiae Baccalaureus*)

Ph.B.J. bachelor of philosophy in journalism

Ph.B.Sp. bachelor of philosophy in speech

Ph.D. doctor of philosophy (Latin *Philosophiae Doctor*)

P.H.D. public health doctor

Ph.D.Ed. doctor of philosophy in education

Ph.G. graduate in pharmacy

Ph.M. master of philosophy (Latin *Philosophiae Magister*)

Phm.B. bachelor of pharmacy

Phm.G. graduate in pharmacy

Pod.D. doctor of podiatry

S.B. bachelor of science

Sc.B. bachelor of science (Latin *Scientiae Baccalaureus*)

Sc.D. doctor of science (Latin *Scientiae Doctor*)

Sci.D. doctor of science

Sci.D.Com. doctor of science in commerce

Sci.D.Met. doctor of science in metallurgy

Sc.M. master of science (Latin *Scientiae Magister*)

Sc.Soc.D.   doctor of social science

S.J.D.   doctor of juridical science

S.M.   master of science (Latin *Scientiae Magister*)

S.Sc.D.   doctor of social science

S.S.D.   doctor of sacred scripture (Latin *Sacrae Scripturae Doctor*)

S.T.B.   bachelor of sacred theology

S.T.D.   doctor of sacred theology

S.T.M.   master of sacred theology

Th.D.   doctor of theology (Latin *Theologiae Doctor*)

Th.M.   master of theology (Latin *Theologiae Magister*)

Vet.M.B.   bachelor of veterinary medicine

V.M.D.   doctor of veterinary medicine (Latin *Veterinariae Medicinae Doctor*)

STATES AND COUNTRIES

U.S. STATES, TERRITORIES, AND POSSESSIONS

	Traditional	Postal
Alabama	Ala.	AL
Alaska	Alaska	AK
American Samoa	Amer. Samoa	AS
Arizona	Ariz.	AZ
Arkansas	Ark.	AR
California	Calif.	CA
Canal Zone	C.Z.	CZ
Colorado	Colo.	CO
Connecticut	Conn.	CT
Delaware	Del.	DE
District of Columbia	D.C.	DC
Florida	Fla.	FL
Georgia	Ga.	GA
Guam	Guam	GU
Hawaii	Hawaii	HI
Idaho	Idaho	ID
Illinois	Ill.	IL
Indiana	Ind.	IN

	Traditional	Postal
Iowa	Iowa	IA
Kansas	Kans.	KS
Kentucky	Ky.	KY
Louisiana	La.	LA
Maine	Maine	ME
Maryland	Md.	MD
Massachusetts	Mass.	MA
Michigan	Mich.	MI
Minnesota	Minn.	MN
Mississippi	Miss.	MS
Missouri	Mo.	MO
Montana	Mont.	MT
Nebraska	Nebr.	NE
Nevada	Nev.	NV
New Hampshire	N.H.	NH
New Jersey	N.J.	NJ
New Mexico	N.Mex.	NM
New York	N.Y.	NY
North Carolina	N.C.	NC
North Dakota	N.Dak.	ND
Ohio	Ohio	OH
Oklahoma	Okla.	OK
Oregon	Oreg.	OR
Pennsylvania	Pa.	PA
Puerto Rico	P.R.	PR
Rhode Island	R.I.	RI
South Carolina	S.C.	SC
South Dakota	S.Dak.	SD
Tennessee	Tenn.	TN
Texas	Tex.	TX

	Traditional	*Postal*
Utah	Utah	UT
Vermont	Vt.	VT
Virginia	Va.	VA
Virgin Islands	V.I.	VI
Washington	Wash.	WA
West Virginia	W.Va.	WV
Wisconsin	Wis.	WI
Wyoming	Wyo.	WY

PRINCIPAL FOREIGN COUNTRIES

Afghanistan	Afghan.	Bhutan	Bhu.
Albania	Alb.	Bolivia	Bol.
Algeria	Alg.	Botswana	Botswana, Bots.
Andorra	And.		
Angola	Ang.	Brazil	Braz.
Antigua	Ant.	Bulgaria	Bulg.
Argentina	Argen.	Burma	Bur.
Australia	Aust., Austl.	Burundi	Burun.
		Cameroon	Cam.
Austria	Aus.	Canada	Can.
Bahamas, The	Bah.	Cape Verde	C.V., CV
Bahrain	Bah.	Central African Empire	C.A.E., CAE, C. Afr. Emp.
Bangladesh	Bangla.		
Barbados	Barb.		
Barbuda	Barbuda, Bar.	Chad	Chad
Belgium	Belg.	Chile	Chile
Belize	Bel.	China	Chin.
Benin	Benin, Ben.	Colombia	Col., Colom.

[388]

Comoros	Comoros, Com.	*Germany, Federal Republic of (West Germany)	F.R.G.,FRG W.Ger.)
Congo	Congo, Cong.		
Costa Rica	C.R., CR	Ghana	Ghana
Cuba	Cuba	Greece	Greece
Cyprus	Cyp.	Grenada	Gren.
Czechoslova- kia	Czech.	Guatemala	Guat.
Denmark	Den.	Guinea	Guinea
Djibouti	Djib.	Guinea-Bissau	Guinea- Bissau
Dominica	Dom.	Guyana	Guy.
Dominican Republic	D.R., DR, Dom.Rep.	Haiti	Haiti
Ecuador	Ecua.	Honduras	Hond.
Egypt	Egyp.	Hungary	Hung.
El Salvador	El Sal.	Iceland	Ice.
Equatorial Guinea	E.G., EG, Eq.Guin.	India	Ind.
		Indonesia	Indon.
Estonia	Est.	Iran	Ir.
Ethiopia	Eth.	Iraq	Iraq
Fiji	Fiji	Ireland	Ir.
Finland	Fin.	Israel	Isr.
France	Fr.	Italy	It.
Gabon	Gab.	Ivory Coast	I.C., IC, Iv.Cst.
Gambia	Gam.	Jamaica	Jam.
*German Democratic Republic (East Germany)	G.D.R., GDR (E.Ger.)	Japan	Jap.
		Jordan	Jord.
		Kampuchea (Cambodia)	Kamp. (Cambod.)

*Preunification.

Kenya	Ken.	New Zealand	N.Z., NZ
Kiribati	Kir.	Nicaragua	Nica.
Korea, North	N.Kor.	Niger	Nig.
Korea, South	S.Kor.	Nigeria	Nig.
Kuwait	Kuw.	Norway	Nor.
Laos	Laos	Oman	Om.
Latvia	Lat.	Pakistan	Pak.
Lebanon	Leb.	Panama	Pan.
Lesotho	Leso	Papua New Guinea	Pap.N.G., Pap.NG
Liberia	Lib., Liberia		
Libya	Lib.	Paraguay	Para.
Liechtenstein	Liech.	Peru	Peru
Lithuania	Lith.	Philippines	Phil.
Luxembourg	Lux.	Poland	Pol.
Madagascar	Madag.	Portugal	Port.
Malawi	Malawi, Mal.	Qatar	Qatar, Qa.
Malaysia	Mal.	Romania	Rom.
Maldives	Mald.	Rwanda	Rwanda
Mali	Mali	Saint Lucia	S.L., SL, St. Lu.
Malta	Mal.		
Mauritania	Maurit.	Saint Vincent and the Grenadines	St.V.&G., St. V&G
Mauritius	Maur.		
Mexico	Mex.		
Monaco	Mon.	San Marino	S.M., SM
Mongolia	Mong.	São Tomé and Principe	São Tomé and Principe
Morocco	Mor.		
Mozambique	Mozam.	Saudi Arabia	S.A., SA
Nauru	Nau.	Senegal	Seneg.
Nepal	Nep.	Seychelles	Seychelles, Sey.
Netherlands, The	Neth.		
		Sierra Leone	S.L., SL

Singapore	Sing.	Uganda	Ugan.
Solomon Islands	S.I., SI	Union of Soviet Socialist Republics	U.S.S.R., USSR
Somalia	Som.		
South Africa	S.A., SA, S.Afr.	United Arab Emirates	U.A.E., UAE
Spain	Sp.	United Kingdom	U.K., UK
Sri Lanka (Ceylon)	S.L., SL, Sri Lan. (Cey.)		
		Upper Volta	U.V., UV
Sudan	Sud.	Uruguay	Uru.
Suriname	Suri.	Vanuatu	Vanu.
Swaziland	Swaz.	Vatican City	V.C., VC
Sweden	Swed.	Venezuela	Venez.
Switzerland	Switz.	Vietnam	Viet.
Syria	Syr.	Western Samoa	W.S., WS
Tanzania	Tanz.		
Thailand	Thai., Thail.	Yemen (South Yemen)	S.Yem.
Tobago	Tob.		
Togo	To.	Yemen (Arab Republic)	Yem.
Tonga	Ton.	Yugoslavia	Yug.
Trinidad	Trin.	Zaire	Zai.
Tunisia	Tun.	Zambia	Zam.
Turkey	Turk.	Zimbabwe	Zimb.
Tuvalu	Tuv.		

SIGNS AND SYMBOLS

ACCENTS

´	acute
˘	breve
¸	cedilla
^	circumflex
¨	dieresis
`	grave
¯	macron
~	tilde

CHEMICAL

‰	salinity
♏	minim
⇅	exchange
↑	gas
A	argon
Ac	actinium
Ag	silver
Al	aluminum
Am	americium
Ar	argon
As	arsenic; astatine
At	astatine
Au	gold
B	boron
Ba	barium
Be	beryllium
Bi	bismuth
Bk	berkelium
Br	bromine
C	carbon
Ca	calcium
Cd	cadmium
Ce	cerium
Cf	californium
Cl	chlorine
Co	cobalt
Cr	chromium
Cm	curium
Cs	cesium
Cu	copper (*cuprum*)

SOURCE: Many of the signs and symbols shown here are from the United States Government Printing Office *Style Manual*, March 1984.

Dy	dysprosium	Os	osmium
Er	erbium	P	phosphorus
Es	einsteinium	Pa	protactinium
Eu	europium	Pb	lead (*plumbum*)
F	fluorine	Pd	palladium
Fe	iron (*ferrum*)	Pm	promethium
Fm	fermium	Po	polonium
Fr	francium	Pr	praseodymium
Ga	gallium	Pt	platinum
Gd	gadolinium	Pu	plutonium
Ge	germanium	Ra	radium
H	hydrogen	Rb	rubidium
Ha	hahnium	Re	rhenium
He	helium	Rf	rutherfordium
Hf	hafnium	Rh	rhodium
Hg	mercury	Rn	radon
	(*hydrargyrum*)	Ru	ruthenium
Ho	holmium	S	sulfur
I	iodine	Sb	antimony (*stibium*)
In	indium	Sc	scendium
Ir	iridium	Se	selenium
K	potassium (*kalium*)	Si	silicon
Kr	krypton	Sm	samarium
La	lanthanum	Sn	tin (*stannum*)
Li	lithium	Sr	strontium
Lr	lawrencium	Ta	tantalum
Lu	lutetium	Tb	terbium
Lw	lawrencium	Tc	technetium
Md	mendelevium	Te	tellurium
Mg	magnesium	Th	thorium
Mn	manganese	Ti	titanium
Mo	molybdenum	Tl	thallium
N	nitrogen	Tm	thulium
Na	sodium (*natrium*)	U	uranium
Nb	niobium	V	vanadium
Nd	neodymium	W	tungsten (*wolfram*)
Ne	neon	Xe	xenon
Ni	nickel	Y	yttrium
No	nobelium	Yb	ytterbium
Np	neptunium	Zn	zinc
O	oxygen	Zr	zirconium

CODE

•	No. 1 6 pt. code dot
•	No. 2 8 pt. code dot
•	No. 3 10 pt. code dot
●	No. 4 8 pt. code dot
●	No. 4 10 pt. code dot
—	No. 1 6 pt. code dash
—	No. 2 8 pt. code dash
—	No. 3 10 pt. code dash
▬	No. 4 8 pt. code dash
▬	No. 4 10 pt. code dash

COMPASS

°	degree
°:	degree with period
'	minute
.:	minute with period
"	second
":	second with period
_"	canceled second

ELECTRICAL

ℜ	reluctance
↔	reaction goes both right and left
↕	reaction goes both up and down
↕	reversible
→	direction of flow; yields
→	direct current
⇆	electrical current
⇆	reversible reaction
⇌	reversible reaction
⇆	alternating current
⇌	alternating current
⇌	reversible reaction beginning at left
⇋	reversible reaction beginning at right
Ω	ohm; omega
$M\Omega$	megohm; omega
$\mu\Omega$	microohm; mu omega
ω	angular frequency, solid angle; omega
Φ	magnetic flux; phi
Ψ	dielectric flux; electrostatic flux; psi
γ	conductivity; gamma
ρ	resistivity; rho
λ	equivalent conductivity
HP	horsepower

SYSTEM FLOWCHART

⬭	punched card
⬭	perforated (punched) tape
⬭	document
Ｑ	magnetic tape
⬭	transmittal tape
▽	off-line storage
⬭	on-line storage
○	display
⬭	manual input
○	sorting and collating
▽	clerical or manual operation
□	auxiliary operation
⬭	keying operation
↔	communication link

PROGRAM FLOWCHART

□	processing
▱	input/output
◇	decision
⬭	program modification
⬚	predefined process
⬭	terminal
○	connector
⬭	off-page connector
⇆⇅	flow direction
□---	annotation

GREEK ALPHABET

Name of Letter	Greek Alphabet	
Alpha	A	a α^1
Beta	B	β
Gamma	Γ	γ
Delta	Δ	δ ∂^1
Epsilon	E	ϵ
Zeta	Z	ζ
Eta	H	η
Theta	Θ	θ ϑ^1
Iota	I	ι
Kappa	K	κ

Name of Letter	Greek Alphabet	
Lambda	Λ	λ
Mu	M	μ
Nu	N	ν
Xi	Ξ	ξ
Omicron	O	o
Pi	Π	π
Rho	P	ρ
Sigma	Σ	σ ς[2]
Tau	T	τ
Upsilon	Υ	υ
Phi	Φ	φ
Chi	X	χ
Psi	Ψ	ψ
Omega	Ω	ω

[1]Old style character.
[2]Final letter.

MATHEMATICAL

—	vinculum (above letters)	÷	divided by
∺	geometrical proportion	∴	therefore; hence
		∵	because
—:	difference, excess	::	proportion; as
‖	parallel	≪	is dominated by
‖s	parallels	>	greater than
≠	not parallels	⌐	greater than
| |	absolute value	≥	greater than or equal to
·	multiplied by	≧	greater than or equal to
:	is to; ratio	≷	greater than or less than

≯	is not greater than	=	equal to
<	less than	~	difference
⊐	less than	≃	perspective to
≶	less than or greater than	≅	congruent to approximately equal
≮	is not less than		
◄	smaller than	≏	difference between
≤	less than or equal to	⇌	geometrically equivalent to
≦	less than or equal to		
≧ or ≥	greater than or equal to	(	included in
		)	excluded from
≤	equal to or less than	⊂	is contained in
≦	equal to or less than	∪	logical sum or union
≩	is not greater than equal to or less than	∩	logical product or intersection
		√	radical
>	equal to or greater than	√	root
		∛	square root
≧	is not less than equal to or greater than	∛	cube root
		∜	fourth root
≜	equilateral	∜	fifth root
⊥	perpendicular to	∜	sixth root
⊢	assertion sign	π	pi
≐	approaches	ε	base (2.718) of natural system of logarithms; epsilon
≒	approaches a limit		
⩗	equal angles		
≠	not equal to	ε	is a member of; dielectric constant; mean error; epsilon
≡	identical with		
≢	not identical with		
Ɱ	score	+	plus
≈ or ≑	nearly equal to	**+**	bold plus
		−	minus

—	bold minus
/	shill(ing); slash; virgule
±	plus or minus
∓	minus or plus
×	multiplied by
=	bold equal
#	number
⅌	per
%	percent
∫	integral
|	single bond
\	single bond
/	single bond
‖	double bond
⑊	double bond
//	double bond
⬡	benzene ring
∂ or δ	differential; variation
∂	Italian differential
→	approaches limit of
~	cycle sine
∫	horizontal integral
∮	contour integral
∝	variation; varies as
∏	product
Σ	summation of; sum; sigma
! or ⌊	factorial product

MEASURE

lb	pound
ʒ	dram
fʒ	fluid dram
℥	ounce
f℥	fluid ounce
O	pint

MISCELLANEOUS

©	copyright
§	section
†	dagger
‡	double dagger
℀	account of
℅	care of
𝍸	score
¶	paragraph
þ	Anglo-Saxon
℄	center line
☌	conjunction
⊥	perpendicular to
″ or “	ditto
∝	variation
℞	recipe
]	move right
[	move left
○ or ⊙ or ①	annual
⊙⊙ or ②	biennial

∈	element of	c̄	mean value of c
℈	scruple	∪	mathmodifier
f	function	⊂	mathmodifier
!	exclamation mark	⊡	dot in square
⊞	plus in square	△	dot in triangle
♃	perennial	⊠	station mark
φ	diameter	@	at

Foreign Money

Country or area	Basic monetary unit		Principal fractional unit	
	Name	Symbol	Name	Abbreviation or symbol
Afghanistan	Afghani	Af	Pul	
Albania	Lek	L	Quintar	
Algeria	Dinar	DA	Centime	
Andorra	French franc	Fr.F.	French centime	
	Spanish peseta	Sp. Ptas.[1]	Spanish centimo	
Angola	Kwanza	Kz	Lwei	
Antigua and Barbuda	Dollar	EC$	Cent	
Argentina	Peso	M$N	Centavo	Ctvo.
Australia	Dollar	A$	Cent	
Austria	Schilling	S	Groschen	
Bahamas, The	Dollar	B$	Cent	
Bahrain	Dinar	BD	Fil	
Bangladesh	Taka	Tk	Paise	
Barbados	Dollar	Bds$	Cent	
Belgium	Franc	BF	Centime	
Belize	Dollar	$B	Cent	
Benin	Franc	CFAF	Centime	
Bermuda	Dollar	$B	Cent	
Bhutan	Ngultruns	N	Tikchung	
Bolivia	Peso Boliviana	$b	Centavo	Ctvo.
Botswana	Pula	P	Thebe	
Brazil	New cruzeiro	NCr$	Centavo	Ctvo.
Brunei	Dollar	B$	Cent	
Bulgaria	Lev	L	Stotinka	
Burma (Myanmar)	Kyat	K	Pya	
Burundi	Franc	FBu	Centime	
Cameroon	Franc	CFAF	. . . do	
Canada	Dollar	$ or Can$	Cent	C, ct.
Cape Verde	Escudo	C.V.Esc	Centavo	
Central African Republic	Franc	CFAF	Centime	
Chad	Franc	CFAF	. . . do	
Chile	Peso	Ch$	Centavo	
China	Yuan	Ұ	Fen	
Colombia	Peso	Col$	Centavo	Ctvo.
Comoros	Franc	CFAF	Centime	

Country or area	Basic monetary unit		Principal fractional unit	
	Name	Symbol	Name	Abbreviation or symbol
Congo	... do	CFAF	... do	
Cook Islands	New Zealand dollar	NZ$	Cent	
Costa Rica	Colon	¢	Centimo	Ctmo.
Cuba	Peso	$	Centavo	Ctvo.
Cyprus	Pound	£ or £C	Mil	
Czechoslovakia	Koruna	Kcs	Haler	
Dahomey	Franc	CFAF	Centime	
Denmark	Krone	DKr	Øre	
Djibouti	Franc	DF	Centime	
Dominica	Dollar	EC$	Cent	
Dominican Republic	Peso	RD$	Centavo	Ctvo.
Ecuador	Sucre	S/	... do	Ctvo.
Egypt	Pound	£E	Piaster	
El Salvador	Colon	¢	Centavo	Ctvo.
Equatorial Guinea	Ekuele	EK	Centimo	
Estonia	Ruble		Kopek	
Ethiopia	Birr	EB	Cent	
Falkland Islands	Pound	£	Shilling	
Faroe Islands	Danish krone	DKr	Øre	
Fiji	Dollar	$F	Cent	
Finland	Finnmark	Fimr	Penni	Pia
France	Franc	F	Centime	
French Guiana	... do	F	... do	
French Polynesia	... do	CFPF	... do	
Gabon	... do	CFAF	... do	
Gambia	Dalasi	DD	Butut	
German Democratic Republic	Mark	DME	Pfennig	Pf.
Ghana	Cedi	¢	Pesewa	P.
Gibraltar	Pound	£	Shilling	
Greece	Drachma	Dr	Lepton	
Greenland	Danish krone	DKr	Øre	
Grenada	Dollar	EC$	Cent	
Guadeloupe	Franc	F	Centime	
Guatemala	Quetzal	Q	Centavo	Ctvo.
Guinea	Syli	GS	Cauri	

Country or area	Basic monetary unit		Principal fractional unit	
	Name	Symbol	Name	Abbreviation or symbol
Guyana	Dollar	G$	Cent	
Haiti	Gourde	G	Centime	
Honduras	Lempira	L	Centavo	Ctvo.
Hong Kong	Dollar	HK$	Cent	
Hungary	Forint	FT	Filler	
Iceland	Krona	IKr	Eyrir	
India	Rupee	Rs	Paisa	
Indonesia	Rupiah	Rp	Sen	
Iran	Rial	Rls^2	Dinar	
Iraq	Dinar	ID	Fil	
Ireland	Pound	£ or £Ir	Shilling	S.,d.
Israel	Shekel	I£	Agrirot	
Italy	Lira	Lit	Centesimo	Ctmo.
Ivory Coast	Franc	CFAF	Centime	
Jamaica	Dollar	J$	Cent	
Japan	Yen	¥	Sen	
Jordan	Dinar	JD	Fil	
Kampuchea	Riel	KR		
Kenya	Shilling	K Sh	Cent	
Kiribati	Australian dollar	A$	. . . do	
Korea	Chon	W	Chun	
Kuwait	Dinar	KD	Fil	
Laos	Kip	K	At	
Latvia	Ruble	R	Kopek	
Lebanon	Pound	LL	Piaster	
Lesotho	Rand	R	Cent	
Liberia	Dollar	$	. . . do	
Libya	Dinar	LD	Milleme	
Liechtenstein	Swiss franc	Sw F	Centime	
Lithuania	Ruble	R	Kopek	
Luxembourg	Franc	Lux F	Centime	
Macao	Pataca	P	Avo	
Madagascar	Franc	FMG	Centime	
Malawi	Kwacha	K	Tambal	
Malaysia	Ringgits	M$	Sen	
Maldives	Rupee	Mal Re	Lari	
Mali	Franc	MF		
Malta	Pound	£M	Cent	
Martinique	Franc	F	Centime	

Country or area	Basic monetary unit		Principal fractional unit	
	Name	Symbol	Name	Abbreviation or symbol
Mauritania	Ouguiya	UM	Khoum	
Mauritius	Rupee	Mau Rs[3]	Cent	
Mexico	Peso	Mex$	Centavo	Ctvo.
Monaco	French franc	Fr	Centime	
Mongolia	Tugrik	Tug	Möngö	
Montserrat	Dollar	EC$	Cent	
Morocco	Dirham	DH	Centime	
Mozambique	Escudo	M. Esc	Centavo	
Nauru	Australian dollar	$A[1]	Cent	
Nepal	Rupee	NRs[1]	Pice	
Netherlands	Guilder	f.	Cent	
Netherlands Antilles	. . . do	NAE	. . . do	
New Caledonia	Franc	CFPF	Centime	
New Zealand	Dollar	$NZ	Cent	
Nicaragua	Cordoba	C$	Centavo	Ctvo.
Niger	Franc	CFAF	Centime	
Nigeria	Naira	₦	Kobo	k.
Norway	Krone	NKr	Øre	
Oman	Riyal	ORls	Baiza	
Pakistan	Rupee	PRs	Paisa	
Panama	Balboa	B	Centesimo	Ctmo.
Paraguay	Guarani	G	Centimo	Ctmo.
Papua New Guinea	Kina	K	Toea	
Peru	Sol	S/	Centavo	Ctvo.
Philippines	Peso	₱	. . . do	Ctvo.
Poland	Zloty	Zl	Grosz	
Portugal	Escudo	Esc	Centavo	
Qatar	Riyal	QRls	Dirham	
Reunion	French franc	F	Centime	
Romania	Leu	L	Ban	
Rwanda	Franc	RF	Centime	
St. Christopher-Nevis	Dollar	EC$	Cent	
St. Lucia	. . . do	EC$	. . . do	
St. Pierre and Miquelon	Franc	CFAF	Centime	

Country or area	Basic monetary unit		Principal fractional unit	
	Name	Symbol	Name	Abbreviation or symbol
St. Vincent and the Grenadines	Dollar	EC$	Cent	
San Marino	Italian lira	Lit	Centesimo	
Sao Tome e Principe	Dobra	Db	Centavo	
Saudi Arabia	Riyal	SRls[2]	Halala	
Senegal	Franc	CFAF	Centime	
Seychelles	Rupee	Sey Rs[2]	Cent	
Sierra Leone	Leone	Le	... do	
Singapore	Dollar	S$	... do	
Solomon Islands	Dollar	SI$	... do	
Somalia	Shilling	So. Sh.	... do	
South Africa	Rand	R	Cent	
Spain	Peseta	Ptas[1]	Centimo	
Sri Lanka	Rupee	Cey Rs[3]	Cent	
Sudan	Pound	£S	Piaster	
Suriname	Guilder	Sur. f.	Cent	
Swaziland	Lilangeni (emalangeni, plural).	E	... do	
Sweden	Krona	SKr	Öre	
Switzerland	Franc	SwF	Centime	
Syria	Pound	£Syr	Piaster	
Taiwan	New Taiwan dollar	NT$	Cent	
Tanzania	Shilling	T Sh	Cent	
Thailand	Baht	B	Satang	
Togo	Franc	CFAF	Centime	
Tonga	Pa'anga	T$	Seniti	
Trinidad and Tobago	Dollar	TT$	Cent	
Tunisia	Dinar	D	Millime	
Turkey	Lira	TL	Kurus	
Tuvalu	Australian dollar	A$	Cent	
Uganda	Shilling	U Sh	... do	
U.S.S.R.	Ruble	R	Kopek	
United Arab Emirates	Dirham	UD	Fil	
United Kingdom	Pound	£ or £stg.	Shilliing	S., d.

Country or area	Basic monetary unit		Principal fractional unit	
	Name	Symbol	Name	Abbreviation or symbol
United States	Dollar	$ or US$	Cent	
Upper Volta	Franc	CFAF	Centime	
Uruguay	Peso	N$	Centesimo	
Vanatu	Franc	FNH	Centime	
Vatican City	Italian lira	Lit	Centesimo	Ctmo.
Venezuela	Bolivar	Bs	Centimo	
Vietnam	Dông	VND	Hao	
Wallis and Futuna	Franc	CFPF	Centime	
Western Samoa	Tala	WS$	Cent	
Yemen (Aden)	Dinar	SYD	Fil	
Yemen (Sanaa)	Rial	Y Rls[2]	. . . do	
Yugoslavia	Dinar	Din	Para	
Zaire	Zaire	Z	Likuta	
Zambia	Kwacha	K	Ngwee	S., d.
Zimbabwe	Dollar	Z$	Cent	

[1]Singular: Pta.
[2]Singular: Rl.
[3]Singular: Re.

MUSIC		♄	Saturn
♮	natural	♅	Uranus
♭	flat	♆	Neptune
♯	sharp	♇	Pluto
		☊	dragon's head, ascending node
PLANETS		☋	dragon's tail, descending node
☿	Mercury		
♀	Venus		
⊕	Earth	☌	conjunction
♂	Mars	☍	opposition
♃	Jupiter	☉ or ☺	Sun

[405]

☾	Sun's lower limb	☾	last quarter
☉	Sun's upper limb	☽	last quarter
☉	solar corona	○	full Moon
⊕	solar halo	☺	full Moon
☾	Moon	⊖	eclipse of Moon
●	new Moon	▽	lunar halo
☽	first quarter	∪	lunar corona
◑	first quarter	⚳	Ceres
☽	third quarter	⚘	Juno
◐	last quarter		

PROOFREADER MARKS

Margin Symbol	Text Marking	Meaning
ℓ	books	Delete.
⦦	book s	Delete and close up.
stet.	evening ~~paper~~ and	Let it stand.
no ¶	studies) (Readers know	No paragraph.
#	talkingand	Add space.
out, sc	sensible who is	Something missing; see copy.
sp. out	② students	Spell out.
◡	semi colon	Close up.
[	[the letter	Move left.
]	the letter	Move right.

Margin Symbol	Text Marking	Meaning
tr	def<del>i</del>ess	Transpose.
‖	‖call the customer and	Line up, or align.
¶	calling. However	New paragraph.
⑦	1984	Question to author.
?	Is it correct	Insert question mark.
!	Incredible	Insert exclamation mark.
|=|	non American	Insert hyphen.
ˇ/ˇ	when he said, some	Insert quotation marks.
⌃	finished moreover	Insert semicolon.
⌄⌃	the following news	Insert colon.
⌃	pens, pencils and	Insert comma.
⊙	this coat	Insert period.
↓	the speakers	Insert apostrophe.
b	ƒin	Change to b.
caps (or ≡)	<u>Reviews</u>	Set in capital letters.
lc	F<del>O</del>REWORD	Set in lowercase letters.
bf (or ⌇)	Typing and dictation	Set in boldface type.

Margin Symbol	Text Marking	Meaning
ital (or —)	<u>Accounting Handbook</u>	Set in italic type.
S.C. (or =)	<u>a.m.</u> or <u>p.m.</u>	Set in small capital letters.
C. + S.C.	<u>Spelling Guide</u>	Set in caps and small caps.
✓✓✓	k✓e✓y✓ topics	Correct spacing.
☐	☐Close the discussion	Indent one em.
(rom.)	*Epilogue*	Change to roman type.
✌	note✌	Set as superior number.
⋀	H⋀O	Set as inferior number.
【 / 】	˄a + b˄	Insert brackets.
€/⋝	˄a + b˄	Insert parentheses.
$\frac{1}{M}$	and statements⌒they	One-em dash.

PUNCTUATION

¡		Spanish open quote	
¿		Spanish open quote	
{ }	braces		
[ ]	brackets		
( )	parentheses	SEX	
⟨ ⟩	square parentheses; angle brackets	♂ or male ♂	

☐ male, in charts
♀ female
○ female, in charts
⚥ hermaphrodite

☞ index
☜ index

GEOLOGIC SYSTEMS[1]

Q Quaternary
T Tertiary
K Cretaceous
J Jurassic
Ŧ Triassic
P Permian
P Pennsylvanian
M Mississippian
D Devonian
S Silurian
O Ordovician
Є Cambrian
pЄ Precambrian
C Carboniferous

SHAPES

◆ solid diamond
◇ open diamond
○ circle
▲ solid triangle
△ triangle
☐ square
■ solid square
▱ parallelogram
☐ rectangle
⊡ double rectangle
★ solid star
☆ open star
L right angle
∠ angle
√ check
✔ check
β German ss
β italic German ss
🖝 solid index
🖜 solid index

WEATHER

T thunder
ⵕ thunderstorm; sheet lightning
< sheet lightning
↓ precipitate
◍ rain

[1]Standard letter symbols used by the Geological Survey on geologic maps. Capital letter indicates the system and one or more lowercased letters designate the formation and member where used.

[409]

←	floating ice crystals		ZODIAC
↔	ice needles	♈	Aries; Ram
▲	hail	♉	Taurus; Bull
⊗	sleet	♊	Gemini; Twins
∞	glazed frost	♋	Cancer; Crab
⊔	hoarfrost	♌	Leo; Lion
∨	frostwork	♍	Virgo; Virgin
✳	snow or sextile	♎	Libra; Balance
⊠	snow on ground	♏	Scorpio; Scorpion
✛	drifting snow (low)	♐	Sagittarius; Archer
☰	fog	♑	Capricorn; Goat
∞	haze	♒	Aquarius; Water bearer
△	Aurora	♓	Pisces; Fishes

About the Author

MARY A. DE VRIES has written dozens of books dealing with writing style and word usage—including *The Complete Word Book* (Prentice Hall) and three Signet editions: *The Practical Writer's Guide, The New American Handbook of Letter Writing,* and *The Complete Office Handbook*—and is currently preparing *The Prentice Hall Style Manual.*